D0154125

The Nobel Peace Prize

THE NOBEL PEACE PRIZE

What Nobel Really Wanted

Fredrik S. Heffermehl

 PRAEGER

AN IMPRINT OF ABC-CLIO, LLC
Santa Barbara, California • Denver, Colorado • Oxford, England

Library of Congress Cataloging-in-Publication Data

Heffermehl, Fredrik S.
    The Nobel Peace Prize : what Nobel really wanted / Fredrik S. Heffermehl.
        p. cm.
    Includes bibliographical references and index.
    ISBN 978-0-313-38744-9 (hardcopy : alk. paper) — ISBN 978-0-313-38745-6 (e-book)
    1. Peace—Awards—History. 2. Nobel Prizes—History. 3. Nobel, Alfred Bernhard, 1833–1896. I. Title.
    JZ5537.H44   2010
    303.6′6—dc22   2010015502

ISBN: 978-0-313-38744-9
EISBN: 978-0-313-38745-6

14   13   12   11   10   1   2   3   4   5

This book is also available on the World Wide Web as an eBook.
Visit www.abc-clio.com for details.

Praeger
An Imprint of ABC-CLIO, LLC

ABC-CLIO, LLC
130 Cremona Drive, P.O. Box 1911
Santa Barbara, California 93116-1911

This book is printed on acid-free paper ∞

Manufactured in the United States of America

*To Alfred Nobel and the political struggle
he wished to support with his peace prize,
and to Bertha von Suttner, who inspired him*

Facts do not cease to exist because they are ignored.
—Aldous Huxley 1927

CONTENTS

LIST OF FIGURES

LIST OF TABLES

PREFACE

This book will surprise many. It certainly surprised the author, turning 70, to see his primary concerns and experiences through life suddenly consolidate into this one project. At age 16, I had grappled with the dilemmas of being called up to serve, to be trained—and potentially ordered—to shoot my peers over the coincidences of history and national borders. Still believing that reason, morality, and concern for what was best—taking everyone into account—must govern the world, I thought that such an unserviceable institution as the military must be abolished in a matter of years. Later I became a business lawyer, interrupted by a most rewarding and interesting year as a postgraduate student at the New York University School of Law, before I started to work full time for peace in the early 1980s.

My understanding of "peace" and how to achieve it was developed during my years as vice president of the International Peace Bureau and of the International Association of Lawyers against Nuclear Arms. As president of the Norwegian Peace Council, I was invited to attend all of the ceremonies and Nobel banquets between 1989 and 2008. I first attended the Nobel ceremony in 1958—and it took 49 years before I suddenly understood the hidden truth about the Peace Prize—that it responded perfectly to the dilemmas I had first encountered at age 16.

The Nobel Peace Prize is the world's most important prize and is—not without reason—the most visible and prestigious. The roll call of winners and human achievement commands admiration. But in August 2007 the prospect of the 2007 prize going to Al Gore prompted me to check Nobel's will and discover how far the prize had deviated from what he must have had in mind when he wrote it in 1895. Part I of this book explains how and why it went wrong, and demonstrates my attempts to make the Norwegian Parliament and the Nobel committee respect the founder's will.

Similar complaints had been voiced often over the years, but my book seems to have been the first time someone officially pointed out that respecting what Nobel had in mind is a binding legal duty. In addition, adherence to his wishes would, more than ever, be to *the greatest benefit of mankind,* the common goal of all five Nobel prizes. The response, however, was unflinching business as usual. Nobel prizes were given to Martti Ahtisaari (2008) and Barack Obama (2009), and the president of Norway's Parliament, Thorbjørn Jagland, became the new Nobel committee chair. The lack of response made it necessary with this book to take the debate to a wider, international public and to extend its scope.

In Part II, I explore how far back the neglect of Nobel's intentions began. Once it proved possible to penetrate the absolute secrecy of the Nobel committee room, a startling wealth of evidence appeared. Nanny Jahn Hayes, daughter of Gunnar Jahn, the Nobel committee chair from 1942 to 1966, provided the revealing extracts from Jahn's private diaries, which are published and discussed here for the first time.

All social change starts with a little group of devoted people. This book is not only my search for the lost Nobel Peace Prize, but also a study of a struggling political idea and its prospects of prevailing against overwhelming forces.

ACKNOWLEDGMENTS

I thank Norwegian Literature Abroad, Fiction and Non-Fiction (NORLA), and the Norwegian Association of Non-Fiction Writers for their financial contributions to my work on the present book. Elisabeth Skjervum Hole and Gunnar Totland (Vidarforlaget) did much to develop my first book on the subject, in Norwegian, in 2008. Scandinavian lawyers Ståle Eskeland, Stig Gustafsson, and Ketil Lund, and British historian Peter van den Dungen read early drafts of the book. Others gave help and encouragement in many different ways: Ingeborg Breines; Elizabeth Chapman; Johan Galtung; Gunnar Garbo; Anton Geist; Alexander Harang; Nanny Jahn Hayes; Fabian Heffermehl; Henning Isoz; Arild Johansen; Knut Johansen; Jørgen Johansen; John Jones; Bruce Kent; Anne C. Kjelling; Evelin Lindner; Tomas Magnusson; Jan Oberg; Doug Pauley; Torild Skard; and Peter Weiss.

Working with Praeger editor Robert Hutchinson in the United States, and with copy editor Michael Duggan in London, provided constant stimulation. Mai-Bente Bonnevie offered good advice and is the main source of inspiration, love, and joy in my life. My warmest thanks to them all.

Testament

Jag undertecknad Alfred Bernhard Nobel förklarar härmed efter moget betänkande min yttersta vilja i afseende i den egendom jag vid min död kan efterlemna vara följande:

Öfver hela min återstående realiserbara förmögenhet förfogas på följande sätt: Kapitalet, af utredningsmännen realiseradt till säkra värdepapper, skall utgöra en fond hvars ränta årligen utdelas som prisbelöning åt dem som under det förlupne året hafva gjort menskligheten den största nytta. Räntan delas i fem lika delar som tillfalla: en del den som inom fysikens område har gjort den vigtigaste upptäckt eller uppfinning; en del den som har gjort den vigtigaste kemiska upptäckt eller förbättring; en del den som har gjort den vigtigaste upptäckt inom fysiologiens eller medicinens domän; en del den som inom literaturen har producerat det utmärktaste i idealisk rigtning; och en del åt den som har verkat mest eller best för folkens förbrödrande och afskaffande eller minskning af stående armeer samt bildande och spridande af fredskongresser. Priset för fysik och kemi utdelas af Svenska Vetenskapsakademien; för fysiologiska eller medicinska arbeten af Carolinska Institutet i Stockholm; för literatur af Akademien i Stockholm samt för fredsförfäktare af ett utskott af fem personer som väljas af Norska Stortinget. Det är min uttryckliga vilja att vid prisutdelningarne intet afseende fästes vid någon slags nationalitetstillhörighet sålunda att den värdigaste erhåller priset antingen han är Skandinav eller ej.

Detta testamente är hittils det enda giltiga och upphäfver alla mina föregående testamentariska bestämmelser om sådane skulle förefinnas efter min död.

Slutligen anordnar jag såsom varande min uttryckliga önskan och vilja att efter min död pulsådrorne uppskäras och att sedan detta skett och tydliga dödstecken af kompetente läkare intygats liket förbrännes i så kalladt crematorinugn.

Paris den 27 November 1895

Alfred Bernhard Nobel

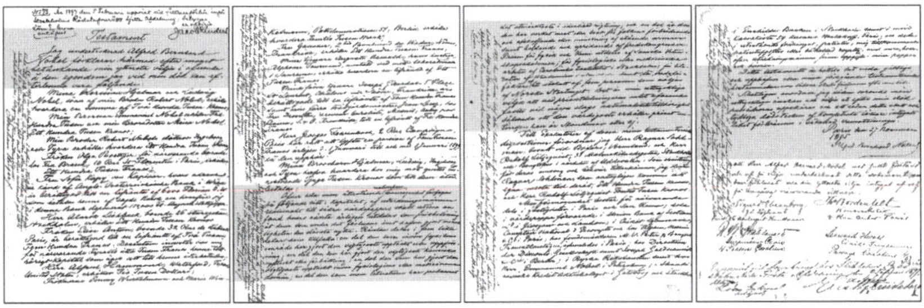

Provisions on the five Nobel prizes
(Translation: The Nobel Foundation):

The whole of my remaining realizable estate shall be dealt with in the following way: the capital, invested in safe securities by my executors, shall constitute a fund, the interest on which shall be annually distributed in the form of prizes to those who, *during the preceding year,* shall *have conferred the greatest benefit on mankind.* The said interest shall be divided into five equal parts, which shall be apportioned as follows: one part to the person who shall have made the most important discovery or invention within the field of physics; one part to the person who shall have made the most important chemical discovery or improvement; one part to the person who shall have made the most important discovery within the domain of physiology or medicine; one part to the person who shall have produced in the field of literature the most outstanding work in an ideal direction; and one part *to the person who shall have done the most or the best work for brotherhood between nations, for the abolition or reduction of standing armies and for the holding and promotion of peace congresses* (Italics added).

Figure 1.1 Alfred Nobel's will, signed in Paris on November 27, 1895. The normal facsimile of the will, regarding the five prizes that bear his name, excludes the remaining three pages where he provided generously for his family and servants. (© The Nobel Foundation.)

Part I

Peace is disarmament.
>—Alfred Nobel, 1895
>(essence of the Nobel will)

Chapter 1

INTRODUCTION

Moscow, August 19, 1991

I awoke to the thunder of tanks rolling through the city streets. During my first visit to the Soviet capital, I was witness to an attempted *coup d'état*. A group of older and not entirely sober officers explained on television why they had mobilized the military forces to "save the Soviet state." The truth was that they wanted to stop Gorbachev's reforms and liberalization. A few hours later, from the balcony of a Russian friend, a history professor, I watched the long column of tanks and military vehicles that rumbled over the square toward the Kremlin. Shuddering, the professor uttered a sentence I shall never forget: "Just imagine what we paid for all of this, and now it's being used against us."

Berlin, October 1990

One year after the fall of the Iron Curtain, I was a guest in the home of an East German. Delighted with his newly won freedom, he brought out a hidden treasure, an album of photographs of life years ago in the *Volksarmee* (People's Army) around the time they built the Wall. One picture was taken from behind a machine gun aimed along an endless, open border lane cut in a dense forest. I asked my host if he had ever pulled the trigger to stop anyone from fleeing across the border. He didn't like the question, but finally he admitted: "We were all so young back then."

These two episodes remind us just how complex the issues surrounding military power are. People believe it is in their own interest to pay for weapons and rearmament. But the military often pursue other ends than people are led to believe. The huge military sector, with its intelligence services and secrecy, claims to protect citizens and democratic governance, but often it will obstruct or interfere in the democratic process.

Nor do the military precautions that states take, ostensibly to protect against enemy nations, provide security for their own citizens. It has become increasingly obvious that security cannot be purchased by acquisition of weapons: the race to gain an advantage in arms buildup and military technology makes the world more dangerous for us all, and makes us all the poorer.

Thus, the idea of military "security" is a dangerous illusion. Each inhabitant of the planet spends nearly $200 per year on military security—but how secure have we become as a result? We continue to pay astronomical sums, even though the military has long been a major—maybe the greatest—threat to mankind, a perpetual threat to obliterate life on earth. One could well ponder how this has come about, but more important is the question of whether we can and should continue in this direction. In general, all too little thought is given to these fundamental issues, and the scope of debate is severely confined.

Every year the world spends on military security three or four times the amount it would take to assure every citizen of the globe a decent standard of living: food, clothing, shelter, clean water, education, and health care. Billions of people live in a state of poverty that could be eradicated with just a tiny fraction of the close to $1,500 billion[1] the world spends each year on the military.

I once mentioned this figure over a cup of tea to India's ambassador in Oslo. His reaction was that it was impossible to eliminate military outlays in a world in which inequality reigned. In 1990, President Bush made it clear that the United States would resort to military force against anyone who might challenge "the American way of life." But can we defend the use of military power as a means of appropriating wealth?

Even in peacetime, the military is an expensive proposition, in terms of money, resources, and pollution. Not to mention the costs if the military is actually used in battle. With more advanced and efficient weapons, the costs have increased dramatically. An American economist, Joseph Stiglitz, has estimated that the war in Iraq will cost the United States $3 billion—and it will cost the rest of the world a comparable sum.[2]

Military spending in peace and war greatly reduces quality of life, and results in endless human suffering, the loss of life and limb, mental pain, and destroyed lives that send shock waves of hate down the centuries. Should it not be possible to better manage relations between people and nations?

Many understand the insanity of war, but as we have seen for centuries, it is not enough that the desire for a peaceful world always has had broad popular support. Although democracy implies that power stems from the people and nearly everyone wants peace, the military manages more often than not to draw the long straw. For critics seeking an end to the perpetual buildup of arms, the uphill political trek is much too steep. Too many people are reaping the benefits and too few are giving adequate thought to the dangers and in what way they are involved in and responsible for that danger. Far too many people are fascinated by "our sons and daughters" in elegant uniforms, a chief source of national pride. Air shows, military parades, and marching bands are more pleasant to think about than bombed-out villages and maimed or orphaned children.

It has become harder to win support for a nonviolent world order in a culture in which the military seems more and more to become a significant social force: The military tradition is long, it is a lucrative business, and it has considerable political power. Millions of people with experience and education are well paid to perform assignments for the military. Huge industries are geared toward producing specialized military equipment, and these industries are difficult to convert to civilian production. People's careers and enormous profits are linked to the continuation of this system. Money talks—and politicians understand the language.

Those who actively oppose this prominent player in society have trouble being heard. It does not matter that the arguments against war and rearmament are convincing. The voices of peace do not get through. The weapons industry and the military dominate in everyday politics. Although governments need to think about ways out of military defense, this is the very last thing they are planning for. No one ever seriously seeks an alternative. The media do not lead their audience in the right direction. Society debates what type of new fighter plane we should choose, but no fundamental debate is had about how we can bring the arms race to a halt.

As a result, few resources are left over for promoting peace. The struggle for peace and disarmament is weakened in large part by the lack of money and people. The fight against militarism can contribute decisively to rescuing the environment, but why is it so much easier to get financial support for the political battle to save the environment than for the battle to promote peace?

Significant resources must be invested in efforts to achieve a new world order, one in which military remedies take a back seat. If these efforts succeed, funds will be available for all the other good causes: the battle against hunger; disease; poverty; pollution; damage to the environment. Demilitarization would offer an enormous chance to address and resolve the causes of mankind's main problems, instead of aggravating them.

Hardly a peace activist alive can have failed to dream at some point that one day the world's richest man might give financial support that really helped—just think if Bill Gates or Warren Buffett had invested massively in promoting peace. But peace workers are realists: They know that the rich uncle is a distant and totally unrealistic dream. Or is it?

Unfortunately, even peace activists have forgotten the story of Alfred Nobel. Was it not the very struggle for sound international relations, not based on military power, that Nobel wanted to support when he wrote his will in 1895? In establishing a prize for "brotherhood among nations . . . [the] abolition or reduction of the military . . . [and the] promotion of peace congresses," could Nobel have had anything else in mind than a prize to promote demilitarization of our world? Stable, durable, peace requires disarmament.

Chapter 2

AN IDEA AHEAD OF ITS TIME

NOBEL: THE MAN AND HIS LEGACY

Many days are set aside for good causes on the international calendar, but few draw attention from the whole world. December 10 is a rare exception. Quite a lot of people know that this day is United Nations' Human Rights Day. Nevertheless, however important the cause, the global tribute to human rights is overshadowed by a project launched by a private individual more than 100 years ago. Alfred Nobel is the man who has managed to place the capitals of Sweden and Norway, Stockholm and Oslo, and himself at the center of world attention on one day of the year, every year, except in wartime, since 1901.

On this day, some of the world's most gifted and brilliant people come to the two Scandinavian capitals to be honored in splendid ceremonies, with friends and family in tow. The ceremonies reach their glittering peak in the presence of royalty. Newspaper and television coverage reaches most parts of the world. In Swedish society, hardly anything is more coveted than to be one of 1,000 people invited to the annual Nobel banquet in the Blue Hall of Stockholm's magnificent *Stadshuset* (City Hall).

Nobel "invented" this day when he was writing his will in 1895 and chose the anniversary of his death as the date for awarding five prizes: one each for three branches of science, one for literature, and one for peace. One year later, on December 10, 1896, he died. As a result, almost every year since 1901 four Nobel prizes, for literature, medicine, physics, and chemistry, have been awarded in Stockholm, and the Peace Prize has been awarded in Oslo.

Quiet reigned in the house where Nobel lay on his deathbed in San Remo, Italy. His stately villa was called *Mio Nido*, My Nest, but it cannot have been very homelike. The world-famous, super-rich inventor was unmarried and had no children. His relatives were notified of his illness, but none of them got there in time. No friend was present to offer comfort: only hired servants were in the house. That Nobel had suffered from loneliness for quite a while can be seen from a letter he wrote nine years before his death, at a time when one of his brothers, Ludvig, had just died of a heart attack and Nobel himself was having frequent attacks of angina, particularly worrisome for someone who traveled as much as Nobel:

> *For the past nine days I have been ill and have had to stay indoors with no other company than a paid valet; no one inquires about me. . . . When at the age of 54 one is left so alone in the world, and a paid servant is the one person who has so far shown the most kindness, then come heavy thoughts, heavier than most people can imagine. I can see in my valet's eyes how much he pities me, but I cannot, of course, let him notice that.*[1]

Nobel was 63 when he died. He had a bustling and productive life behind him, always on the go, always absorbed in his work, mainly inventions in chemistry and technology. He had a home and laboratory in several countries, and he kept in touch with many people. Nobel handwrote 50 letters a day. He kept files and did his own bookkeeping and was distinctly "hands on" in everything he did. At his death, he had 355 international patents, and he was a world magnate in the industrial and financial field.[2]

Loneliness was hardly due to a lack of social skills: Nobel's charm and eloquence often had been of great advantage in business transactions and negotiations. But the deep absorption in his work had a downside: he often had been lonely.

Nobel's lifestyle was impressive. He owned beautiful houses, but lived modestly just the same. The laboratory was his most important room, and to create and invent was his passion. He was gifted in many ways: he not only was inventive, but also had the commercial talent necessary to translate ideas into practical—and profitable—production. Nobel handled both the legal and commercial aspects of his many projects himself, more to ensure that his ideas were put into practice than to earn huge amounts of money. But his skills and work ethic did yield big profits: he was one of the richest men of the era when he died.

The quiet surrounding his death came to an emphatic end a month later, when Nobel's will was made public. Most of the assets he left would go toward establishing five international prizes that would reward

Figure 2.1 Alfred Nobel on admission card to the 1887 World Exhibition, Paris. (© The Nobel Foundation.)

the most useful contributions to mankind in medicine, physics, chemistry, literature, and peace. The first four prizes would be conferred in Sweden, while a five-member committee chosen by Norway's Parliament would confer the fifth, the Peace Prize.

Nobel had made a generous gift to mankind, but the surprising will received a mixed reception. It caused a sensation and was discussed in the world press. Nobel's relatives were indignant and protested, but they were not alone in contesting the will.

Sweden's King Oscar II was dismayed that every year large sums of hard currency would leave Sweden. The king thought Nobel had been the victim of misguided visionaries and misconceived internationalism. The fact too that the Norwegian Parliament would be responsible for awarding the Peace Prize had repercussions on the tense and fragile relationship between Sweden and Norway, which at around this time was in the final stages of the process leading to dissolution of the union between the two countries. "Unpatriotic," said the king, who was so angry that he intervened and asked Nobel's relatives to do their best to quash the will.

The will raised a major practical question: Considering Nobel's nomadic life, which country was the correct venue for settlement of his estate? In some countries, the deceased's citizenship determines where the settlement of an estate takes place; in other countries, it is the last place of residence. Nobel had owned homes in five countries, but what did he really call home? This confusion could have huge consequences. How could one decide which country had the authority, the jurisdiction, to settle the estate?

Alfred Nobel had grown up in Sweden and lived there until he was nine years old. That was when his father, an architect, engineer, and weapons designer, went bankrupt, and the whole family moved to Russia, where the father helped the czar in producing land mines. Subsequently, Nobel never lived in Sweden for any length of time, but he always remained a Swedish citizen. He died in Italy, but he had been able to afford a series of estates all around Europe. He shuttled between his various homes: a large villa in the center of Paris, another in San Remo in Italy, the Björkborn manor in Bofors, Sweden, as well as smaller houses in Laurieston, Scotland, and Krümmel, Germany. All of these properties had laboratories or were located near factories he owned or developed. There was a yearly pattern in the way he circulated among the homes: he spent a few months in one house before he moved to the next, motivated by work and climate—and by his health, which was fragile all his life. He suffered from depression and had a weak heart during the last decade of his life.

The will would turn out to be somewhat incomplete. It called for Nobel's assets to be sold and a fund established. It went on to describe the five prizes and the purpose of each, and who would be authorized to confer them, but it provided few answers to important practical and administrative questions. Much was unclear about how the yearly prizes would be awarded. Nothing was said about organizational structure or how the money was to be managed. The quick sale of everything Nobel owned—factories, villas, patents, and other assets—affected many people and interest groups, and it created uncertainty and alarm. Several of Nobel's relatives ran into trouble when Nobel's investments in their joint ventures had to be supplemented with fresh capital at short notice.

A lot of people turn up when there's money to be had. Before long, a crowd of lawyers was on hand. People came with suggestions, wishes, and claims, and several lawsuits were threatened. Demands from officials, relatives, employees, business partners, and other interested parties made for a uniquely complicated challenge. And the answers involved different countries and legal systems. Even a legal expert in international business and estate settlement would have faced the challenge of his lifetime in the effort to rescue assets for the planned prizes, securing a surplus and avoiding an endless series of legal actions.

Yet it was not a first-class lawyer who had been entrusted with responsibility for putting into effect Nobel's last will. Nobel had decided to rely on two very young engineers. The main responsibility was laid on the shoulders of a co-worker Nobel had known for only a few years, Ragnar Sohlman. Born in 1870, he was only 25 years old in 1895, when the will was written. An industrial empire was about to be liquidated. There would be negotiations with powerful people in financial circles, with states, kings, and parliaments, and arrangements had to be made with everyone who had more or less justified demands and expectations.

Nobel was competent in many fields, but he had been forced to spend a little too much time on trials and attorneys over the years. This was probably the reason he did not involve himself with attorneys when he wrote his will, which could have easily spoiled his plan for the prizes. He had failed to check whether the five authorities that he had chosen to confer the prizes were willing to take on the task. A rejection, just one, could have invalidated the will. What was lacking was an existent foundation or legal person that could receive proceeds from the sales and manage the assets. A legal entity had to be established first—and rules had to be laid down for it and for the prizes. A settlement in France could have invalidated the will. The prizes also could have been lost if Nobel had overestimated Sohlman's abilities.

How gigantic the challenges were, and how superbly Sohlman met them, is a story full of excitement. After a few years in Nobel's employ in different parts of Europe, Sohlman returned home to Sweden to manage the estate, but he was summoned immediately for military service—and not excused—due to the military tension building up between Sweden and Norway a few years before the breakup of the union in 1905. Sohlman, however, was able to negotiate special arrangements. He was allowed to rent three rooms in a private home within the military camp to be used as offices for himself, a bookkeeper, and an office manager, so that he was able to administer the Nobel estate in his spare time. The regiment had just one telephone. It was reserved for officers, but soldier Sohlman was constantly called to the phone for talks with bank managers in Paris, London, and Stockholm, and with cabinet ministers and other people of high standing. The need to áct, and act vigorously, is evident from his own account:[3]

> *My immediate return to Paris was necessitated by telegrams and letters from Consul General Nordling, informing us that Hjalmar and Ludvig Nobel and Count Carl Gustaf Ridderstolpe, an in-law, had arrived in Paris to investigate the situation with a view to a possible court action against the will.*
>
> *Immediately after my arrival we therefore began to transfer the Nobel securities from the bank in Paris, partly to London and partly to Stockholm . . . in insured postal packages, which had to be presented at a special Expédition des Finances at the Gare du Nord . . . Securities to the value of not more than the above [insurance limit] of two and a half million francs were then withdrawn daily for a week from the vaults of the bank and taken to the Consulate General's office where they were listed, tied up in bundles, wrapped up and sealed. In the afternoon they were taken to the Gare du Nord . . . Since the actual transfers to and from the Consulate General involved certain risks of hold-ups and robberies, special precautions were taken and care was exercised to avoid attention . . . after the securities had been packed in a suitcase we took an ordinary horse-cab first to the Consulate General, then to the Gare du Nord. With a loaded revolver in my hand I sat in the cab prepared to defend the suitcase in case a collision with another carriage had been arranged by robbers—at that time not an unusual occurrence in Paris.*

It would have been easiest for Sohlman to ask the banks to send the stocks and bonds in the usual manner, but he feared this would attract attention and potential trouble, for example, with the French tax authorities, who were interested in inheritance tax on the assets in France. In a bold maneuver, Sohlman had managed to outsmart both France and the heirs. When Nobel's relatives invited Sohlman to dinner to try to convince him that Paris was Nobel's home and the right place for an estate settlement, they were in for a surprise. The relatives could hardly believe their own ears when they were informed that a lawsuit in France would be a waste of time: the stocks and bonds were no longer there.

French lawyers for the relatives regretted bitterly that they had not impounded the stocks and bonds in time.[4] Sohlman's course of action may seem both brazen and cunning, but he explained why he had a clear conscience—that is, if the issue was decided in favor of France in a French court, France would tax the estate, and the relatives would succeed in invalidating the will on the basis of strict rules in French inheritance law. It was entirely clear to Sohlman that Nobel had not foreseen the possibility of such an outcome. He had written the will in Swedish, used two Swedish engineers as witnesses, named two other Swedish engineers as executors, and had asked Swedish and Norwegian institutions to take responsibility for conferring the prizes. In conclusion, Sohlman wrote:

> Had [Nobel] in any way conceived that the house in Paris could be viewed as his legal domicile, he would have shipped the stocks and bonds out of the country, just as we did. While he was alive, he constantly transferred the stocks and bonds from one place to another.

THE FOUNDATION IS ESTABLISHED

These episodes tell us a lot about Sohlman's efficiency, intelligence, and initiative. He had the ability to see what was essential, to cut through to the core. No doubt he deserves much of the credit for the fact that the assets were not eaten up by lawsuits and attorneys' fees. One of the most important steps he took was to show great generosity and thereby settle all the various disputes. The estate employed good lawyers, but they were held tightly in check and had to yield to Sohlman, who preferred a moderately expensive settlement to a very costly trial.

Sweden's King Oscar II did more than just be unexcited about the will; he disliked it so much that he supported the fiery campaign mounted by Swedish media. The Nobel family tried to quash the will and reach a settlement where the funds would be divided among the family and the four Swedish institutions mentioned in the will. The Peace Prize was the most endangered. It was a thorn in the eye to Swedes who thought the funds ought to be used to promote Swedish culture and science, not be placed in the hands of a committee appointed by Norway's Parliament. This, it was claimed, would hurt Swedish interests and the relationship with Norway.[5]

At one point, the King summoned Alfred Nobel's nephew, Emanuel Nobel, to the royal palace to ask the family to help get his uncle's will annulled. Especially unfortunate was the Peace Prize, which, according to the king, would lead only to problems and controversies: "Your uncle has come under the influence of visionaries and especially of women [sic]." But Emanuel answered, "Your Majesty, I do not want to submit my brothers and sisters to eminent scientists upbraiding us for taking money that should have gone to them."[6] After the hearing, when Emanuel told his lawyer that he had refused to help the king, the lawyer insisted that they leave Stockholm before nightfall to save their lives. The lawyer was Russian; his fear says a lot about life under the czar.

Emanuel Nobel would come to play a decisive role in the outcome. He vigorously opposed any attempt by the family to thwart his uncle's last wishes, and as a result, a settlement was reached between the family and the will administrator. The relatives of Alfred had nothing to complain about: both of Alfred's brothers had earned fortunes from their businesses and their children were left considerable sums of money in the will, and they received an extra million Swedish crowns when they agreed to accept the terms of the will.

What in the end convinced the French authorities to accept Swedish jurisdiction over the estate, the factor that especially impressed the French judges, was that Nobel had transferred his saddle horses to Sweden shortly before he died.[7]

As a result of the estate managers' negotiations with Nobel's heirs, with the institutions that would confer the prizes, and with the Swedish authorities, a foundation was set up and its Basic Statutes (*Grundstadgar*) were approved by all parties and by the king. In the opening words, this document states the goal of the foundation—it repeats the will's wording concerning the prizes—and in addition notes that the relatives have renounced any further demands, and any attempt to influence the management of the Nobel Foundation, on the following conditions: (1) the procedural rules for conferring the prizes are followed, (2) all the prizes are conferred at least once every five years, (3) the prizes must be for at least 60 percent of the sum the committees have at their disposal, and (4) each prize is not shared among more than three recipients. It is not permitted to file a challenge against decisions to confer a prize, and the committees are not allowed to lodge dissenting views.

As of 2009, Nobel prizes have been awarded to a total of 761 people and 20 organizations. Some of them received a Nobel prize more than once. Since 1969, the Nobel Foundation has treated an economics prize instituted in 1968 by the Swedish central bank in memory of Nobel as a regular Nobel prize, but these 41 quasi-Nobel prizes have not been included here. The five prizes have been withheld only 49 times, mainly during and to some extent between the two world wars. Presumably as a result of its political nature, the Peace Prize has been withheld more often than the others, a total of 19 times, but only six times in the 60 years after 1948, and never after 1972.

Many important and useful inventions are linked to Nobel's name: weapons, explosives, and gunpowder make up a considerable part. For him personally these creations must have been accompanied by thoughts and second thoughts about his responsibility as an inventor, out of a genuine wish to contribute to a better world. It is scarcely an exaggeration to say that his last "invention"—the Nobel prizes—is in this respect his very best. The prizes are discussed year-round, around the world, including the awards themselves, those who receive them, those who may receive them, and those who should have received them. Media coverage is enormous, and the prizes are analyzed in books and articles. To a degree seldom seen, the prizes and the name *Nobel* have become an established international institution.

We have, accordingly, a lot to thank Nobel for. But the Nobel Foundation's financial managers also deserve gratitude for their success in defending the monetary value of the prizes through changing times. (Much of the considerable loss during the economic crisis in 2008 was recovered in 2009).

Over the years, the Norwegian Nobel committee, its secretaries, and advisers have succeeded in securing for the Peace Prize a unique reputation. The laureates constitute a rare selection of impressive men and women. Ideas, visions, valuable experiences, and hopes for the future are conveyed during the ceremonies, both in speeches praising the prize winners and in their own speeches—the statutes call them Nobel *lec-tures*. All this can be gleaned from books and anthologies and, in recent years, from the Internet.[8] Together, it constitutes a unique and invaluable wealth of effort and achievement, a highpoint in international culture.

Through his prizes, and above all the Peace Prize, Nobel is still at work worldwide, more than 110 years after his death. At least that is what we are told. But how true to Nobel are the prizes bearing his name? Questions have been raised regarding all five prizes, but not one has been as persistently controversial as the Peace Prize. And yet, surprisingly, one issue seems never to have been addressed, even if it is of pivotal consequence: the will as a legal instrument. A study in the light of law reveals fundamental flaws and discrepancies between Nobel's intention and what has become of the Peace Prize, which in our time belongs to Nobel only in name.

Chapter 3

INTERPRETING NOBEL'S WILL

WHAT DID NOBEL INTEND IN 1895?

More than 100 years have passed since Nobel wrote his testament, and it is necessary to examine what consequences the enormous changes in the world may have for the Peace Prize. The task of the Nobel committee is, today as one century ago, to carry out Nobel's intentions with the will. This makes it mandatory, first to examine what Nobel actually had in mind that autumn day in 1895, when he signed his will at the Swedish-Norwegian club in Paris, in the presence of two Swedish engineers who attested his signature. Next we have to examine whether, and how, his intentions for the Peace Prize can be realized in the 21st century.

A will is a legal instrument subject to a comprehensive system of principles and binding law that regulate its interpretation and implementation. The execution of estates is guided by the *dead hand*, a legal expression reminding us that the text cannot be rewritten or changed.

What are the implications of this for the Norwegian Nobel committee? The committee and its members are obliged to understand and implement the law pertaining to wills. If uncertain about mandate and applicable rules, a cautious trustee should consult lawyers. What, then, will a lawyer say about the Nobel testament and its interpretation? Would his or her opinion be definite or uncertain? Would it make the will difficult to implement?

What the common reader perceives as a reasonable, natural, and useful or meaningful understanding is normally a good point of departure. Whether the testator writes the will with or without the help of a lawyer, the intention has been—as much as possible—to use unambiguous and clear language.

Most often the testator will have succeeded in finding words that give a precise and adequate description of his intentions regarding the estate. The intention of the testator is the primary point in the interpretation of wills. The text should be read with one single thought in mind, that is, what the testator intended at the time the words were written. In cases in which it can be proved that the text does not conform to the intention of the testator, his thoughts may override a normal reading of the words used. In Nobel's case, however, both the circumstances surrounding the will and its history provide strong evidence that the words used conform to the intention of Nobel. The words adequately reflect the content of the will and are binding for posterity.

This is the elementary law of testaments. The word *will* is simply a precise linguistic expression of the very idea of the document. In Norway, as elsewhere, the purpose of the document is to express the intention, resolution, and wish of the testator. In his book on Norwegian inheritance law, Norway's leading authority on the subject, Professor Ragnar Knoph, wrote:

> [T]he interpretation of wills shall be entirely subjective and in eminent degree individual; what shall apply is what *this* testator meant in *this* situation by *these* words in *this* connection. [Emphasis in original.][1]

This fundamental rule on the interpretation of testaments is just as valid today, and it has been confirmed and quoted in later textbooks, for instance in Professor Peter Lødrup's textbook on inheritance law.[2]

The will

Nobel's last testament was dated and signed on November 27, 1895, in the presence of two witnesses. It was drawn up in Swedish, which was by no means a given. Nobel could just as well have expressed himself in French, German, English, Russian, or Italian. The part establishing the Peace Prize had this wording:

> [O]one part to *the person* who shall have done the most or the best work *for brotherhood between nations, for the abolition or reduction of standing armies and for the holding and promotion of peace congresses.* [Official translation by the Nobel Foundation, Stockholm. Emphasis added.]

As a point of departure, it is opportune to note that for the Peace Prize Nobel made use of three expressions: *brotherhood, disarmament,* and *peace congresses*. This interpretation must address a time dimension with two components. First, we must ascertain Nobel's precise individual and subjective meaning, that is, find out what was on his mind that late November day in 1895. Second, his ideas have to be translated from 1895 to the present time. In addition, non-Swedish audiences will need translation from the Swedish original text into other languages.

The general background offers immediate and important clues, helpful to the understanding of what *this testator* had in mind. One has to consider the man and the character: Alfred Nobel himself; his international life; his originality, inventiveness, and creative power; and his optimistic belief in the future. The time he lived in is part of the picture of the man—typical of *la belle époque* were great inventions and a strong belief that ideas can change and improve the world. Nobel possessed both the will and the courage to embark on big projects. Above all, Nobel was an internationalist, at home in the world rather than in any single state. In a letter he wrote, "My home is where I work, and I work everywhere."

The international orientation of Nobel is the key to understanding his Peace Prize. He wished to confront the nationalism prevalent in the era.[3] Without this perspective, his way of relating to the world as a whole, it is difficult to see any realism in his vision for peace. Military forces are the creation of individual states and can appear rational and defensible only from the perspective of states that find themselves trapped in a tradition of competitive power struggles.

Those who think only within the scope of the nation state, and take international power play for a given and forever unchangeable fact, will consider disarmament a complete impossibility. Nobel did not view the world from the perspective of a frog, but rather of a bird: as a system for the world armaments and national military forces make little sense. The law of the jungle is not a recipe for a secure and functioning international system. This was Nobel's outlook, and it coincided with the central ideas of the peace movement of the era. Because this view squares well with the concepts he chose to express his intentions, his internationalist mind-set should direct our reading of the will.

Then there are *these words*. One must consider the words Nobel used in 1895 in the light of Swedish usage at the time. Even more important, however, is Nobel's own usage and his ideas, interests, and concerns at the time he wrote the will.

Another factor mentioned by Knoph is *this connection*, the general situation circumscribing the Peace Prize. Here there are important circumstances to consider. The Peace Prize is one of five prizes for which the common denominator is a desire to change and improve the plight of humanity. The prizes in medicine, physics, and chemistry reflect the optimistic spirit of the time—that progress and great discoveries would be a blessing for humankind—and the prize for literature reflect a belief that authors could contribute in charting the course forward.

Thus all five prizes have the same elevated purpose: Nobel wished to serve humanity and improve the world through great inventions and important, useful, and fresh insights. Laureates should not only have cultivated their garden with care, they also ought to have broken new ground, have been innovative, or have shown the road to progress and improvement. Like the four other prizes, the Peace Prize should be given to persons who had *conferred the greatest benefit on mankind* in the field of abolishing armaments and wars.

To understand the mental universe of Nobel, it is essential to be aware that in his time world peace was a much less remote dream than it is in the 21st century; an end to militarism was written about and discussed, and it involved wider society (both for and against). The cause of peace had many supporters in parliaments and governments, and huge peace congresses were organized to transform the dream into reality. As late as 1920, the Swedish minister of war, Per Albin Hansson, emphasized that he was not a militarist, "and I have no intention of becoming one. I intend to remain a champion of disarmament, and I consider the abolition of armaments not a remote dream but something for which one should work honestly, energetically, and incessantly."[4]

Nobel's three criteria for the Peace Prize

Nobel expressed his idea of the greatest benefits for mankind in the different fields he wished his prizes to cover with the words *invention* and *improvement* for the science prizes and *in idealistic direction* for the literature prize. In the area of peace, Nobel makes use of three expressions: *brotherhood among nations, abolition or reduction of military forces* (*stående armeer*—standing armies—is the term he used in Swedish), and promoting *peace congresses*. It is not enough to interpret each of these criteria separately; one also should consider that they may be interconnected and must be read as a whole.

With the term *peace congresses* (*fredskongresser* in Swedish) Nobel obviously is referring to the great gatherings that started in the 1890s to achieve a better-organized world, replacing military force and power intrigues with trust, cooperation, and binding international law. At the time, efforts for lasting peace flourished as never before. In the early 1890s, the International Peace Bureau and the Inter-Parliamentary Union had been established; the will was written three years after the (privately organized) peace congress in Bern, Switzerland, in 1892, and four years before the (official) peace congress at The Hague in the Netherlands in 1899.

These early peace congresses envisaged law and disarmament as ways to avoid wars—the peace movement sought fundamental change and improvement in international relations. Through international law and justice, the peace congresses wished to create a new world order of trust that would make armaments and wars obsolete.

But fierce opposition surfaced against this road toward security. Here is one description of the 1899 conference:

> In the debate on ending armaments two world views were clearly exposed: Those who believed in the road of trust and cooperation were opposing those praising the old belief that nothing other than weapons can solve international conflicts. This latter category did their best to sabotage the deliberations.[5]

The concept "standing armies" Nobel used is a typical example in which the two words Nobel actually used must be read in the light of the language, the discussion, and realities of the time. The issue at the time was whether military forces should be "standing" or "on call." By wishing abolition of *standing armies* Nobel rejected the idea of a permanent military institution as part of societies. This idea, of course, also covers the later advent of air forces, missiles, space weapons.

As long as military forces and weapons exist, risk is always present. Abuse, human error, system error, and accidents may unleash a major war. Nobel was familiar with the vision of the peace movement—that the greatest progress for mankind was to be rescued from the scourge of militarism and wars. There is no reason to believe that Nobel had lesser ambitions when he—in response to constant urging from people within the same peace movement—established his Peace Prize.

There were then, as there always are, two fundamentally different ways to approach peace and security, two competing political ideas, two totally opposite approaches, the choice of one excluding the other. A basic, momentous fact is this: *In making his will, Nobel took a position and chose one of the two sides. He wished to see disarmament replace military power games.* This is a fundamental, determining feature of his prize for peace.

Brotherhood among nations—the best translation?

The third expression Nobel used—"brotherhood among nations" (*folkens förbrödrande*)—seems to square well with the two other criteria (disarmament and peace congresses). Neither in 1895 nor in our time will demilitarization be possible without good international relations, where nations unite in mutual trust to create a better-organized world.

Unfortunately the *brotherhood* criterion seems to have presented the Nobel committees with irresistible temptation. Increasingly, it has been used to justify rewarding anything that is good and kind and can help to make the world a better place. A recent example occurred when the committee chair, Ole Danbolt Mjøs, in defending the shared Al Gore/ IPCC environment prizes of 2007, read "brotherhood" as meaning "that we must survive on the planet . . . this must be the most important form of brotherhood or sisterhood . . . this is a broad category."[6] Explaining his personal 2007 usage, without concern for what Nobel must have had in mind, Mjøs revealed a lack of elementary insight into his legal responsibility as custodian of the will.

Nobel wished for a brotherhood of *folken*, clearly meaning "nations" (as in *Folkeforbundet* the League of Nations). "Peoples" is preferred by Irwin Abrams, the leading international authority on the history of the Peace Prize,[7] but "nations" is the word used in English by the Nobel Foundation. What was this "brotherhood" that Nobel wished to emerge among "nations"? Like the other four Nobel prizes, the aim was to stimulate major leaps in civilization—that is, fundamental changes in the international system not just the less specific "friendship and kindness between people."

The interpreter should step into the shoes of Nobel and ask what he most probably wished to express by "brotherhood among nations" and the inescapable answer is this: At the end of the 19th century, Nobel, disgusted by the cost of armaments and the destruction and suffering in recurring wars, wished for a completely new kind of brotherhood, a fundamental reform of the way nations relate to each other—they must cooperate, unite, and stop fighting wars.

This view is amply confirmed in a peace history book by the Swedish author and peace activist P. A. Fogelström.[8] The book shows Swedish usage around the former turn of the century and how the three Nobel criteria are the overriding themes in the history of the peace movement. For example, in 1893, a broad alliance of people petitioned the Swedish king, cabinet, and parliament to build the security of nations on international law and take every opportunity to enter into agreements on mandatory arbitration, that is, submitting differences to a neutral, impartial umpire. In all disputes between "Sweden and other civilized states" the ideas of peace should be promoted rather than continuing to be weighed down by the "increasingly costly military burdens."[9]

Without a doubt, *brotherhood* and a new system of international justice at the time were linked with disarmament. One of many examples of this is found in Fogelström's account of the World Peace Congress in Sweden in 1910. The congress wanted

> immediate and considerable alleviation, and in the near future complete abolition, of the insufferable burdens of the war machinery, to the benefit of the culture and the brotherhood of humanity, inasmuch as the legal aspects of the international relations between the states of Europe had now fundamentally been solved through the court of arbitration at The Hague and established treaties on arbitration.[10]

In 2008, British historian Douglas Bulloch published an article analyzing Nobel's will, his concept of peace, and the policy of the Nobel committee. Discussions of Nobel's three criteria have been rare. Although he introduces interesting perspectives, Bulloch does not seem overly concerned with precisely what Nobel had in mind when he sees the three criteria as no more than "help . . . to get some idea of" what Nobel might have understood by the concept of peace.[11] To Bulloch "fraternity between nations . . . [evokes] a system of norms by which to arbitrate disputes between states impartially." This seems too modest. We have to presume that Nobel had in mind a more fundamental change of the international political-military system.

Considering whether the translation of the Swedish expression *folkens förbrödrande* into English, should use "between nations" (as the Nobel Foundation and the Norwegian committee do) or "among nations," I concluded that the latter must be the better solution, since *between* points more to a situation between two. Then I rejected both, having discovered that "*of* nations" would be closer to the genitive "s" that Nobel used.

Next came a bigger surprise. The official translation into English, *fraternity,* seems to miss an important aspect. The Swedish word *förbrödrande* is not, like brotherhood or fraternity, about something existing, it is either about *change* or the *result of change.* The distinction between *fraternity* and *fraternization* exists in all Latin languages. In the three Scandinavian languages it is *broderskap* and *förbrödrande,* and in German we have *Bruderschaft* and *Verbrüderung.*[12]

The English expression "fraternizing with the enemy" has a derogatory meaning, but the *Oxford Dictionary* defines "fraternize" as to "form a friendship with someone, especially when one is not supposed to." The word "confraternization" is further described as "fraternization together, recognition of each other as brethren." Pointing to change, not just reinforcing a preexisting condition, the word seems to have the right associations. In the 21st century, "confraternization" sounds odd in English, but it was in use in the 19th century,[13] and thus it seems ideal for the translation of an 1895 document. It will be used in this book.

Three criteria make organic whole

Nobel seems to have written the will in solitude. The help to interpret it that can be gleaned from circumstances around the final will of 1895 is limited to comparison with two wills Nobel had written two years earlier, and to the testimony of the two Swedes who witnessed the signing in 1895. But we have the text itself, and ample context and history, which together justify reading the three criteria as being both interconnected and making an organic whole.

One point in favor of reading the three criteria as parts of a whole can be found in the conjunctions Nobel used. He chose the words "and" and "plus," writing, "worked the most and best for (A, confraternization) *and* (B, disarmament) *plus* (C, peace congresses)." Between the three criteria Nobel did not use "or" (A or B or C), which would have made the three criteria more independent—but not mutually exclusive.

No one seems to have entertained the idea that Nobel, by using the words "and" and "plus," meant to require that laureates must have shown merit in all three criteria. Still, a reading of the three terms as a whole makes them more understandable and meaningful; the three criteria shed light on, and get meaning from, each other. Such a reading is strongly indicated by the fact that together they reflect the program of the peace movement in 1895.

Fortunately, it is not for us to speculate whether *we* see links and connections between the words used in the will, the task is to find out how Nobel saw this, what he may reasonably or likely have intended. As a matter of fact, the three criteria together form a holistic program for a new and demilitarized world order, the words together are a clear reflection of the program of the peace movement, and without a doubt this was Nobel's intention.

The following section on Bertha von Suttner will show how closely the three criteria are interrelated. Also the word *confraternization* cannot be given a free and modern interpretation, it must be read and understood in light of the platform and program of the peace movement of the 1890s.

Bertha von Suttner

In his textbook on inheritance law, Professor Ragnar Knoph underlined the fact that interpretation of the language used in wills aims to find the true meaning of the words, but then he qualified his statement:

> In themselves, however, words have no meaning whatsoever. They can only get their meaning as symbols for the thoughts, conceptions and feelings that the user attaches to them in his mind. To construe the content of these symbols is to understand them and reproduce them with the help of other, known, symbols; that is the task of the interpreter.[14]

As a consequence, we have every reason to take a closer look at Suttner and whether the prize resulted from her entreaties for financial support. Her hope clearly was that Nobel would leave a substantial amount for her work. An earlier will in 1893 included a legacy of 1 percent of the total estate to Suttner's Austrian peace society, which in the final 1895 will became instead a prize for "the abolition or reduction of armies."

The tireless work of Suttner (1843–1914) in the last three decades of her life sought an end to the war games and the shifting alliances of monarchs that had tormented Europe during the 19th century. The honor and glory for rulers and officers concealed unspeakable suffering, death, and misery on the battlefield. In 1876, Bertha von Suttner, her last name still Kinsky, worked for Nobel in Paris. In the week that they spent together, she learned to appreciate his attitudes and to enjoy discussing the world with him.

Nobel had appointed her to serve him as secretary and housekeeper, but he also may have entertained a hope that he finally had found the woman in his life. She, however, had to answer him that her heart was not free. After only a week of service, Nobel had to leave Paris for an urgent business matter in Sweden, and just a few days later Bertha Kinsky, selling a piece of jewelry to pay the hotel bill, also left Paris and the planned work for Nobel to marry Arthur von Suttner in secret and flee from his family, which was opposed to the *mésalliance*.[15]

Nevertheless, a lasting friendship with Nobel had been established; the two kept corresponding for the two decades that passed between their first encounter and the death of Nobel. Toward the end of Nobel's life Suttner made him seriously interested in the cause of peace, but it would be wrong to say that she introduced the theme to him. On the contrary, Nobel had had to relate to dilemmas of war and peace since childhood, when his father was arms constructor to the Russian czar, and he had conceived many of his inventions in the military field.

Swedish Nobel historian Henrik Schück, in *Nobel: The Man and His Prizes,* describing Nobel's lifelong interest in peace points to his fancy for the English poet Percy Bysshe Shelley in his younger years. Schück—finding the pacifist ideas of Nobel unrealistic—seems to have wished to reduce the influence Suttner had had on the will, but all he achieves is to confirm how, to Nobel, peace was a lifelong concern.

Nobel having sowed the seed, Suttner gradually developed an interest in the cause. During the 1880s, it grew to an intense, burning devotion and she became the era's leading champion of peace. Now it was she who put pressure on Nobel to do more for the cause. To someone wishing to map Nobel's *thoughts, views, conceptions, and feelings* (according to Knoph the key factors to determine the content of a will) nothing is more enlightening than his friendship and correspondence with Suttner.

Her book *Die Waffen nieder!* (*Lay Down Your Arms,* 1889), a scathing criticism of the military, and the wars and power intrigues between powerful nations, became one of the greatest international bestsellers of the 19th century. In April 1890, Nobel wrote an enthusiastic letter to thank Suttner for her book: "It is said that there are two thousand languages . . . but surely your remarkable work must be translated into all of them. It ought to be read and reflected upon by each and everyone." And Nobel looked forward to "the honor and the pleasure to press your hand in mine—the hand of an amazon who so valiantly wages war against war."

Figure 3.1 Bertha von Suttner, c. 1890. (© The Nobel Foundation.)

Not only do the three criteria make up the nucleus of the 1890s peace movement program; Suttner had discussed them with Nobel in a number of letters. He created the prize *in response to Suttner's intense appeals* and Nobel immediately informed her when he had written his will in 1895. Suttner responded with enthusiasm: "Whether or not I am still alive by then does not matter; what you and I have given will live on."

This exchange is of momentous importance to determine the character of the Peace Prize. One could just as well say that this is the "Lay Down Your Arms Prize," Its most distinctive content, the part that had made Nobel hesitate for so long before taking the step, can be summed up in one word: disarmament. The preconditions for this to happen—a new level of international law and order, cooperation, and trust—are formulated through the two other expressions he used: "confraternization" and "peace congresses."

Where did the uncertainty over Nobel's intent come from?

In their correspondence, Nobel and Suttner grappled with ideas on how to bring about world peace. Once, when the baroness had told Nobel that his dynamite factories were not entirely innocent, Nobel replied, "Perhaps my factories will put an end to wars sooner than your congresses; on the day when two army corps may mutually annihilate each other in a second, probably all civilized nations will recoil with horror and disband their troops."[16]

From time to time, the Nobel *apparatchiks* have invoked this and similar statements from Nobel as proof that his attitudes were unstable and changing; he never could decide on the best course to end war. Nobel may have had moral qualms over his inventions of new and more potent explosives for military use, such as *ballistit*, a type of "slow dynamite" that gives high exit speed with lower pressure in the barrel, thus making it possible to reduce the weight of firearms considerably. Again and again, Nobel fantasized about a weapon so strong and dangerous that it would put an end to war.

It is, indeed, a fact that for all the numerous ideas on peace over the span of his life, and however fascinated by the ideas of Suttner, it took Nobel several years to embrace the visions of the peace movement. In conversations and letters, he expressed doubts about the peace movement's chances of success, and he wished to be reassured that the movement had a serious, viable program.

When it comes to interpreting his will, however, this mixed picture is not a difficulty. What counts is the will, not his earlier vacillations. It is Nobel's intentions at the exact point in his life when he drew up and signed his 1895 will that have to be respected. The pivotal nature of wills is reflected in the strict requirements of form that must be met. A valid testament requires almost a small ceremony. The personal signature of the testator, in the presence of two witnesses who must cosign the document, creates awareness that the period of deliberation is over, that this is a serious and decisive moment, outside and above everyday discussion and reflection.

As a result, what counts in the final analysis is not the many shifting and contradictory utterances from Nobel during his lifetime. The will is conclusive evidence that Suttner had managed to convince Nobel to "do something" for the peace movement. He did overcome his doubts

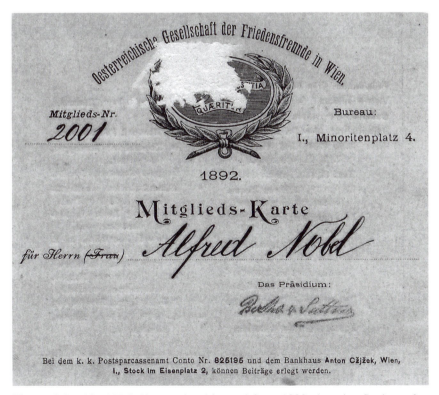

Figure 3.2 Alfred Nobel's membership card from 1892, Austrian Society of Friends of Peace. (© The Nobel Foundation.)

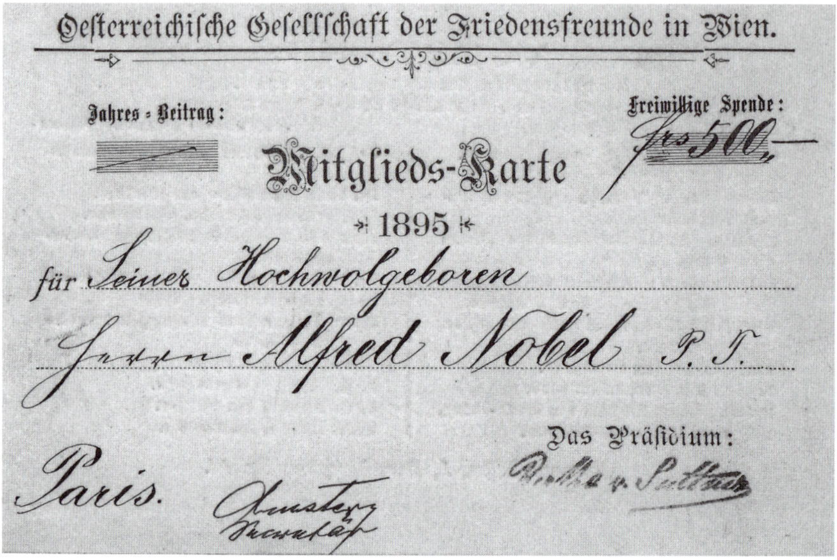
Oesterreichische Gesellschaft der Friedensfreunde in Wien.

Jahres-Beitrag: Freiwillige Spende: Frs 500,–

Mitglieds-Karte

1895

für Seiner Hochwolgeboren

Herrn Alfred Nobel P.T.

Das Präsidium:

Paris.

Figure 3.3 Alfred Nobel's membership card from 1895, Austrian Society of Friends of Peace. (Courtesy of The Swedish National Archives.)

and concluded that the ideas of Suttner and the peace movement were realistic enough to make it worth making money available. Nobel's intention was to enable the peace ideas and movement to grow. This wish, not altered or revoked before his death, is legally binding for all posterity.

The various thoughts that Nobel expressed before and after the testament may be of some interest, or help, to get a fuller picture of his intentions, but only as supplement, not to alter the basic purpose on which he settled. One example: On several occasions, Nobel expressed a wish that his money should become useful as financial support for the future work of the peace movement, and more generally he told the two witnesses that he wished to "give promising persons such complete independence that they would in the future be able to devote their whole energies to the work."[17]

Abrams, who has studied the Nobel Peace Prize since 1937, is of the opinion that Nobel was worried the prize could end up with people who would use it as a golden opportunity to stop working: "On the other hand I wish to help the dreamers, as they find it difficult to get on in life."[18]

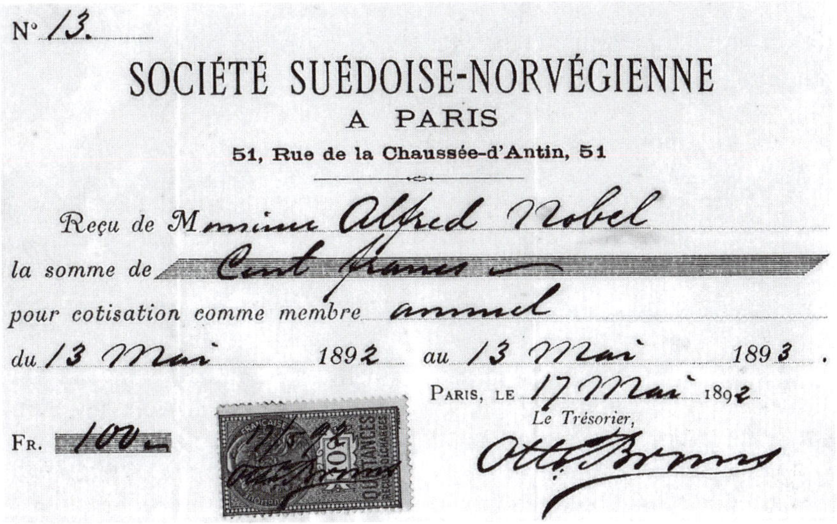

N° 13.

SOCIÉTÉ SUÉDOISE-NORVÉGIENNE

A PARIS

51, Rue de la Chaussée-d'Antin, 51

Reçu de Monsieur Alfred Nobel

la somme de Cent francs

pour cotisation comme membre annuel

du 13 Mai 1892 au 13 Mai 1893.

Paris, le 17 Mai 1892

Le Trésorier,

Fr. 100

Figure 3.4 Alfred Nobel's membership card, Swedish-Norwegian Club, Paris. (© The Nobel Foundation.)

Nobel used friends in the Swedish-Norwegian Club in Paris, two young Swedish engineers, to serve as witnesses to the will. They remembered Nobel's strong wish to facilitate the lives of dreamers,

> those noble and idealistic poets and inventors whose high promise is so often lost because they are impractical and without means. Nobel had spoken of lightening the everyday burdens for these creative souls, so they could make the contribution of which they were capable.[19]

The witnesses found it necessary to voice a public protest in 1914. In the press, they objected to the direction the prizes had taken, with many prizes being awarded to people who were already famous.[20]

The statement that Nobel wished to support dreamers is not easy to reconcile with the strong elitism inherent in his will, mentioning those who had "*done the most and the best work*" Abrams feels that the prizes, contrary to Nobel's original intention, have not been used as much to encourage future work for peace and disarmament as Nobel would have hoped; many of the recipients have not needed the money and have given it away—the prizes serving to make them philanthropists rather than being used to fund their own service to mankind.[21]

With little doubt, it was important to Nobel that the Peace Prize would stimulate further work for peace by being a useful source of financing.

Why Norway?

The three criteria laid out in the will (confraternization, disarmament, and peace congresses) are sufficient proof of the nature of the peace work Nobel wished to support. But incisive study of the text of the will lays bare two additional circumstances that remove any trace of doubt:

> The prizes for physics and chemistry shall be awarded by the Swedish Academy of Sciences; that for physiological or medical works by the Karolinska Institutet in Stockholm; that for literature by the Academy in Stockholm, and that *for champions of peace* by a committee of five persons to be elected by the Norwegian *Storting*. It is my express wish that in awarding the prizes no consideration whatever shall be given to the nationality of the candidates, but that the most worthy shall receive the prize, whether he be a Scandinavian or not. [Emphasis added.]

What can have been Nobel's motive when he chose to leave it to the Parliament of Norway to elect a Nobel committee that would award the Peace Prize? Much speculation has surrounded this question, with different suppositions—for instance, that Norway at the time still was in union with Sweden, and should have a role in his plan for the prizes; and that he admired the famous Norwegian writer and champion of peace Bjørnstjerne Bjørnson, as well as Norwegian literature.

But no one seems to have seen the most obvious answer to the question: What must the main concern of Nobel himself have been? His need was to find trustee/s who would ensure that the purpose of the will could be fulfilled far into the future.

Why then might the Parliament of Norway be entrusted with a prize against militarism? The reasons were there—in ample measure. The Norwegian Parliament at the time, with the liberals (*Venstre*) as the dominating party, was in the vanguard of European parliaments actively promoting the peace policies of the period.[22]

In those years of increasing friction in the union between Norway and Sweden, *Stortinget* advocated arbitration of disputes between states to replace wars. Norway had been one of the first countries to allocate money to the peace movement—for instance, to the International Peace Bureau (IPB).

In the first years, nobody seems to have been in doubt and both *Stortinget* and the Nobel committee knew very well that Nobel had chosen Norway for its reputation as a leading protagonist of peace ideas. Announcing the first two Nobel Peace Prizes, in Parliament on December 10, 1901, President Carl Christian Berner spoke of Norway as a country and a people with a strong wish for peace, adding:

> At various times *Stortinget* has gone on record in favor of the signing of peace and arbitration treaties with foreign powers, in order to prevent settlement of possible disputes by armed force and to ensure just solutions through peaceful means. We may well believe that this need which motivates the Norwegian people, this ardent desire for peace and good relations among nations, is what influenced Dr. Alfred Nobel to entrust to the parliament of Norway the important responsibility of awarding the prize, through a committee of five.[23]

Similarly, during the ceremony in Parliament on December 10, 1906, President Gunnar Knudsen) expressed the following opinion:

> [I]t is appropriate to recall that the Norwegian parliament was one of the first national assemblies to adopt and to support the cause of peace. The cause of peace, gentlemen, looked very different 10 years ago than it does today. Peace was looked upon as a utopia, and the champions of peace as well-meaning but enthusiastic idealists who could not be taken seriously in practical political work since they did not understand the facts of life. That situation is now entirely changed, since in later years leading statesmen and even heads of state have taken the matter in hand: the cause of peace has a fundamentally improved standing in the general opinion.[24]

This was a time when both Parliament and the Nobel committee knew what they were doing—and why. The confusion is of more recent date.

"Champions of peace"—a new criterion!

In the few cases in which posterity has been interested at all in what Nobel intended, attention has focused on the three criteria (confraternization, disarmament, and peace congresses). They are the results of a conscious purpose, Nobel struggling with the language to define his intention. But Nobel was most helpful when he summed up elsewhere in the text which recipients he had in mind. It was a moment of jubilation when

I discovered one single word in the will, innocent and forgotten—but very revealing of Nobel's actual intention.

In the section in which Nobel describes the bodies that he wished to award the annual prizes, he used the expression *champions of peace* (*fredsförfäktare*) of those *Stortinget* should help him award the prize to. The word is special, even though used in Nobel's will it still today has not found its way into the Swedish dictionaries. It seems to have been created by Nobel then and there to describe the type of winners he had in mind. This is decisive guidance in defining the content of the will: nothing less than a new criterion, the sum of the three other.

While *fredsförfäktare* is not found in Swedish dictionaries, these dictionaries do contain both the verb *förfäkta* and the noun *förfäktare*, in German *verfechten* and in Norwegian *forfekte*. The idea is to promote something, fight for something. The most interesting definition of the verb *förfäkta* is the following: "Eagerly advocating a certain opinion."[25] Nobel actually created both a new word and a new prize for *those who eagerly advocate peace*.

The official Nobel Foundation translation into English is *champions of peace*. Nobel must have had in mind active preventive work where the struggle for peace is the core of the effort, not a peripheral and unintended by-product. "Is this person a champion of peace?" is a most useful control question to decide whether someone deserves and is qualified to receive the Nobel Peace Prize.

With the emphasis that Ragnar Knoph placed on the subjective thoughts of the testator as the decisive consideration, the question to be asked is this: What kind of people did Nobel have in mind when he used *fredsförfäktare* as a descriptive label? No doubt it must have been people like Bertha von Suttner, the woman who had written 70 letters to him with increasingly clear appeals to help the peace cause financially.

In her memoirs, Suttner described a decisive meeting with Nobel in August 1892. In connection with the Fourth World Peace Congress held in Bern that year, she and her husband were Nobel's guests for three days at a hotel in Zurich, Switzerland. As president of the Austrian Society of Friends of Peace, Suttner discussed her struggle for peace with Nobel and brought up the issue of financial support, reminding Nobel of how he, responding to her earlier pleas, had sent money to the Austrian Peace Society, and had sometimes asked her to share this money with the IPB (the "bureau in Bern").

Nobel responded that he had no doubts about the cause and its legitimacy, but he did have doubts about the chances of succeeding and the way to proceed. But he declared himself willing to be convinced: "Teach me, convince me." If she succeeded in doing so, he would "do something big" *(etwas Grosses)* for the movement.[26] Suttner promised that from then on she would keep Nobel constantly informed through her magazine *Lay Down Your Arms* (same name as her book, *Die Waffen nieder!)* and other publications. She would not only try to teach him, but also to win his enthusiasm. According to Suttner, Nobel said, "If I could only be convinced that the organization *(die Liga)* could bring the goals closer, I would give a considerable amount—but first I shall have to be thoroughly informed in the matter."[27] Following this meeting, held three years before the will was written, Suttner seems to have stepped up her efforts to keep Nobel updated on the goals and activities of the peace movement.

Suttner wrote in her autobiography:

> Nobel owned a tiny aluminium motor boat, in which we took delightful trips around the lake . . . and talked about a thousand things between heaven and earth. *Nobel and I even agreed that we would write a book together, a polemic against everything that keeps the world in wretchedness and stupidity.*[28] [Emphasis added.]

Words as those marked by italics here, about profound changes of the world, are relevant to proving the intention of a testator.

Nobel's sympathy for the peace movement is confirmed in the collection of his correspondence with Suttner, published by Edelgard Biedermann (2001). On a number of occasions Suttner thanked him for money received to support her peace work—and asked for more. In a letter after Nobel's death, to Alfred Fried (Nobel laureate 1911), she writes of the serious loss of the man who "over the years has given up to 10,000 francs to my association."[29] Also, in the last year he lived, in March 1896, Nobel sent money to Suttner: "Fine, I shall transfer one thousand florins to your association in Vienna, and then you may transfer half of it to the bureau in Bern (IPB). You can see that I do as you wish."[30]

By *champions of peace* Nobel must have had in mind the wider circle of Suttner's partners in the struggle, people active in the peace societies of the period, for example the Austrian Friends of Peace and the many protagonists of the International Peace Bureau[31] and the Inter-Parliamentary Union. These peace activists have a vast number of successors, people that continue to struggle—with knowledge, skill,

Figure 3.5 Alfred Nobel's aluminum yacht, the *Mignon*. (© The Nobel Foundation.)

personal sacrifice, and resolve—for the same vision as the peace movement in Nobel's time. In short, the intended recipients are available—and they are more than willing to receive the prize. In fact, they need it badly to finance the work it was meant to support.

Nobel did not call it a "peace prize"

The work of interpreting a will deals with the language found in the text—often so much so that other words, just as important, may be overlooked: the words that are *not* used. Over the years much has been written, said and thought about *the Peace Prize*. Again and again, thought and discussion in the Nobel committee has revolved around how "a peace prize in a modern age" ought to be defined. This discussion could have been quite useful—had it not been for the fact that Nobel himself never used the expression "peace prize."[32]

It seems this designation has a long history and most probably was created in the year immediately before the first prizes (my research in

December 2009 with language institutes and lexicographers in Norway has not brought up any use before the year 1900). Increasingly the committee has allowed itself license to base its work on free speculation over an arbitrary label, *peace prize* (*fredspris*), rather than the term *champions of peace* (*fredsförfäktare*) that Nobel used. It is a fundamental flaw to create a new word and interpret that instead of those found in the will, but this has been standard practice during the last 40–50 years. From a legal point of view, this is nothing less than a major and elementary blunder.

An example of a Nobel committee in free fantasy, giving the *Peace Prize* a life of its own, was evident when committee chair Egil Aarvik, in his speech for Lech Walesa (1983) called it "a natural development . . . to consider the peace prize in the light of the UN Declaration of Human Rights," and that, by the Walesa award, the committee "once again draws the attention of the world community to its own [!] definition of the concept of peace."[33]

Interpretation—the determining factors

To sum up: the goal of the interpretation of a will is to find out what the testator intended, the purpose he or she had in mind. To describe the recipients he had in mind Nobel created a Swedish word, *fredsförfäktare* ("champions of peace"). Under the law it is both improper and illegal for the Nobel Committee to ignore the specific expression that Nobel actually used, *champions of peace,* and instead give its own content to the much less specific term "peace prize." The committee is guilty of an unauthorized change of its mandate.

The interpretation of a testament, determining its content, is all about what the testator intended. The Nobel committee is left with six criteria to help it understand what Nobel had in mind and his idea of the most deserving and legitimate recipients of the Nobel Peace Prize. First, there are two general expressions that apply to all five Nobel prizes:

during the *expired year*

has *conferred the greatest benefit on mankind*

Then there are four particular expressions regarding the Peace Prize:

the *champions of peace*

the *confraternization of nations*

the *abolition or reduction of standing armies*

the *holding and promotion of peace congresses*

The concepts *confraternization, disarmament,* and *peace congresses* are interdependent and mutually helpful to understand what a *champion of peace* is. Although the other prizes are intended for persons who have "invented," "discovered," "improved" (physics, chemistry, medicine), or "produced" (literature), Nobel used the word "worked" (*verkat*) to explain what he expected the champion of peace to have done. This seems to exclude work with a more indirect and incidental bearing on peace. Even if the word *work* might appear to indicate practical activity, it is highly unlikely that Nobel wished to exclude intellectual activity and prizes rewarding bright and innovative ideas and thinking.

In the search for Nobel's intention it is late-19th-century Swedish and his own use of language that counts. Further clues are the belief of the era in innovations that would change the lot of mankind and Nobel's life and background, which made him see the needs of the world rather than narrow national interests. Then there is the particular history behind the will, especially his contact with Suttner and his promises to do something great for her peace movement. His trust in Norway as the most suitable executor must have been occasioned by the fact that the Norwegian parliament was the leading protagonist of arbitration, neutrality, and alternatives to military force in the 1890s.[34] The fairly correct understanding of the mandate in the early decades, both in Parliament and in the Nobel Committee, is another strong indicator of his original intention.

In current usage, the purpose of the Nobel Peace Prize may be summed up as honoring work toward the establishment of a "peaceful, demilitarized international community through negotiation between nations." It is an idea whose time has come.

TRANSLATING NOBEL'S INTENTION FROM 1895 TO 2010

Having determined the purpose Nobel had in mind in 1895 we then need to translate this purpose to the present time. The task is to rediscover and recognize, as closely as possible, Nobel's own intention in the modern world and formulate it in the usage of our time. Very often wills become outdated or irrelevant over time, but 115 years later Nobel's approach to peace and security is a more urgent necessity than ever before. The error of the Nobel committee is not in adapting to a modern age, but in failing to understand the point of departure for this exercise. What they should have developed was Nobel's idea of peace, not their own.

Considering the need for democracy, human rights, justice, environment, energy, and resource conservation, I would be the last person to contest that we need a broad concept of peace work. Many activities have a bearing on peace. But the prize Nobel established was not for *peace* in general, it was a prize for *people who do determined work in certain ways and certain fields to end war.*

What forms and directions does this work take in our time, and how should the 1895 intention of Nobel be modernized and updated? Because the words in the will echo the program of the peace movement in the 1890s, the goals and ideas of this movement are the best source to understanding what Nobel had in mind.

Regarding the word *armies*, my conclusion was that the purpose is to abolish a permanent (standing) military establishment. "Armies" refers to military forces and weapons of all kinds, military and supporting activities in general, military industry, and arms trade. With one exception: a military force intended to protect and defend a *confraternization* of nations.

Many of the ways to achieve the goal of peace through disarmament are modern, ideas unknown to Nobel; early warning and skills in resolving conflicts by nonviolent means are ways to reduce the risk of military confrontation.

In his 2008 article, Douglas Bulloch of the London School of Economics states that *abolition or reduction of standing armies* is common usage in the 19th century "for arms control measures." Bulloch seems to overlook the fact that "arms control" is a lesser ambition than the "abolition or reduction" of military forces that Nobel expressly advocated. In my view, the word "control," the prevailing concept in the last four decades, is illustrative of language controlling modern political thought. Until 30 to 40 years ago, "disarmament" was a common term in international diplomatic discourse; an obligation of "general and complete disarmament" was for instance adopted in Article VI of the 1968 Treaty on the Non-proliferation [and disarmament] of Nuclear Weapons.

Gradually, in the course of a few decades, "disarmament"—the distinctive idea of the Nobel testament—has become ostracized from the debate. Anyone wishing to appear with it now had to discuss "arms control." This reduction of acceptable vocabulary may result from a change in the political situation, but it also serves to maintain and strengthen a new way of thinking—as described by George Orwell in his novel *1984*: "Control the language, and you control the thoughts."

Nobel Secretary Geir Lundestad claimed in an article in 2007 that "the peace congresses soon ended,"[35] a statement revealing how the committee lacks contact with or interest in the peace movement. Peace congresses continue to be held; their size and scope make them hard to overlook. One hundred years after the 1899 peace congress at The Hague, civil society organized a new peace congress: The Hague Appeal for Peace, with 10,000 participants.[36] True enough, this conference did not receive much coverage in the media, but—even if the general public was not informed—the secretary of the Nobel committee must have been, since he handles all nominations. The Hague Appeal was indeed nominated,[37] but the committee did not select this *peace congress* for the 2000 award.

Similarly, one must wonder how the Nobel secretary (and committee) could avoid seeing the value of the series of peace congresses initiated in 1982 by the Britons E. P. Thompson, Mary Kaldor, Dan Smith, and Ken Coates under the name END (European Nuclear Disarmament). The annual END congresses over the east-west divide in Europe— aimed at getting rid of the Iron Curtain, removing nuclear weapons, and ending the split between blocs in Europe—certainly were worthy of a Nobel Peace Prize. A number of leading figures in the European peace movement—Wim Bartels, Mient Jan Faber, and Bruce Kent—had put in a major effort by the time the last END congress was held in 1991—at about the same time the Iron Curtain fell.

These types of congress are organized by civil society organizations (CSOs), often in cooperation with or supported by national governments. They cover a broad spectrum, from the Peace Forum in Barcelona in 2004[38] to the World Peace Forum in Vancouver 2006.[39] A Norwegian example of more specialized initiatives was the big international conference Higher Education for Peace at the University of Tromsø in 2000, with the university rector (and later Nobel chair) Ole Danbolt Mjøs at the helm.[40] Nobel saw the importance of peace congresses: Why is the committee almost blind to them?

Peace congresses at the start of the last century were large-scale international efforts to create a common understanding of the need to abolish armies and wars. In the 21st century, such work takes new forms, for instance, the use of international media. When Australian television documentary maker and author John Pilger tries to mobilize anger at wars and the arms trade, reaching the whole world, this is a modern parallel to the *peace congresses*. The U.S. economist Ruth Leger Sivard did an enormous job for 22 years writing her yearbooks *World Military and Social Expenditures* (1974–1996), with statistics and articles. They powerfully document the costs of militarism, the dangers and the damage done. The figures, tables, and texts she distributed demonstrated a huge effort to disseminate knowledge and build a broad consensus against militarism and war.

This work goes to illustrate that it is not difficult to be loyal to Nobel—interesting and qualified candidates are available. The *peace congresses* of the 1890s come in many shapes in our time.

Chapter 4

THE EXECUTION OF NOBEL'S WILL

DUTIES OF THE NORWEGIAN PARLIAMENT AND THE NOBEL COMMITTEE

In response to the wish of Nobel, the Parliament of Norway, *Stortinget*, announced, on April 26, 1897, that it had accepted the responsibility and would take on the task described in the will. The prize was not to be awarded by Parliament itself, but by an independent "body of five members elected by *Stortinget*."

Three months later, Parliament adopted rules of procedure for the election of the five-members committee, based on six-year terms and renewing half of the members (two or three) every three years.

During the first four decades after 1901, insight, interest, and involvement in peace politics were necessary qualifications to be appointed to the committee. No doubt the seats were attractive, thus the first Nobel committee in 1897 included the country's most prominent politicians. In those first decades, both prime ministers and foreign ministers would bask in the glory of Nobel by taking up seats on the Nobel committee.

The committee has had a stable composition, particularly in the first five decades. In the course of 109 years, it has had only 53 different members. Twelve people have been in the chair. Aase Lionæs, in 1949, became the first of 10 women on the committee. Since 2009, four of the five committee members are women. Hans Jacob Horst and Aase Lionæs are the only members to have served for 30 years.

Despite the fact that during the committee's first five years Norway was a nation potentially heading for war, the first Nobel committees showed reasonable loyalty to Nobel and the purpose of his prize. The parliamentary records of the first decades contain many a serious discussion of candidates for committee membership and whether their merits were suitable and sufficient. The clear goal was to compose a committee well qualified in the peace issues that Nobel had tasked the committee with.

One can, however, also find stray interventions in the debates suggesting that some parliamentarians were driven more by personal and party interests than by the wish to be faithful to Nobel's will, a tendency that came to a head in 1948. In that year, for the first time, the committee seats were shared between the parties according to a mathematical formula reflecting their strength in the latest election. Established practice since then is that the election committee of the Norwegian Parliament will automatically accept the names put forward by the political parties. Parliament does nothing to describe the task or the desirable qualifications. It is most regrettable that Parliament has abandoned its obligation to perform a free, overall evaluation to secure a varied and competent committee.

Over the years, both the Parliament of Norway and the cabinet have gradually marked a clearer distance to the committee. Parliament has clarified that its only task is to elect the committee members. Politicians who are active in Parliament or cabinet cannot serve. The practice of having the committee announce the winner(s) in Parliament was discontinued after only five years. The annual reports from the Nobel committee are no longer debated in Parliament.

To further underline its independence, "parliament" was removed from the name, which since 1917 has been called the Norwegian Nobel committee. Yet with the high incidence of senior politicians on the committee, it is difficult to establish credible independence from Norwegian politics.

The committee selects its own chair and deputy chair. It hires staff, a secretary for the committee, who also serves as director of the Nobel Institute, consultants to help screen the candidates, and other staff.

The Nobel committee has a fixed calendar, where the deadline for nominations is a key date. Nominations must be postmarked no later than February 1. The right to submit candidates is restricted to people within certain categories, parliamentarians and cabinet ministers; academics within law, history, and philosophy; leaders of research institutes within peace and foreign affairs; Nobel laureates; and others. The details are summarized in appendix 1. If they come within these categories, people from all countries of the world may nominate.

Each year the committee holds its first meeting in February to review a full list of the nominees, with short résumés for each of them. This discussion ends with a short list of around 20 to 30 names that the committee wishes to examine. It has at its disposal four to five experts in history, law, economics, and political science to write evaluations. Both before and after the summer recess, new meetings are held to narrow down the list and seek agreement on a winner—one name or a prize divided among no more than three. The final decision is made in time to announce the outcome on the second Friday of October.

Tight secrecy

An obstacle to evaluating the Nobel committee's work is the strict secrecy. Under the bylaws the list of nominees is a close secret, the committee's voting is secret, the minutes are secret, and under the rules, the minutes shall not contain anything on discussion, only the final decision. In addition, the committee urges all who make nominations not to publish the names of their candidates in the media.

The secrecy is surprisingly efficient—close to leak-free—and it lasts for a long time. The veil is lifted only after 50 years, but the information open to public access is still rather limited. The list of nominated candidates is published (now on nobelprize.org), and it is possible for those who can show cause to get permission to see nomination letters and evaluations. It is strictly forbidden to record dissent in the minutes.

Secrecy is normally an unfortunate practice, but not always. There are some good reasons why the committee is under strict instructions not to disclose internal strife. How good would it feel for the winner to have made it with a three-two vote? Unfortunately, it is a common experience that secrecy combined with power tends to lead to corruption and abuse. This arguably has happened with the Nobel prizes as well: the scarcity of information spells uncertainty and limitations for anyone wishing to evaluate the quality of the choices the committees have made.

No doubt the lack of public insight and discussion has served to immunize the committee against criticism. The lack of transparency is to a large degree a formality, however, since the public gets to know a lot. An important part of the task of the committee is to attain the highest possible visibility to the laureates. As far as possible, the public should understand why the winner was selected. The point of the prize is, after all, to spread ideas and inspiration. For this reason, the committee's motives and reasoning have always been explained in the speeches held in honor of the laureates. At every announcement since 1971, the committee has offered a short text on the winner and the motives behind each particular award.

In 2001, a history of the first 100 years was written for the centenary celebrations. The Nobel committee opened its files for three selected historians to analyze documents, nominations, and correspondence concerning prizes—more than 50 years old.

On rare occasions, the outside world has gotten inside the committee room. Committee members have given interviews. A veteran parliamentarian, Hanna Kvanmo, in an interview shortly before her death, told of an intense tug-of-war, but "as a rule we have been able to reach agreement in our discussions. There has to be a consensus, no way around that."[1] Considering the political profile of committee members in later years, consensus as a strict principle will effectively rule out candidates promoting the ideas on peace that Nobel wished to support.

The political antagonism in the committee has at times been too large to contain: in a couple of cases, members have resigned from the committee, with harsh criticism of their colleagues and their decision.

A strict principle of consensus should not be taken for granted; even if the committee seeks to reach consensus, credible, but unofficial, sources say committee members at times disagree with the majority decision. The 1973 Peace Prizes for then–U.S. Secretary of State Henry Kissinger and the Vietnamese peace talks negotiator Le Duc Tho perhaps must have been the most unpopular ever. That year, a majority of three voted for Kissinger and Tho. One of them even wished to give the prize to U.S. President Richard Nixon, and Kissinger was his compromise solution. The other two members (Einar Hovdhaugen and Helge Rognlien) voted for Dom Helder Camara, the Roman Catholic Brazilian archbishop and hero of nonviolent struggle for social justice. During the first two meetings, they did not reach agreement. In the third, and last, meeting they started with a new vote, with the same result as before-and that was the outcome.

The tension in the committee burst into the open when committee chair Aase Lionæs, put under pressure by reporters, told the media that the Kissinger/Tho decision had "not been difficult." The minority of two, who had voted against the decision, were so unhappy with being named in public as supporters of the decision that they left the committee. One of the minority, Einar Hovdhaugen, was so disgusted that he chose to blow the whistle—but not very spontaneously. After considering the matter for 12 years, he published a caustic eight-page article on the patterns and procedures he had observed as a member of the committee. After being bulldozed by the majority for Kissinger, and having been advised by the chair on dress code at the ceremony, he fumed as he traveled home:

> Stupefied, depressed and with worried forebodings I boarded the evening train for my ride home. I had been a member of innumerable committees during my lifetime and I was accustomed to thorough discussion and evaluation. The working style that I met in the Nobel committee was unknown to me.[2]

In the article, Hovdhaugen disagreed in particular with the voting system, and was of the opinion that a majority ought not to select candidates about which there was disagreement. As the statutes do not permit registration of dissent, he felt the committee's practice was outdated, not in conformity with generally accepted principles: a majority should never choose a laureate who challenges the conscience of other committee members. Because it is always an open question which candidate is "the best," it ought to be possible to find someone acceptable to all members. It seems likely that this criticism led to a stronger emphasis on consensus.

PRIZES TRUE TO NOBEL—OR COMMITTEE WAYWARDNESS?

How has the Peace Prize developed in the course of more than 100 years? How loyal have the committees been to Nobel's will? Only an individual evaluation of all prizes awarded can determine the measure of respect that the Nobel committee has shown to Nobel and the content of his will.

Great changes in society during a century and more may seem to complicate the evaluation, but they are not so much of a problem as one might think. The Nobel testament was indeed visionary; his original purpose is much more important in an age when continuation of life on the planet requires that we remove the weapons before they remove us.

The laureates in most cases have done extraordinarily important work deserving the highest respect, praise, and attention, and the honor received cannot and should not be taken away from them. But the point is that the prize given in Nobel's name also has to show respect for Nobel and his specific ideas when making the will.

My goal in the following is to examine the Nobel committee's work rather than the merits of the laureates. The evaluation is based on the Nobel committee's words, as far as possible, particularly in the speeches in honor of the laureates. The question I have evaluated is whether or not the committee has included language sufficient to show that the award is honoring the methods and fields of peace work that Nobel wished to support. I also consider whether it is tenable to call a laureate a *champion of peace* (*fredsförfäktare*) in Nobel's sense of the word. When I first discovered the significance of this word I called it a fourth criterion, but in actual fact Nobel, through this one word, sums up the three criteria (confraternization, disarmament, peace congresses), so it may just as well be called the first criterion.

Notes on some of the committee decisions

In the years between 1901 and 2009, the Nobel Peace Prize was awarded 119 times, to 96 individuals and 23 organizations (some organizations more than once). During each of the two world wars, 1914–1918 and 1939–1945, no Peace Prize was awarded (the decision to award the 1944 Nobel Peace Prize to the Red Cross was taken in 1945). In 19 years, the committee chose not to make an award.[3] For almost four decades now, since 1973, the prize has been awarded every year.

The prize shared between the United Nations and Secretary-General Kofi Annan in 2001 was the last to be clearly justified with tenable arguments. Since then, there have been many conspicuous examples of laureates who can only remotely be called *champions for peace* in the sense that Nobel used the expression: Al Gore has spoken occasionally against nuclear weapons, but that was not the reason he was awarded the Nobel Peace Prize. When did Gore or the United Nations Panel on Climate Change (prize winners in 2007) speak out against military resource depletion and military pollution as important components of climate problems?

Mohammad Yunus (2006) provides microcapital to many, but when did he challenge the billions allocated to war machinery and its entrepreneurs? What about Wangari Maathai's forest planting (2004)? Shirin Ebadi's human rights defense in Iran (2003)? Brave, impressive, outstanding people—but were they Nobel's idea of *champions of peace*?

The Nobel committee deserves praise for having reminded the world, through a series of prizes, of the seriousness of the threat that nuclear weapons pose to our common security. The prizes to Mohammad El Baradei and the International Atomic Energy Agency (IAEA) in 2005 had relevance to the content of the will—but many who struggle for the abolition of nuclear weapons are worried over the conflicting aims of the IAEA. It promotes the use of nuclear power and technology, yet at the same time it tries to ensure that know-how and fissionable materials do not fall into the wrong hands—a risk clearly exacerbated by its first aim.

In the case of the IAEA, the Nobel committee gave its blessing to an organization with a debatable, many would say counterproductive, role in the struggle against the doomsday weapon. But El Baradei had, with courage and purpose, made the most of a difficult international responsibility. The prize encouraged him to dare criticize the nuclear powers that tend to discuss only the nonproliferation obligations of everyone else and never to take their own duties seriously. Under the treaty on nonproliferation and nuclear disarmament (1968), the nuclear weapon states have a legal obligation to enter into negotiations leading to the abolition of all nuclear weapons.

In my examination of the committee language, I found that the committee has seldom backed the specific peace agenda contained in the will. On only six occasions has the speech for the laureate given express confirmation of Nobel's intention with the Peace Prize: Mikhail Gorbachev (1990), Philip Noel-Baker (1959), Norman Angell (1933), Aristide Briand and Gustav Stresemann (shared, 1926), Christian Lange and Hjalmar Branting (1921), and Bertha von Suttner (1905).

The following awards were so distant from Nobel's idea of "champions of peace" that they must be considered serious mistakes: Yasser Arafat, Shimon Peres, and Yitzhak Rabin (shared, 1994); Anwar al-Sadat and Menachem Begin (1978); Henry Kissinger and Le Duc Tho (1973); George C. Marshall (1953); Austen Chamberlain and Charles G. Dawes (shared, 1925); Elihu Root (1912); and Theodore Roosevelt (1906).

Among the prizes clearly deserved are those for work for international law and order. The UN Charter no doubt has its weaknesses, and failing loyalty to the world organization seriously undermines its results and potential. Most of the prizes for the United Nations and its predecessor, the League of Nations, were solidly based on the will. People in the service of the League of Nations and the United Nations or their special agencies have received a number of Peace Prizes over the years. Still, these prizes often have been made on primarily humanitarian grounds and have failed to respect the intention of Nobel: UN High Commissioner for Refugees (1954, 1981); the International Labor Organization (1969); UN Children's Fund (1965); Nansen International Office for Refugees (1938); Fridtjof Nansen (1922); and John Boyd Orr (1949).

The committee leader's speech for Nansen in 1922 described his formidable talent and his effort for refugees. His humanitarian emergency relief was historic, but neither the speech for the laureate nor the speech by Nansen shows him as entitled to the Peace Prize under the Nobel criteria. The committee could have done better, it could have emphasized Nansen's contributions to peace during the dissolution of the union between Norway and Sweden in 1905 and for the strongest possible League of Nations in the period from 1919 to 1920, but the committee failed to place the Nansen prize within the Nobel criteria. That said, it must have had a favorable effect. In the speech, Nansen held one year later to honor the new laureate, Nansen warmly embraced Nobel's ideas.

A considerable distance from the idea of the Peace Prize has been apparent in the acceptance speeches from those who received humanitarian prizes. For instance, when the UN Children's Fund (UNICEF) received the prize, the unbearable situation of children in wars was not mentioned at all, although war, a hell for everybody, is even worse for children.

The problems with the Nobel prizes to UN agencies also apply to other humanitarian prizes such as Médecins sans Frontières (Doctors Without Borders, 1999) and the International Red Cross (1963, 1944, 1917). Their contribution to the alleviation of suffering is of the highest value, but they do not strive actively and as a matter of principle against war itself.

Neither Elie Wiesel (1986), Mother Teresa (1979), Georges Pire (1958), nor the agronomist Norman Borlaug (1970) can be called *champions of peace* in the sense Nobel used the word.

In several cases in which the committee failed by not giving proper reasons for the award, the laureates themselves paid tribute to the idea of the Peace Prize in their Nobel lecture or became untiring champions of peace of the kind that Nobel wished to foster. Some examples include Albert Schweitzer (1952) and Ralph Bunche (1950). Desmond Tutu (1984) and Mairead Corrigan (1976) have both done much to challenge militarism and war.

The prize that went to Rigoberta Menchú Tum (1992) bore unmistakable symbolism in the historic year when "the world" celebrated the

500th anniversary of Christopher Columbus and his "discovery" of America. I was enthusiastic about this award when it was given in 1992, but after becoming aware of Nobel's intention I see that however deserving of a Peace Prize, she was not a champion of the deep international reform Nobel had in mind.

Some awards are too local in scope to comply with the international-ist visions of Nobel, as for example the prizes for Carlos Belo and José Ramos-Horta (1996), and Albert Lutuli (1960). The Nobel committee repeatedly has called attention to nonviolent struggles to legitimize an award. But is nonviolence alone sufficient? In some cases, it is a prag-matic tool in a concrete situation, while others fight actively for nonvio-lence as a general principle. Nonviolent struggle can take such particularly convincing or innovative forms that it is an example for others. In such cases, the Nobel committee should say just that in its presentation of the winner.

Geir Lundestad, the Nobel director, has made amends for the failure to honor Mahatma Gandhi, by again and again calling it a clear error. In his article on Nobel, Bulloch maintains that with the 1989 prize to the Dalai Lama the committee also wished to make good its mistake with Gandhi. In his Nobel speech that year chair, Egil Aarvik compared the Dalai Lama to Gandhi and said that "the Nobel committee had noticed that many wonder why Gandhi never got the prize" and that it tended to share their view.[4]

It would be of great interest to see a study of how often the people Nobel had in mind were nominated, but more remote or even directly disqualified, people were preferred by the committee. An analysis of this type, based on a correct understanding of the will, ought to be done. Because of the secrecy surrounding the Nobel committee, it will be nearly impossible to analyze reliably champions of peace passed over in the last 50 years, but it is clearly possible to document some of them.

A glaring example is that organizers of peace congresses have been ignored by the committee, despite express mention of them in the will. When, 100 years after The First Hague Peace Congress, more than 10,000 activists participated in The Hague Appeal for Peace, Cora and Peter Weiss and Bill Pace were at the helm of the effort. Both Cora Weiss and The Hague Appeal for Peace were nominated. With more sense both for Nobel's idea and the modern peace movement, the com-mittee would not have awarded the 2000 prize to Korean statesman, Kim Dae-jung.[5]

One of the first two Peace Prizes, awarded in 1901 to Henry Dunant, founder of the Red Cross, was met with heavy criticism. I have maintained that the Peace Prize to Dunant was a mistake, given not for the prevention of war but for the alleviation of suffering. During the work on this book, I have seen some reason to doubt this negative view. Although Dunant's name was primarily connected with the Red Cross, several accounts describe him as an active member of the peace movement for a number of years. Thus, it would have been possible for the committee to justify the prize as within the scope of the will. The texts of the speeches for the earliest recipients, including that for Dunant, are missing. It is reasonable to assume, however, that the prize was motivated by the public perception, and that Dunant received the prize for the wrong reason, as the founder of the Red Cross.

Bertha von Suttner, the one who knew Nobel's intention with the prize better than anyone, voiced a negative reaction when the Peace Prize went to Dunant. She also, however, drew public attention to his membership and activity in the peace movement.

Grading of the committee: Pass/fail, 1901–2009

In 2008, I did a full evaluation of the Nobel committees and the reasons they have given for prizes up to 2007. Table 4.1 shows the list of all the Peace Prizes since 1901, with my evaluation of the committee's loyalty to the will. With two added since 1907, the total number awarded is now 120. The question that has been posed—and answered by a yes or a no—is whether the committees have explained their choices and described the laureate that is reasonably in compliance with Nobel's will. The result, that 50 of the 120 prizes did not fit the will, is a rough image, but sufficiently clear to permit conclusions.

In most cases, the determination was clear. In other cases—as in all grading—the determination rested on a best judgment, or at least next-best judgment. Because of the scope of the material, it was possible only to make an evaluation of how the committee explained the prize, not to make a full assessment of the decision in relation to the will. A stricter demand, requiring both good reasons *and* tenable grounds, would have resulted in a higher incidence of "fail."

For prizes that are not in compliance with the will, I have at times used the term "committee prizes" to denote illegitimately awarded prizes, that is, the committee has misused the Nobel name for purposes outside his intention. At the Web site of the Norwegian Nobel

Table 4.1
Nobel Peace Prize winners, 1901–2009

1901	Frédéric Passy, (Henry Dunant)	1936	Carlos Saavedra Lamas
1902	Élie Ducommun, Albert Gobat	1937	Robert Cecil
		1938	(Nansen Intl. Office for Refugees)
1903	Randal Cremer	1944	(Intl. Committee of the Red Cross)
1904	Institute of Intl. Law	1945	Cordell Hull
1905	Bertha von Suttner	1946	Emily Greene Balch, John R. Mott
1906	(Theodore Roosevelt)		
1907	Ernesto Teodoro Moneta, Louis Renault	1947	Friends Service Council, American Friends Service Committee
1908	Klas Pontus Arnoldson, Fredrik Bajer	1949	(John Boyd Orr)
1909	Auguste Beernaert, Paul Henri d'Estournelles de Constant	1950	Ralph Bunche
		1951	Léon Jouhaux
		1952	(Albert Schweitzer)
1910	International Peace Bureau	1953	(George C. Marshall)
1911	Tobias Asser, Alfred Fried	1954	(Office of the UN High Commissioner for Refugees)
1912	(Elihu Root)		
1913	Henri La Fontaine	1957	Lester Bowles Pearson
1917	(Intl. Committee of the Red Cross)	1958	(Georges Pire)
		1959	Philip Noel-Baker
1919	Woodrow Wilson	1960	(Albert Lutuli)
1920	Léon Bourgeois	1961	Dag Hammarskjöld
1921	Hjalmar Branting, Christian Lange	1962	Linus Pauling
1922	(Fridtjof Nansen)	1963	(Intl. Committee of the Red Cross), (League of Red Cross Societies)
1925	Austen Chamberlain, Charles G. Dawes		
		1964	Martin Luther King
1926	Aristide Briand, Gustav Stresemann	1965	(United Nations Children's Fund)
1927	Ferdinand Buisson, Ludwig Quidde	1968	(René Cassin)
		1969	(Intl. Labour Organization)
1929	Frank B. Kellogg	1970	(Norman Borlaug)
1930	Nathan Söderblom	1971	Willy Brandt
1931	Jane Addams, Nicholas Murray Butler	1973	(Henry Kissinger), (Le Duc Tho)
		1974	Seán MacBride, Eisaku Sato
1933	Norman Angell	1975	Andrej Sakharov
1934	Arthur Henderson	1976	(Betty Williams), (Mairead Corrigan)
1935	Carl von Ossietzky		

(*continued*)

Table 4.1 (*continued*)

1977	(Amnesty International)	1995	Joseph Rotblat, Pugwash
1978	(Anwar al-Sadat),		Conferences on Science
	(Menachem Begin)		and World Affairs
1979	(Mother Teresa)	1996	(Carlos Filipe Ximenes Belo),
1980	Adolfo Pérez Esquivel		(José Ramos-Horta)
1981	(Office of the UN High	1997	Intl. Campaign to Ban
	Commissioner for		Landmines, Jody Williams
	Refugees)	1998	(John Hume), (David Trimble)
1982	Alva Myrdal, Alfonso	1999	(Médecins Sans Frontières)
	García Robles	2000	(Kim Dae-jung)
1983	(Lech Walesa)	2001	United Nations, Kofi
1984	(Desmond Tutu)		Annan
1985	Intl. Physicians for the	2002	Jimmy Carter
	Prevention of Nuclear War	2003	(Shirin Ebadi)
1986	(Elie Wiesel)	2004	(Wangari Maathai)
1987	Oscar Arias Sánchez	2005	Mohamed ElBaradei,
1988	United Nations		(International Atomic Energy
	Peacekeeping Forces		Agency)
1989	The 14. Dalai Lama	2006	(Muhammad Yunus), (Grameen
1990	Mikhail Gorbachev		Bank)
1991	Aung San Suu Kyi	2007	(Intergvmtl. Panel on Climate
1992	(Rigoberta Menchú Tum)		Change), (Albert Arnold (Al)
1993	Nelson Mandela, F.W. de		Gore Jr.)
	Klerk	2008	(Martti Ahtisaari)
1994	(Yasser Arafat), (Shimon	2009	(Barack Obama)
	Peres), (Yitzhak Rabin)		

Names in parenthesis: not justified (as evaluated by the author in accordance with Nobel's will). In nineteen years no peace prize was awarded.

Committee (http://nobelpeaceprize.org), the laureates are grouped in decades. Grouped by decades, my evaluation of the committee's arguments for their choices is visualized in Table 4.2.

For the first four decades, up to 1940, the committee's reasons for 35 out of 41 Nobel prizes met Nobel's criteria, meaning that 85 percent of the prizes were justified with reasons bringing them within the purpose of the prize. In those early years, the memory of the will was fresh and the mentality had not much changed since the 1890s. The line of laureates in those first years provides strong confirmation of my interpretation of the will in chapter 3 of the type of winners for which the prize was intended.

Table 4.2
Number of awarded and not justified Nobel Peace Prizes by decade

	Awarded	Not justified	Not justified (%)
1901–1910	15	2	13%
1911–1920	7	2	29%
1921–1930	11	1	9%
1931–1940	8	1	13%
1941–1950	8	2	25%
1951–1960	8	5	63%
1961–1970	9	6	67%
1971–1980	13	8	62%
1981–1990	11	4	36%
1991–2000	17	10	59%
2001–2009	13	9	69%
	120	**50**	

As evaluated by the author in accordance with Nobel's will.

In the years after 1944, overall compliance has been barely over half the prewar level. Only 35 of the 79 Nobel prizes are sufficiently justified between 1944 and 2001, leaving a score of 44 percent. Even with a generous margin for error in my assessments, the result is unmistakable: 1945 brought a considerable change. In the postwar period, respect for the testament of Nobel has dropped significantly. Thus, we have every reason to look into possible explanations for such an astounding decline in loyalty toward Nobel and his intention with the Peace Prize.

Chapter 5

THE PEACE PRIZE IN DANGER

A CALL TO ORDER

The Nobel Peace Prize enjoys great international prestige: the Parliament of Norway plays a key role; a solid committee and administration emanates trust and reliability. It took a long time for the idea to dawn on me that anything so important and visible could be managed with anything less than impeccable observance of the law.

In the wake of the prize to Wangari Maathai (2004), the theme "environment" was suddenly called a new dimension of the prize. Although a highly attractive prize for environmental work may be needed, apart from the legal aspect, does that make the prize Nobel instituted for peace and disarmament any less needed? Would not the struggle to end militarism and wars also, in preeminent degree, contribute to rescuing the environment?

When in the summer of 2007, Al Gore was increasingly being mentioned as a prime candidate to win the Peace Prize, it made me take a fresh look at the will. Just a swift glance at Nobel's will—and a normal, straight reading of his own words—was enough. It struck me how far the prize had strayed from its purpose, and the result of my reading became an article in the leading Norwegian daily, *Aftenposten*, on August 14, 2007, entitled "The Peace Prize in Danger." The paper had highlighted my main conclusion: "The Nobel committee must immediately rethink its task and responsibility as managers of the Nobel Peace Prize."

In this first expression of criticism, I further pointed out, in clear, unambiguous terms, that Nobel had established

a peace prize, not a prize for the environment, not for economics and also not for humanitarian work. If the five members appointed by parliament lose sight of this, it will undermine the character and status of the prize. Even if there are many views of what peace is, the committee is in no way free to choose laureates according to its own free judgment . . . Nobel endeavored a radical system change in international politics, he wished to discover the paths that could lead to a world without war and abuse of power.[1]

Every year, while present at the announcement of the Peace Prize, I have been asked to comment in Norwegian and international media. I have been friendly and always found something positive to say. Now I realized that my media comments had been much too kind for much too long, and I directed a strong appeal to the Nobel committee and each of its members, stressing their personal "moral and legal responsibility to respect the testament of Nobel." A particular responsibility rested on the chair of the committee, Danbolt Mjøs, and an important practical responsibility lay on the shoulders of the committee secretary, Geir Lundestad.

"Many roads to peace"

In the article in *Aftenposten*, I primarily called for a reevaluation of policy, not for a specific response, and I did not get one either. I looked forward to the announcement two months later of the Peace Prize(s) for 2007 with great anticipation, hoping the committee would had given serious consideration to the call for a change of policy.

The committee's response came on Friday, October 12, 2007, at precisely 11:00 A.M., when the heavy oak doors of the Nobel Hall opened and the chair of the committee, Professor Mjøs, strode forward to announce: "The Nobel Peace Prize for 2007 will be shared between Al Gore and the Intergovernmental Panel on Climate Change, IPCC."

My appeal to respect Nobel had not had much effect on the committee. But all my later studies into the subject have confirmed that first appeal in August 2007. The media was also unfazed, and met the 2007 award with the usual friendly coverage, Norwegian and international editors expressed grandiloquent opinions on the Nobel committee having made a reasonably good or useful decision, a courageous, unsurprising, relevant choice, and so on. For the very first time, my comments were critical. In a news release to Norwegian and foreign media, I stated:

> Given his idea of peace and his goal in founding the peace prize, Nobel may have come to regret that he entrusted the Norwegian parliament with the award. It is not loyal to Nobel's testament to use a very general concept of peace, . . . [since] there is no doubt that his intention with the

prize was to pursue a more fundamental change: a world without militarism and war.

I was not alone, the prize for 2007 was criticized from many quarters. Lundestad defended the award in *Aftenposten* of October 17, 2007. Aware that many felt that over time the concept of peace had become too broad, he wrote: "The committee thinks that there are many roads to peace."

Clear, revealing—and irrelevant. Of course there are many roads to peace, I could not agree more, but the Nobel committee demonstrates a fundamental misunderstanding: It has forgotten that its task is to bestow Nobel's prize, not its own. In *Aftenposten* of October 18, 2007, I therefore responded:

> The legal obligation of the committee is to interpret Nobel's will of 1895, understand its meaning and carry it into effect. In *Aftenposten* of October 17, the Nobel Institute director Geir Lundestad reveals that he must have failed to give the committee proper legal orientation in the matter.[2]

The Nobel director offered no further response. The signal seemed clear: this is how we do this, it is how we intend to continue, and we have nothing more to say. A thorough legal evaluation of the issues would not come from the committee. It would have to come from others.

Chapter 6

AFTER WORLD WAR II: POLITICS DISTORTING THE PRIZE

LAWMAKERS MUST RESPECT THE LAW

To make a will is to make up one's mind, but a testator is free to change his or her mind at any time. Death, however, makes the will final and fixed. A bequest for the eradication of leprosy must be used against leprosy. If at a later point leprosy is eliminated, it will be possible, with proper public approval, to use the funds for a new purpose, for example, the eradication of tuberculosis. No one has approved a change to Nobel's will. The scourge of war has not been eradicated; the target of the testament has not been reached. The military has not been abolished; instead the world seems caught in a destructive pattern that too many take for granted and see no escape route from.

Chapter 4 laid bare the steep decline in loyalty to Nobel. After World War II, with a new and broad political consensus in favor of military, the prize ceased to be a tool to promote peace politics. Possible explanations have to do with organization, individuals, and a change in the general climate in Norway regarding security policy.

In 1897, the testament of Nobel was a sensation. The claims from the family made it urgent to get the Nobel Foundation established; there was no time to lose and little time to consider matters of principle, responsibility, and the potential consequences. In addition, the options were restricted: If the Parliament of Norway had refused, not only the Peace Prize but also the other Nobel prizes could have failed to come into existence.

The idea of tasking a Parliament with the implementation of a will may have been typical of the innovative and unconventional mind of

Alfred Nobel. But it was a new and untried solution. Politicians are trained to conduct politics; they wish to accomplish as much as possible on behalf of their political program; they seek power and position. How should everyone in Parliament understand and keep remembering, decade after decade, that their task was not to give or make law, but to abide by it—just like anyone else who assumes a role in the execution of a will?

For a number of years, they nevertheless did reasonably well. In the years before World War II, interest in the work of the peace movement remained a minimum requirement to become a member of the committee. This was expressed in several debates in Parliament and reflected in the actual composition of the Nobel committees, which during the first couple of decades were dominated by leading parliamentarians from the Liberal party (*Venstre* in Norwegian, meaning "left"). The committee members either belonged to or had ties with the peace movement. The author Bjørnstjerne Bjørnson, a prominent Norwegian and leading figure on the European peace and rights scene, was one of the members in the first decade.[1]

In a debate on the election of new committee members in 1903, there were objections to a law professor. One parliamentarian did not accept expertise in international law as sufficient qualification to get elected: "What has he [Professor Hertzberg] achieved in the service of peace and confraternization among nations that should entitle him to a seat on the committee? Should he be allowed to displace many others who have for years worked to serve this cause?"[2]

Most of those elected to the Nobel committee remained members for decades, in most cases until their death,[3] and most often they were leading protagonists of peace work, both at the national and international level. A key person among the Liberals, Hans Jakob Horst, active in the international struggle among parliamentarians for peace, was a committee member from 1901 to 1931. In 1913, one parliamentarian, Bernhard Hanssen, was proposed and, after a heated debate, elected by 61 to 42 votes. Hanssen was a shipowner and president of the Norwegian Peace Society and was a veteran when he left in 1938, after 25 years on the committee. The Norwegian Peace Society had been founded during the Liberal Party convention in 1895. Had it not been for the role that the Liberals played as a dominant party in Norway and proponents of the cause of peace, Nobel probably never would have entrusted Norway with the Peace Prize.[4]

A temptation for *Stortinget* to favor party interests over peace politics, however, seems to have been present almost from the beginning.

Already in the 1913 Parliamentary debate, protesters felt a need to defend the integrity of the committee—it would weaken the idea of democracy to distribute the seats between the parties on the basis of proportionality, which is the normal way with parliamentary committees. Here we had "a committee that should be elevated miles above party interests and party quarrel."[5] A lawyer and eager champion of peace, Carl Bonnevie, stated:

> The socialist representative Mr. Buen expressed the opinion that this election should not be a party matter. That is a statement I think will find much support also in our party, and that we will feel as an obligation. In my view the non-socialist parties would incur a considerable responsibility by making the selection of members a party matter.[6]

This line still held for another 35 years, but in 1945, Norway entered a postwar period of strong belief in military measures. "Never again an April 9" (the date of the German invasion of Norway in 1940) became a main slogan in debates on defense and security matters in Norway. This was to last for 50 years, until Norwegian military forces, under the new North Atlantic Treaty Organization (NATO) treaty of 1999, started to fight abroad and a slogan reminding Norwegians of the horrible experience of attack by a foreign power became less useful.

In the years following 1945, a general promilitary sentiment reigned, and the majority in Parliament seems to have felt it was entirely justifiable to place people with a military mind-set on a committee that should strive for the direct opposite. The obvious result was a committee much less qualified and less willing to implement Nobel's intention. The friends of defense had replaced the friends of peace.

Nobel committee transformed

These considerable political changes coincided with the resignation or death of the veterans on and around the Nobel committee. A wealth of knowledge and continuity was lost in 1946, when Ragnvald Moe retired after 36 years as committee secretary. This came on top of similar losses toward the end of the 1930s. In 1936, the minister of foreign affairs, Halfdan Koht, suspended his membership—two weeks before the announcement of the prize (for 1935) to Carl von Ossietzky. Christian Lange died in 1938. Two other members who were leaders in the internationalist struggle for peace also retired in the 1930s, after 32 and 33 years on the committee: Hans Jacob Horst in 1931 and Bernhard Hanssen in 1938.

Table 6.1
Number of awarded and not justified Nobel Peace Prizes
by committee chair

		Awarded	Not justified	Not justified (%)
1901–1921	Jørgen Løvland	24	4	17%
1922–1941	Fredrik Stang	17	2	12%
1942–1966	Gunnar Jahn	22	10	45%
1967	Bernt Ingvaldsen	0	–	–
1968–1978	Aase Lionæs	14	10	71%
1979–1981	John Sannes	3	2	67%
1982–1989	Egil Aarvik	9	3	33%
1990	Gidske Anderson	1	0	0%
1991–1999	Francis Sejersted	16	9	56%
2000–2002	Gunnar Berge	4	1	25%
2003–2008	Ole Danbolt Mjøs	9	8	89%
2009–	Torbjørn Jagland	1	1	100%
		120	**50**	

As evaluated by the author in accordance with Nobel's will.

All members of the Nobel committee have the same vote and in principle count equally, but presumably the committee chairs always have had a somewhat greater influence than other members. The committee chair presents the winner, delivers the speech to honor the laureate, and defends the decision in the media. It is important that the chair is comfortable with the choice.

The three first committee chairs all served between 19 and 25 years and together cover a full 65 years, from 1901 to 1966. Later committee chairs normally have served eight years, one served 11, and two lasted only one.

Since World War II, the peace movement as such has not been directly represented on the committee, according to Abrams.[7] Even if prizes that fail to respect the will belong primarily in the post–World War II era, also some earlier statements demonstrate poor understanding of the committee's task. In the speech to honor Kellogg (1929), committee member Johan Ludwig Mowinckel resorted to pure fiction, ignoring both the text of the will and what Nobel actually intended:

> Alfred Nobel himself had no illusions as to the difficulties and the complexity of work for peace. For this reason he placed no strict limitations

on his Peace Prize; any serious and noble effort to advance the cause of peace could qualify . . . It is thus in full accord with Alfred Nobel's conception of work for peace that no restrictions are imposed on the manner in which it is performed. Nor can it be otherwise. For in this work, both hand and heart are required.

Similar cases of bold, lofty—completely free and frivolous—speculation by committee chairs as to Nobel and his intention have occurred again and again over the years. Committee Chair Aase Lionæs revealed similar confusion in her speech for Norman Borlaug (1970). Borlaug, whose achievement was to have developed new, efficient types of high-yield grain, was not easy to call a *champion of peace*. Lionæs opened her speech by stating that Nobel in his will had stipulated the conditions that had to be met by a recipient of the prize, and that

> paragraph one[8] states, *inter alia,* that the award of the prize shall be made to the person who, during the preceding year, "shall have conferred the greatest benefit on mankind."

To defend the award to Borlaug, she invoked a general direction for all Nobel prizes as an independent and sufficient criterion for the Peace Prize, a bizarre maneuver that pretended to be an interpretation of the will.

The speech by committee chair Egil Aarvik in 1983, for Lech Walesa, seems to reveal a committee considering itself entitled to forget Nobel and design its own prize:

> The guidelines given to the committee in Alfred Nobel's will stipulate that the presentation of the peace prize is the responsibility of the committee alone, and cannot be influenced by outside forces. Thus the Nobel peace prize can never be more—or less—than a hand stretched out to individuals or groups who give expression to the longing for peace and freedom felt by all the peoples of the world, wherever they live. We believe that it is in the spirit of Alfred Nobel's legacy that the peace prize should be a gesture of solidarity with those who, in the service of peace, campaign for humanity's highest ideals.

There have been few explanations of the legal aspects and the intention of Nobel when he wrote the testament. But the committee gave an exemplary rendition of the legal obligations in the speech for Gorbachev (1990), as will be explained in chapter 7.

Table 6.2
Number of awarded and not justified Nobel Peace Prizes
by committee secretary

		Awarded	Not justified	Not justified (%)
1901–1909	Christian L. Lange	14	2	14%
1910–1945	Ragnvald Moe	29	5	17%
1946–1973	August Schou	26	14	54%
1974–1977	Tim Greve	6	3	50%
1978–1989	Jakob Sverdrup	14	7	50%
1990–2009	Geir Lundestad	31	19	61%
		120	**50**	

As evaluated by the author in accordance with Nobel's will.

DO THE SECRETARIES MATCH UP?

A competent secretary should provide a committee with correct information on applicable rules and ensure proper awareness of the framework surrounding the decisions. Members change and have other commitments, and being on the Nobel committee is but one of many obligations for most members. In practice, they have to be able to rely on a competent and loyal administration to ensure the quality of their work. The secretary must have studied the formal requirements and be able to help the committee respect its mandate.

Have the various Nobel secretaries been up to the task? My study of how they have viewed their role, and Nobel's will, would seem to indicate that the secretaries after 1946 carry much of the responsibility for the misconceptions that have developed since. The first two secretaries, Christian Lange and Ragnvald Moe, both had good scores: close to 90 percent of the prizes adhered to the testament in the 44 years they served. During the period of the third secretary, August Schou, serving 28 years from 1946, the score dropped to around half that of his predecessors. The latest secretary, Geir Lundestad, serving since 1990, has an overall score of 40 percent. There is, however, a sharp drop from 47 percent in the first 10 years of his period, to 28 percent in the latter 10 years. How commercial interests have been significant in this deterioration, and the likely role of the secretary, will be addressed in chapter 8.

Before 1946: Two secretaries in 45 years

Christian L. Lange was secretary during the first nine years of the Nobel Foundation's inception; Ragnvald Moe served for the next

36 years. Both had history and languages as their educational background. Both shared visions that were close to Nobel's peace vision. After his years as secretary, Lange continued as a consultant to the committee. During the last years of his life, from 1934 to 1938, he was a member of the committee. Most awards were in compliance as long as these two were central to the Nobel system.

Hardly any Norwegian has done more competent and comprehensive lifelong work for peace than Lange, a knowledgeable and industrious man who must have had greater influence on the Peace Prize than anyone else. He was a key organizer of interparliamentary peace work and a delegate to the League of Nations. Having so active a champion for peace through the first 37 years, so congenial with Nobel, and combining key roles in the work of the Nobel committee with a central role in international peace work was essential to ensuring a good start and a reasonably good track record up to World War II.

The Peace Prize that Lange received in 1921 is among the most deserved in the history of the prize. He used his lecture to expound "internationalism" as a rational basis for interaction between states. To Lange pacifism was a moral demand, but as a practical policy he advocated internationalism, which was the theme of his doctoral thesis in 1919. How well Lange was suited to realize Nobel's will was borne out in his Nobel lecture, in which he outlined "the theoretical basis for the work that is now being done for international peace and justice." To attain the goals of the antimilitarists, we need a new social and political theory on how states should organize their mutual relations. About *internationalism*,[9] Lange said:

I shall discuss "Internationalism," and not "Pacifism." The latter word has never appealed to me—it is a linguistic hybrid, directing one-sided attention to the negative aspect of the peace movement, the struggle against war; "anti-militarism" is a better word for this aspect of our efforts. Not that I stand aside from pacifism or anti-militarism; they constitute a necessary part of our work. But I endow these words with the special connotation (not universally accepted) of a *moral* theory; by pacifism I understand a moral protest against the use of violence and war in international relations. A pacifist will often—at least nowadays—be an internationalist and vice versa. . . .

Internationalism is a *social* and *political* theory, a certain concept of how human society ought to be organized, and in particular a concept of how the nations ought to organize their mutual relations.

Lange is to date the only person to have been secretary and later committee member, and the only laureate to have sat on the committee.

The next secretary, Ragnvald Moe, was not a peace activist, but he had a correct understanding of the purpose of the will. The connection between the prize and the peace movement is reflected already in the title of his 1932 book *Le prix Nobel et le mouvement pacifiste 1890–1930* ("The Nobel Prize and the Peace Movement 1890–1930"). Moe makes a point of paramount importance as evidence for the precise intention of the testator, when he links the change of wording Nobel made in the final will (1895) with the program of the 1890s peace movement.

Moe points out that in the first will (1893) Nobel mentioned only one criterion—arbitration among nations—as a condition for the Peace Prize. In the final will (1895) Nobel, "to better encompass all aspects of the work of the peace movement," included the three criteria— confraternization among nations, disarmament, and promotion of peace congresses—because he wished for *"a wider description, more adequately covering all the different aspects of the work of the peace movement of the 1890s"* [emphasis added].[10]

This is a momentous remark, in which Moe in clear terms pointed out where, and in what political landscape, any person wishing to determine the intention and content of Nobel's testament will have to search.

1946: A new secretary rewrites Nobel history

Unfortunately the clear understanding that Moe had had of the purpose of the prize was lost in 1946, when August Schou took over as secretary. In his chapter "The Peace Prize," in a book published in 1951 to celebrate the first 50 years of the Nobel Prizes, Schou reveals a defective understanding of the testament. He mentions that Bertha von Suttner had considerable influence when Nobel got the idea to include a peace prize but that she exaggerated the scope of this influence in her autobiography. Here she claims that her ideas in every respect became decisive for Nobel's view of the peace cause, but, Schou writes, a closer review of their extensive correspondence "shows that this is not correct."[11]

Schou also discusses what he calls "Alfred Nobel's attitude to the peace question." Doing so he reveals a capital mistake as to how the Nobel committee must relate to the shifting thoughts Nobel had on the problem of peace during the full course of his life. Schou failed to see that it was what Nobel had in mind signing his will that counts. Quotations from other periods may deepen or supplement the text, that is, they may help to understand but not to alter or squander the purpose of testator. Schou and his successors have done a grave mistake when they have considered it an open question what Nobel actually intended with his will.

The text leaves no doubt: Schou cannot have given the Nobel committee correct guidance on the content, purpose, and limitations of the testament.

The same basic failure was to be repeated by later secretaries. In the short unpublished manuscript *Alfred Nobel and the Peace Movement* Jakob Sverdrup, secretary from 1978 to 1989, describes different ideas from the whole of Nobel's life and then concludes: "We have seen how Alfred Nobel studied different possibilities for a peace policy without finding any convincing answer."[12] Sverdrup has the testament, how can he claim that Nobel found no answer?

It may appear that Sverdrup was on the right track when he continues by writing that Nobel had decided one of his prizes "should go to the cause of peace" and that in January, 1893, he made Suttner aware of his plan. However, Sverdrup ends his reasoning with these words:

Had Bertha von Suttner nevertheless managed to convince Alfred Nobel that her road was the right one? I do not believe that one can get closer to this than to note that her ideas and activities undoubtedly influenced Nobel when he formulated his last testament. It has to be added, of course, that a short wording in a will cannot reflect Nobel's entire thinking around the problem of peace.

Anyone with elementary knowledge of inheritance law will be staggered. A will is not about a persons "entire thinking" but on the decision made at the point of writing it. Sverdrup was victim to the same misunderstanding as Schou.

Like Schou, Sverdrup dealt with the task on the basis that the intention of the will was an open question. The next secretary, Tim Greve, a ranking career diplomat, is unlikely to have questioned an interpretation of the will that suited Norwegian foreign policy. Lundestad, since 1990, has definitely embraced the view held by Schou and Sverdrup. All secretaries since 1946 seem to have thought the same. It gave them a comfortable freedom, but it fell short of their legal obligations as custodians of a will.

All periods read history to suit their purpose

It is easy to attribute ill will to people who act in ways one dislikes. During my investigation of how the Peace Prize has been managed, I have done my best to prefer the explanation that individuals and societies have a selective memory. All humans tend to note and remember those parts of reality that best suit their attitudes and needs, and to overlook and forget those that do not fit.

In an interview with the *New York Times*, Francis Sejersted, the revered committee chair of the 1990s, stated that "awarding a peace prize is, to put it bluntly, a political act."[13] That makes me remember a conversation I had under the Communist regime in Prague, with an academic at the Czechoslovak Institute of Contemporary History. When I asked him what he was doing, his answer was, "I do nothing, since contemporary history is politics, and it is dangerous to express any thoughts regarding politics in this country."

This expert on contemporary history lived in a most un-free society, where orthodoxy was enforced by explicit means. But is the problem limited to totalitarian societies? It is important to realize how strongly the minds of people everywhere are governed by the culture in which they live.

One example may illustrate this. The police are supposed to protect citizens against injury and danger. Once, in the 1980s, I wrote a letter to alert the chief of police in Stavanger, Norway, of a great danger: a U.S. submarine carrying nuclear weapons would soon make a port call at his western coastal city. There was no reply. Responding to a reminder some months later, the police chief confirmed having received the letter. It had not occurred to him, however, that he could do anything about the matter; he had seen my warning as a joke.

His reaction reveals a paradox of sorts. Whenever a gas canister has gone astray, the Norwegian police will turn out with blue lights flashing and sirens blaring. Ships with dangerous cargo are kept away from the most populated areas. But confronted with a danger that potentially could have leveled the district and poisoned large parts of southern Norway, it did not even cross his mind to do anything.

The example illustrates how military security policy is an exempted arena. Here nothing functions—not normal freedom of thought, not sense of reality, legal order, morality, logic, politics, public opinion or humanity. The military have great power, even decisive power, over minds and societies. With his Peace Prize, Nobel wished to do something to break this tradition, but strong political forces in society managed relatively soon to neutralize the challenge and render the prize politically harmless.

During my inquiries into the history of the Peace Prize, I quite often have found it hard to imagine that the neglect of Nobel could have happened in good faith, but I have tried to excuse it as a gradual development of the committee's ambitions and appetite in incremental steps. I hoped the betrayal of Nobel was the result of many small steps and presumably innocent adaptations.

Lange, Lange, and Schou

Nineteen hundred and forty-five was a dramatic year in Norway. Five years of German occupation were over and a new era was about to start: The whole country had to be rebuilt and restored. Much had to be put in place, many cards reshuffled. The war had changed attitudes to the military. A few were more determined than ever in their opposition to the military and war, but for the great majority, the occupation by a foreign power became a decisive argument for a strong military defense. It became common to reproach the friends of peace for naïvety in the 1930s. Many leading politicians had spent years in German camps as prisoners of war. A strong belief in military defense and close ties with the United States and Great Britain took a firm hold and has dominated Norwegian politics ever since.

At the Nobel Institute and in the Nobel committee, the nucleus of stable peace "veterans" was gone. They would have to be replaced by new people at a time when the national mood had moved away from the ideas of Nobel. The result was that the ties with Nobel and his ideas were weakened.

Surprisingly, the prize lost direction even though the man who took over as secretary of the Nobel committee from 1946, Schou, must have been well prepared to ensure continuity. Schou had assisted the first of his two predecessors, Lange, with the second part of the three volumes on the history of internationalism and he completed the third volume alone. As a result, Schou must have been familiar with Lange's thinking about peace.

Other important factors, however, pulled in the opposite direction. Close friends of Schou—Halvard Lange (son of Christian) and Finn Moe—were influential in shaping Norwegian foreign policy after the war. Schou had studied history with Halvard Lange, who later became minister of foreign affairs (from 1946 to 1965). An active pacifist in his younger years, Halvard abandoned this stance under the threat from Nazism and became central to Norway's entry into NATO membership in 1949. As a member of the national board of the Labor Party, Lange may have influenced the appointment of Schou. During the 19 years that Lange served as foreign minister, it must often have been useful to have a close friend as the Nobel secretary. The position that no connection exists between the Peace Prize and Norwegian foreign policy must have been particularly hard to defend in those years. Norway is a small country.

Norwegian military and security policies in 1946 took big steps away from Nobel, but in principle, a testament is not affected by political trends. True to this principle, everyone has kept insisting that they respect the will, while in fact it was fully in line with Norwegian foreign policy to make the prize "apolitical" and irrelevant as an agent for disarmament. The Cold War spelled disaster for Nobel's Peace Prize.

1948: PARTIES IN—PEACE POLITICS OUT

In particular, one occurrence served to emasculate the prize as a tool for peace politics. Ownership to the seats on the Nobel committee was turned over to the parties after a debate in *Stortinget* in 1948 to elect new members to the Nobel committee. A strong controversy over the election method resulted in the system being changed. Down went the free, comprehensive evaluation to ensure that the committee, viewed as a group, had a varied background and competence. Instead, the selection was in effect delegated to the political parties. Following a simple mathematical formula, based on their strength in the previous election, the political parties were given one or more seats on the Nobel committee. The role of Parliament as such became an automatic, empty routine.

This shift, changing in the process the character of the prize, resulted from a new political balance. After the war, the Labor Party held an absolute majority for several decades. By insisting on the new formula, Labor secured more seats on the Nobel committee.

The Parliamentary Records (Stortingsforhandlinger) for November 29, 1948, show that the opposition in Parliament saw the danger, but protests were in vain. A leading Conservative, C. J. Hambro, said, "[up to now] it has never happened that members elected to the Nobel committee have been removed if they were willing to serve a new term." Hambro further underlined that Nobel had shown confidence in the Parliament of Norway, and that in elections for the Nobel committee, Parliament always emphasized qualifications, placing "much importance on selecting, as members of the committee, individuals who were particularly suited by their general political and historical insight and knowledge of languages and their ability to follow international work."

Several members of Parliament (MPs, including Lars Vatnaland and Oscar Olsen) agreed with Hambro that the Nobel committee was different from those established for Parliament business. They understood that the Nobel committee was not a body that should negotiate national political compromises: It had a private task to implement a given peace policy. It would be unfair and unfortunate to compose the committee according to party lines. One MP (Oscar Olsen) showed both precision and foresight in his intervention; he held that the Nobel committee should "work independently of partisan politics and party consideration." The new system of election need not necessarily lead to party politics playing a role in the work of the committee, he said, "but it is the very election where these factors may come into play, that can have an unfortunate effect."

The view of Labor was that "a stronger influence than before for the labor movement in the Nobel committee cannot in any way be against the spirit or the interests that Nobel and his donation should promote."

Labor won the vote, but the opposition has been proven sadly right in its warning. What Labor failed to see (or respect) was this was not a committee to formulate political compromises, but one that should serve the will of a private person. The need was not for a representative cross-section of political views, but for the best and most dedicated expertise in the field of peace and disarmament.

As a result, since 1948, the parties have used coveted seats on the committee to reward their own veterans. The unavoidable effect has been that Nobel and the purpose of his testament paled.

Grave consequences of Parliament's new line

That the opposition had a point in 1948 was confirmed 55 years later by the history professor Francis Sejersted. In an interview this member, and for nine years the chair, of the Nobel committee, criticized the voting system of 1948, and his views were endorsed by an editorial in *Aftenposten*, on March 2, 2003:

> [Sejersted] pointed out that a practice has developed where seats on the committee a little too often have been a partisan show of honor to politicians who have finished their careers. This will not only lead to committees with a high average in age, but also to a situation where no one in Parliament takes responsibility for, or has control over, the composition of the Nobel committee as a whole. No one co-ordinates such important factors as the background and experience, age and sex of committee members; it is the political "meat-weight," as some call it, that counts.
>
> The whole composition of the Nobel committee is determined by the results of the national elections, and the more or less sensible person-preferences of the parties. Such partisan criteria will often exclude independent intellectuals and experts on foreign policy, and in addition have the effect that members are chosen as individuals without taking into consideration how the committee will function in its entirety.

Without a doubt, the change has been unfortunate, removing competence and interest in, and respect for, Nobel's thinking about peace. When the political parties started to "own" their seats on the committee, the Peace Prize was redefined. It became the prize of the committee, which developed the mind-set that "peace is what the Nobel committee wishes, at any given point in time, to consider as peace."[14] With the prevailing attitudes in Parliament, the prize ceased to challenge the military sector it was intended to abolish.

The task given by Nobel fell into the wrong hands, as most Nobel committee members were averse to, and often clearly against, any idea of military disarmament. The list of committee members invites a question, I wrote in *Nobels vilje*: Has the committee during the 65 years since 1945 had one single member who could properly be called "a champion for peace," any member who has defended peace through disarmament, and seen this idea as more important than NATO membership, or than other good causes, such as human rights, democracy, or environment?

The composition of the committees has had adverse consequences beyond the annual awards, for example, in the employment of secretaries and consultants who assist the committee in its work.

The lists of applicants for posts in the institute are, like everything else with this committee, kept secret. One example can nevertheless be reported: the employment in 1990 of the present committee secretary,

Lundestad, a historian with warm enthusiasm for the United States and NATO. He was preferred over another applicant, Ingrid Eide, a pioneer in peace research who had worked with Johan Galtung to establish the Peace Research Institute of Oslo (PRIO). She had been active in the struggle against nuclear weapons, and was an academic and a politician with experience as deputy cabinet minister.[15]

As to peace politics, Eide was as closely in line with Nobel as Lundestad was remote, and she was not behind anyone in qualifications. This raises an uncomfortable question: Do the chances of being employed as Nobel secretary decrease the closer the applicant is to Nobel and the idea behind the will?

The new system Parliament introduced to elect committee members led to failure at all stages: committees on which none of the members stood for the idea of the Peace Prize have given the prize to the wrong winners; they have employed the wrong secretaries, advisors, and staff; and these again have produced internal and external information, articles on, and studies of the prize that do not promote the intended purpose of Nobel.

In short, since 1948, the world has not been given the Nobel Peace Prizes it deserves—and was entitled to. Not only have the Nobel committees betrayed Nobel and violated the law, but also the Norwegian lawmakers have broken the law. For a national assembly, familiar with enacting laws, it seems to have run against instinct to be bound to respect the laws rather than enacting them.

The legal aspects of appointing the Nobel committee—the obligation to obey the law and respect the will—are clearly borne out in a legal opinion by the professor of law Torstein Eckhoff in 1973.[16] He considers Parliament to be "free to decide both in the question of *who* shall be elected, *how* the election shall be prepared (who is entitled to propose candidates and so on), and for *how long* a term the election shall apply" [emphasis in original]. But the professor takes care to remind us that at all points the content of the testament must be respected.

Through my book *Nobels vilje* Parliament was told that initially it had understood its task correctly and, until the change of procedure in 1948, had felt an obligation to elect Peace Prize committees that fit the purpose. Parliament could not in effect renounce its authority by delegating the selection of members to the parties, reducing its own role to a mere formality. This is a consequential error, and it is essential to revert to the original system and elect people with the needed qualifications and attitudes to the task.

LEGAL QUALITY CONTROL NEGLECTED

The committee secretaries have all been educated in history, letters, or international affairs. Their unfamiliarity with the binding rules of law that apply to wills was not a problem in the first 45 years, when the two secretaries were in full agreement with Nobel and his intentions. The second secretary (Moe) not only had his predecessor (Lange) around for most of his 37 years in office, but in his last 18 years, the committee chair was a highly respected jurist (Fredrik Stang). The secretaries since 1946 have neither understood the concept of peace in the Nobel will, nor have they been familiar with the relevant legal principles.

In the years since 1946, a number of jurists have been elected to the committee.[17] It is not unlikely that some may have felt a degree of unease over what Nobel must have meant with the disarmament language he used to describe the Peace Prize. If so, they seem not to have been tempted to react against a practice that suited their attitudes toward security and defense policies. And most of the lawyers were only deputy members and hardly ever called to serve.

Despite all the capable lawyers that have been involved, nothing indicates that a thorough legal interpretation of the will's purpose was ever conducted. As lawyers, they should have had a keener awareness of the obligation not to infringe on the rights of the intended beneficiaries and to actively pursue peace work of the type that Nobel wished to support. The beneficiaries have a protected legal right to enjoy the support Nobel intended to give their work. Their right was violated every time the prize was awarded to individuals or causes that are peripheral, or not at all relevant, to the purpose of the prize.

NOBEL COMMITTEE DEFINES ITS OWN PRIZE

Committee Chair Aase Lionæs showed a striking lack of awareness that Nobel himself had defined the prize and that her task was to implement his wishes in her 1974 speech to honor Sean MacBride and Eisaku Sato. She mentioned that in the course of 70 years, discussions about the committee's decisions had been impossible to avoid:

> This is testimony of how difficult it is to define the concept of peace. The Nobel committee in its awards has sought out winners who have

made a contribution in the most different fields. They have been politicians at the negotiating table, defenders of human rights, experts in international law, the rebel, the humanist, the idealist, the pragmatist, the dreamer. They have all been personalities surrounded by controversy.

A later Nobel chair, Egil Aarvik, once explained the weight that the Nobel committee at that time was beginning to give to human rights: "The will does not state this, but it was made in a different time. Today we realize that there can be no peace without full respect for freedom."[18]

Why create unnecessary difficulties? Why lay waste to Nobel's own words on what he wished to achieve with the prize? The committee makes many such expressions of its wish to adapt the prize to a new era. In this process, the concept "peace prize" is being given a life of its own, even if Nobel himself did not use the expression. At some point, a serious misunderstanding has arisen: In violation of its mandate, the committee started to define its own concept of peace instead of respecting the antimilitarist letter and spirit of the will.

Some may think that the fact Nobel left the task to a political body could justify a political approach. Nothing supports such a view. Nobel must have considered Norway's Parliament as the best ally he could find. When he enlisted Parliament, it was not as a political organ, not as a state organ under the Norwegian Constitution, but as helpers to select the best possible board for a private foundation with certain, identified aims.

While boards of foundations normally are mindful of the bylaws and are aware that illegal payments are a punishable crime, the Nobel committee increasingly has allowed itself license to do as it likes. How far the committee has moved in making the prize its own and ignoring Nobel was expressed by Lundestad in a particularly ostentatious manner in a newspaper article on October 17, 2007. He confirmed that many prizes had had a "more or less clear connection with Nobel's definition." Rather than regretting this, Lundestad warmly defended the committee line: "*Our understanding* of war and conflict has deepened. The environment and climate will, just like human rights, soon prove to be an obvious element of the analysis" [emphasis added].

What about *Nobel*'s understanding and his rather precise definition? Repeatedly, the committee shows in plain language that it considers itself free to shape a "peace prize" as it likes. An article by Lundestad on the Peace Prize from 1901 to 2000 is particularly revealing: In Lundestad's view, the prize would not have been such a success had it not been for the decent, even highly respectable, record the Norwegian Nobel committee has established in its selections over these 100 years. One important element of this record has been *the committee's broad definition of peace*, enough to take in *virtually any relevant field* of peace work

. . . although the Norwegian Nobel *committee never formally defined "peace," in practice it came to interpret the term ever more broadly.* [Emphasis added.][19]

The idea expressed here, that it was up to the committee to "formally define peace," reveals a gross misunderstanding of the mandate and the law. In *Nobels vilje,* I presented Parliament with a serious complaint, writing that neglect of the express and specific peace idea of Nobel had become consistent and total and that the Norwegian trustees behaved as if Nobel had placed money at their free disposal. Their disrespect of Nobel and the law was blatant and had continued in the face of repeated, articulate protest. To use a political majority to take money that rightfully belongs to a political opposition group is blameworthy and undemocratic. If the board of a foundation misappropriates funds, it is a matter that normally comes within the realm of criminal law. In a letter to all parliamentarians weeks before they were to elect the new Nobel committee in November 2008 I reminded them of their responsibility under law. The result was . . . resounding silence.

BURYING AWKWARD HISTORY

Fundamental link with peace movement obscured

Full and precise awareness of the role that Suttner played when the Peace Prize came into existence would be an obstacle to any political wish to dilute and redirect the prize. In view of the precise and solid book of Nobel Secretary Moe, in 1932, it was not easy to write the peace movement out of the Nobel history, but it was done rather successfully. The Nobel Foundation itself had confirmed the connection early, in 1905, in a brochure printed when Suttner herself received the Peace Prize: "It was also she who introduced Nobel to the peace movement, she asked him to come to the peace congress in Bern (1892), and she saw to it that Nobel, for the future, was kept informed of the peace movement."[20]

The secretaries after 1946 tuned down the role of Suttner and accentuated anything that could create an impression of discord between Nobel and pacifist people, organizations, and ideas. A number of such remarks appear in texts by August Schou and Jakob Sverdrup. But the two draw unwarranted conclusions from Nobel's skeptical and critical remarks on the peace movement.

In fact, what Nobel confirms through his letters and statements is how dedicated he was to the peace ideas of the period, and his strong hopes that they would prevail. He is uncertain as to practical solutions, skeptical about strategy, and he warns that the peace movement must not be too absolute and impatient. All that is true, but far too many have overlooked the pivotal point: Nobel *shared the goals of the peace movement* of a world without military and war.

The distance thus created in the postwar era between the Peace Prize and Suttner must have had its effect. When the memory of Suttner and her life achievement was forgotten, so was the master key to properly understanding the nature and content of the Peace Prize. One who worried about this was Norwegian author Gerd Grønvold Saue, former chair of the Norwegian Peace Council and board member of the International Peace Bureau (IPB). In 1991 she published the biographical novel *Fredsfurien* (*The Peace Shrew*), in which she noted as a fact that Suttner worked to win over Nobel for the peace movement and that "beyond doubt the Nobel peace prize is a result of the efforts of Bertha von Suttner." Saue's book was important in arousing renewed interest in Suttner and it helped to remedy some of the incorrect ideas that had taken hold in both Norwegian and Swedish Nobel circles in the postwar period.

One has to wonder how it was possible for the secretaries after World War II to lose touch with the history of Nobel and what he intended with his will. Much had been written about this—there were several clear protests from the peace movement against being pushed aside. Above all, the secretaries after 1946 must have overlooked the insight that was obvious to the two earlier secretaries. In vain did Ragnvald Moe even leave to his successors a solid book with clear documentation of Nobel's purpose: to support the peace movement.

In the book, Moe mentioned that *le pacifisme* (the cause of peace/the peace movement) had become the chief preoccupation of Nobel (*sa pensée dominante*) toward the end of his life.[21] Nobel thought that nations should consider that anything was better than war, Moe wrote. To better contribute to the struggle against war and militarism, Nobel had employed a diplomat and written to him that he would be happy if he could at least be of some use to the cause of peace. If he could do something for the work of the peace congress (1892), his purse would be open.[22] In 1895, the "peace congresses" were mentioned in his will.

Moe further mentions that Nobel, only 10 days after signing his last testament, asked a nephew to check the possibility of buying the liberal Stockholm paper *Aftonbladet*. He wished to have a paper that, as he put it, "is inspired by liberal ideas and opposed to armaments and other remnants of medieval times."[23]

As one can see, much of the material in Moe's book supports and amplifies his conclusion that Nobel chose the particular wording of his last will because he wished to cover *"all the different aspects of the work of the peace movement of the 1890s"* [emphasis added].[24]

This is an observation of paramount importance and it is interesting to see how in his book Moe gives the same descriptions of Nobel's changing thoughts on peace that Schou and Sverdrup would later repeat. Like them, he describes Nobel's shifting views of the peace movement in the course of his life. Unlike them, however, Moe was able to distinguish what counted, and he saw that it was the conclusion Nobel had arrived at when he signed his testament that was, and continues to be, relevant.

Moe had studied the intention of Nobel, and expressed in precise, unambiguous terms the legally binding content of the Peace Prize. How could his successors manage to forget what Moe had written, and ignore the elementary and fundamental rules on legal interpretation that he had described so clearly?

Confusion over choice of Norway

Nobel had conferred the task of awarding the Peace Prize on the Parliament of Norway because, at the time, it was a leading proponent of the peace cause. To begin with, this was common knowledge. The doubts that developed after 1946 over his motive for choosing Norway weakened understanding of the specific types of peace work that Nobel wished to support.

August Schou's reasoning about this can be seen from a text he wrote in 1950:

> There is no reliable testimony to explain why Nobel gave the Norwegian *Storting* the right to choose the peace prize committee. Some people have declared that Nobel's thought was that this in itself would bring about a relaxation of tension in the Swedish-Norwegian Union conflict which had just become acute at that time. There is, however, nothing to indicate that Nobel was particularly concerned with this conflict. . . . Another explanation put forward is that the regulation was a recognition of Stortinget's positive attitude to international work and especially to the cause of arbitration; though here too *there is no real proof*. The only conclusion

left is that Nobel's stipulation with regard to the Peace Prize was based on his general admiration for Norway's contributions to literature in the second half of the 1800s, and especially his admiration for Bjørnstjerne Bjørnson. [Emphasis added.][25]

As we see, Nobel Secretary Schou concludes that it was Nobel's sense for Norway's intellectual life that counted most when he entrusted the task to the Parliament of Norway. But we have every reason to ask: Is there really a need to require "real proof" for the most obvious motive in such a situation—that the testator wishes to secure a loyal and reliable realization of the testament?

Similarly the current secretary, Lundestad, fails to see the most obvious motive for choosing Norway: "Nobel may have been aware of the strong interest of the Norwegian *Storting* (Parliament) in the peaceful solution of international disputes in the 1890s. He might have, in fact, considered Norway a more peace-oriented and more democratic country than Sweden." Lundestad continues and concludes as follows: "Finally, Nobel may have been influenced by his admiration for Norwegian fiction, particularly by the author Bjørnstjerne Bjørnson, who was a well-known peace activist in the 1890s. Or it may have been a combination of all these factors."[26]

Lundestad seemingly fails to see that the peace and demilitarization thinking of the period is reflected in all three of the factors he mentions, and to realize what a powerful signal this is about the specific type of peace thinking that prompted the Nobel testament.

How has it been possible for postwar secretaries to overlook the attitudes that prevailed in the early years of the Peace Prize? In those days, many leading politicians expressed, in unambiguous terms, what they saw as Nobel's motive for the choice of Norway. The first committee chair, Minister of Foreign Affairs Jørgen Løvland, said in his speech at the opening of the Nobel Institute in February 1904 that Nobel "left the award of the peace prize to the Norwegian Parliament without doubt because it—more than any national assembly—had shown an active interest in the cause of peace in its new forms of arbitration and the inter-parliamentary conferences, in which Nobel places such high hopes."

In recent years Stenersen, Sveen, and Libæk, the three historians who in 2001 published a centenary history of the Nobel Peace Prize, have given a more probable analysis. These historians hold that the most important factor in Nobel's choice of Norway must have been the special interest in peace politics shown by the Parliament of Norway, and its moral and financial support for the peace movement. The writers also mention that Nobel considered "the parliament of Norway as particularly capable of selecting an impartial and competent committee."

It is highly regrettable that none of the Nobel secretaries since World War II seem to have understood this primary motive for choosing Norway—and what it can tell about the precise purpose of the prize.

"Always a broad concept of peace." Really?

Following the 2007 Peace Prize for climate work, the Nobel committee secretary, Lundestad, defended the choice in a newspaper article opening with a bold and sweeping statement: "The Nobel committee has always practiced a broad concept of peace." He made a similar comment when an early draft of this book was sent to the Nobel committee to make the members aware as early as possible of my discoveries. On behalf of the committee, Lundestad reacted as follows:

> The committee has made note of the points of view that you offer regarding the wording, in Alfred Nobel's will, on the criteria for awarding the Nobel peace prize. A long discussion may be conducted on how these criteria should be understood. We wish, however, to assert that *all committees since 1901* have adopted an interpretation different from the one you put forward as the only correct one. [Emphasis added.][27]

The claims that "all committees since 1901" have disagreed with me and that, under my interpretation, prizes outside the terms of the will would "cover all periods of the history of the prize," are incorrect. They ignore that the first two decades reflect an almost unfailing loyalty to the peace work that Nobel had in mind. In the first decade, with the exception of Theodore Roosevelt (1906), all the laureates had been partners with or cooperated with Bertha von Suttner, promoting different aspects of the peace movement's program: Frédéric Passy (1901) was a versatile pioneer in organizing work for peace; Albert Gobat and Élie Ducommun (1902) were involved with the interparliamentary union; Randal Cremer (1903) championed arbitration as an alternative to war; the Institute of International Law (1904) strove for an international order based on the rule of law; Bertha von Suttner (1905) needs no explanation; Ernesto Teodoro Moneta and Louis Renault (1907) were both active in the organization of peace congresses; Klas Pontus Arnoldson and Fredrik Bajer (1908) were organizers for peace; and

Auguste Beernaert and Paul Henri d'Estournelles de Constant (1909) worked for arbitration.

Several of these laureates from the first decade had been central in the work of the IPB. In 1910, the IPB itself was awarded the prize. Then the jurist Tobias Asser was honored for international cooperation and the pacifist Alfred Fried for his writing and organizing for peace (1911); Henri La Fontaine (1913) was an expert on the role of international law in the struggle for peace, and he led the peace congress in 1912. During World War I, the committee did not award a Peace Prize, before a good new beginning in 1919, with the prize going to Woodrow Wilson for his role in creating the League of Nations. After him, the jurist Léon Bourgeois (1920) won the prize, for promoting international law and order and compulsory arbitration. Hjalmar Branting and Christian Lange shared the prize for 1921, Branting for mobilizing the working class against war and the peaceful dissolution of the Swedish-Norwegian Union, and Lange for the achievements described in chapter 7.

The current secretary, Lundestad, runs into big problems when he asserts that the Nobel committee always practiced "a broad concept of peace" (that is, never felt restricted by the will, and never paid any attention to the specific purpose that Nobel had in mind). This claim is contradicted by many, including his predecessor, Sverdrup in an unpublished manuscript found in the Nobel Library:

> [T]he list of awards up to World War I is dominated by names that played an active role in the Inter-Parliamentary Union and the peace movement—of the 19 peace prizes of that period the great majority went to individuals or organizations that were active within the framework drawn up by the two congresses.[28]

A more authoritative expression of the same view is found in Stenersen et al. (2001) who write that the prize benefited from a good start: "It secured a firm footing prior to the First World War: the Nobel committee chose mainly to reward people central to the international peace movement, individuals who had lived with peace work throughout their adult lives." The authors fail to see this as resulting from a proper understanding and due respect for the purpose of the will however, noting only: "This added credence to the awards in their first phase."[29]

The prizes of the first two to four decades contradict the claim that the committee has "always" used a broad interpretation of peace. As a historian Lundestad must know that he contradicts the views of his predecessors and of the Nobel historians. Even worse, he contradicts himself. If his position in 2007 is true, why did he write the following in 2001:

> With this composition of the Nobel committee in mind, the list of the Nobel laureates for the years 1901 to 1914 comes as no big surprise. Of the 19 prizes awarded during this period, only two went to persons who did not represent the Inter-Parliamentary Union, popular peace groups or the international legal tradition.[30]

Lundestad is right in confirming that to begin with almost all prizes went to the peace movement but why did it not strike him that the many prizes for the peace movement—and the many friends of peace on the early committees—both reflected a correct understanding of the legal obligations of loyalty to Nobel and the will that prevailed in the early years?

Role of historians

Several of the historians who have written about the Peace Prize have strengthened misconceptions over the purpose of the prize, presumably due to lack of legal insight. Routinely, they have described deviations from Nobel's intent as introducing a new category of prizes—for instance in the fields of human rights, democracy, and the environment. When Nobel historians, such as Abrams, refer to new categories without questioning their legitimacy and relation to Nobel's will, they contribute to the impression that each Nobel committee is free to ascribe to Nobel's prize the content it wishes.

Abrams seems to have described what the committee has done, but never seriously to have raised the question of what it is entitled to do: What is the proper interpretation of the will? And does the Nobel committee have a free hand to read any content it likes into the will? In the foreword to the first edition of his main work on the subject, Abrams continues, noting that the prizes have not brought peace on earth, he explains that the Nobel committees "have acted from a different conception . . . [and] acknowledged efforts of all sorts to tighten human bonds, recognizing that this must be the basis for any enduring political organization of peace."[31] Another example of a compliant attitude is this:

> They have made his prize the most prestigious in the world for those who have, in Nobel's words, conferred *"the greatest benefit on mankind"*

in the field of peace, as the Norwegian Nobel committee has broadly conceived of this.[32]

Abrams divides the Peace Prizes into the following categories: 31 of the 107 prizes between 1901 and 2001 went to the "the organized peace movement"; 21 were "humanitarian"; 4 to "international jurist"; 35 went to "statesmen and political leaders"; and 15 went to work for "human rights."[33]

Abrams further mentions that scholars have faulted the committee for its lack of "a clear peace theory." In his view, "in the long run it is all to the good that the committee has held no one theory of peace and has been free to use its own discretion."[34] Abrams seems, like almost everyone else, to have forgotten that Nobel himself had formulated a "clear theory" for his Peace Prize. As a result he fails to discuss whether it is, in fact, "Nobel's prize" that the committees have handed out.

The general working style of Nobel may appear to some as an argument to grant his trustees extensive freedom. Abrams and others have mentioned that the two witnesses cosigning the 1895 will gave testimony that Nobel used to give instructions and then show great confidence in the ability of individuals to carry them out. Nobel gave a task to people he trusted, told them what he wanted done, and then left it to them, at their own discretion, to carry it out.

This, however, is not a tenable argument to defend the liberties that later Nobel committees have taken. Trustees were given a "mission." Nobel did not bother too much with detail and procedure, but he would have expected the outcome to be as he had described. We have to believe that as a capable, professional leader he counted on his helpers to do their best to comply, not to redefine the task to their own liking.

Abrams, furthermore, without seeing any difficulty, accepts a broad understanding of the concept *brotherhood among nations*. He notes that the Swedish original (*folkens förbrödrande*) "conveys a stronger sense of forging bonds between peoples" than does the English translation—the problem that led me to propose "confraternization" as the best translation. Abrams's interest in the will seems only cursory; he moves on to endorse the committee's understanding of "the spiritual and material foundations on which any enduring peace must rest," and then writes: "Some of the most acclaimed awards have gone to work inspired by a faith in human brotherhood."[35] Having just mentioned that "brotherhood" does not adequately echo the idea of "forging bonds between nations" in the words Nobel used, Abrams moves on to express a particular fancy for prizes inspired by "human" brotherhood.

Another example of questionable history writing is a commentary by Øyvind Stenersen on the 1935 Peace Prize to Carl von Ossietzky. Ossietzky was an active pacifist who had challenged the Nazi regime by publishing information on German rearmament in contravention of the 1919 Treaty of Versailles that ended World War I. With great courage, he risked his life for the central idea behind the Nobel Peace Prize. Even though it is hard to see any reason to speak of a new category of prizes here, Stenersen writes:

> But the Ossietzky prize was a radically new departure. It signified that the Nobel committee was seeking to advance the cause of peace by supporting fighters for fundamental democratic rights under oppressive regimes. The decision marked a new interpretation of Alfred Nobel's will, which prepared the ground for the later human rights awards that made taking sides in ongoing conflicts necessary.[36]

Prepared the way for human rights awards? How and why could it happen that a prize, more at the center of the purpose of the will than most, rewarding a courageous protest against military rearmament of aggressive Nazi Germany, is understood as a new category of prizes - "a radically new departure" even?[37]

NORWAY'S FOREIGN POLICY INTERESTS

The speech in honor of the 1953 Nobel peace laureate praised a man guided above all by two words: honor and self-sacrifice,

> that would take him over larger areas of the earth and the oceans and under the skies than any commander has traveled before him, and let him see more battlefields and a greater devastation than any general has seen before him, and let him plan and direct larger armies and fleets and air-forces than history has ever known.

The terms the committee used to praise the great U.S. Gen. George C. Marshall were indeed florid—well suited to signal a Peace Prize totally disconnected from its original intention. A prize to prevent wars should not reward successful fighting. Was it just too tempting for Norwegian politicians after World War II, through a Nobel for Marshall, to place an apple on the teacher's desk with a deep bow to the United States?

If so, it was neither the first nor the last time. No country has harvested more Nobel Peace Prizes than the United States, and "with every reason" Halfdan Koht said, delivering the committee's speech in 1931 for two great champions of peace, Jane Addams and Nicholas Murray Butler: the United States had the most laureates, but it also had decisive influence in questions of war and peace over the previous 77 years. Koht's next words would seem even more pertinent to the 21st century:

> America wields greater power over war and peace than any other country on earth. All who yearn for a lasting peace must therefore look to America for help. . . .
>
> It must be said, however, that the United States is not the power for peace in the world that we should have wished her to be. She has sometimes let herself drift into the imperialism that is the natural outcome of industrial capitalism in our age. In many ways she is typical of the wildest form of capitalist society, and this has inevitably left its mark on American politics.

Koht, then a professor of history, became Norway's minister of foreign affairs four years later. American diplomacy is known to have the memory of an elephant, and it is likely that his words on behalf of the Nobel committee became a liability he could not foresee when they were spoken.

Peace Prize historians Libæk, Sveen, and Stenersen—in several monographs on decisions of the Nobel committee in three different periods before 1939—have pointed to a number of cases in which the prize was used to promote Norwegian foreign policy interests. Stenersen notes that the articles by his colleagues show that the Nobel committee up until 1932 "preferred candidates with liberal viewpoints in line with the goals of Norwegian foreign policy."[38] In their centenary history, the three sum up: "The committee's decisions reflect liberal Western values of high standing in the past century."[39]

In the almost unbroken line of laureates from the peace movement during the first two decades, there are two conspicuous exceptions: the prizes for U.S. President Theodore Roosevelt (1906) and the prize for U.S. Secretary of War, later secretary of state, Elihu Root (1912). How could Roosevelt, a man with a mind-set completely the opposite of Nobel's "champion of peace," possibly win? This is the first instance of misuse to promote Norwegian foreign policy interests, and it is a most illuminating one.

The counterarguments were well known. Koht, in his written statement as advisor to the committee, had mentioned that Roosevelt
believed too much in war as "an instrument of progress for mankind"
and quoted a strong protest from the American peace movement against
Roosevelt as "somebody who believes in war and works actively in
favor of war and more armament, to turn boys into trigger-happy soldiers, and generally to strengthen the spirit of war in all possible ways."
Roosevelt, Koht wrote, saw U.S. expansion as "a great blessing for all
mankind, and even though it may take place with armed force and
injustice, he believes that it will ultimately create peace and
happiness."

It has been standard routine for the Norwegian political establishment
to deny any connection between the award of the Peace Prize and
Norwegian foreign policy, but in 1906 such assurances were particularly unconvincing. Jørgen Løvland was Nobel chair and simultaneously
the foreign minister. Norway had won her independence only one year
earlier, and Løvland worried for the future of the country. He felt certain that the arms race between Germany and Great Britain would lead
to a naval war near Norwegian waters. Even if Løvland relied primarily
on a close relation with Britain, he may have felt that, as he said,
Norway "needed a large, friendly neighbor—even if he is far away."[40]

If it was common in those years to believe that Norwegian "independence" rested on the United States, this belief seems even stronger
today. In a book by Johan Galtung, a pioneer of modern peace research
published in 2008, *Norge sett utenfra* (*Norway Seen from Outside*), he
lists a number of people who were at least as qualified as many of those
who won a Nobel: (1) José Figueres, president of Costa Rica, for abolishing the army; (2) Jean Monnet and Robert Schuman of France, for
creating peace by making former Nazi Germany a "member of the family" in the European Community; (3) Presidents Sukarno, Nasser, and
Tito (of Indonesia, Egypt, and Yugoslavia) for the Nonaligned Movement, the refusal to be members of two blocs on a potentially disastrous
collision course; (4) Premiers Jawaharlal Nehru and Zhou Enlai (India
and China) for creating five pillars of peaceful coexistence between the
world's largest countries in population terms; (5) Urho Kekkonen, president of Finland, for the 1975 Helsinki Conference on Security and
Co-operation in Europe (CSCE); (6) Olof Palme, prime minister of
Sweden, for the Five Countries initiative for denuclearization; (7) the
churches in Leipzig, then East Germany (the German Democratic

Republic), particularly the Nikolai-Kirche, for the Monday demonstrations in 1989 that ended the Cold War on November 9, 1989; (8) Pope John Paul II, for untiring work on reconciliation through apology, and for dialogue across religious borders; and (9) German theologian Hans Küng for his work on a global ethic bridging religions.[41]

Galtung is not in doubt as to why these peacemakers and Gandhi, the greatest of all, never got their Nobel prizes: incompatibility with the foreign policy of a Norway aligned with the United States—and, as a very loyal ally, not intending to pursue the antimilitaristic purpose of Nobel's will at all.

Can this reasoning by Galtung really be correct? Isn't the Norwegian political elite all for the European Union (EU) and the CSCE? Galtung's response to these questions[42] is that Norwegian foreign policy has long been based on military strength coming first and foremost from the United States. That is why so many Nobel Peace Prizes support the official United States. To secure support for high military budgets in the Western Hemisphere, resistance from within the Soviet bloc had to be unthinkable. Leipzig did not fit, Galtung wrote, "the result was reconcilable with Norwegian foreign policy, but not the method—why should we be members of NATO if such a dissolution from within could happen?"

The general impression of alignment with official Norwegian policy is also confirmed to a large extent by Lundestad, in his article on the Peace Prizes 1901–2000:

> The Norwegian government did not determine the choices of the Norwegian Nobel committee, but these choices reflected the same mixture of idealism and realism that characterized Norwegian, and Scandinavian, foreign policy in general.

It was to free the world from military ravage at the expense of ordinary people that Nobel established his Peace Prize. In 1897, the president of Norway's Parliament declared that the country felt honored and gave a solemn promise to the memory of Alfred Nobel to carry out the task entrusted to Norway "in the peace work of the future." By failing to respect his will, his great vision for mankind, Parliament has wronged Nobel, to the detriment of humanity. A Nobel committee loyal to narrow Norwegian foreign policy interests cannot do much to rescue mankind from the yoke of militarism and war.

COMPOSITION OF THE COMMITTEE

In view of the many peace advocates and activists in parliaments at the time, in particular in Norway, it is a natural assumption that Nobel expected the Nobel committee to be composed mainly of pacifists or sympathizers. This was, indeed, a condition that Norway's Parliament took seriously in the first 40 years.[43]

Political parties seek power, and to place their people in as many positions as possible. The Nobel committee, however, is *not* a political body but must have a composition that is relevant to the task, considering what Nobel wished to achieve. Just as with the committee, the will is a legally binding obligation also to the lawmakers to select a committee of the people best suited to implement Nobel's peace vision.

It is a betrayal of Nobel's trust to use the attractive seats of the committee as a reward to retired parliamentarians. In particular it is objectionable to appoint politicians who have spent their whole political life supporting a security policy, where NATO and a strong military have been principal tools.

In my first book on the Peace Prize, published early October 2008, I appealed to the

> members of the Nobel committee, as well as potential candidates for the 2008 renewal, [to] consider whether he or she is able and inclined to stand up for Nobel and his intention with the peace prize and ask themselves: am I in the vanguard of the struggle for a new law-based international (global) order and disarmament? If the answer is "No," the most decent and fair answer would be to withdraw.

What this appeal achieved will be dealt with in Part II.

Chapter 7

FROM 1990: THE PRIZE UNDER POLITICAL AND CORPORATE CONTROL

A NOBEL "BUSINESS" DEVELOPS

Under the dynamic leadership of Nobel Director Geir Lundestad, the Peace Prize has developed in the last 20 years. Through various measures, worldwide attention has increased. While this is in principle a good thing, it has its downside: it has required a much bigger staff, considerable operating costs—and funding.

An obvious strength of the Nobel prizes was their financial independence. The enormous funds donated by Nobel meant absolute independence and integrity, a full freedom for the five prize-giving bodies to follow the will and select laureates without extraneous considerations.

Until the policy of expansion and additional side-activities pursued during Lundestad's tenure, the Norwegian Nobel committee did not even handle the prize money: the checks went from Stockholm directly to the laureates. The administrative costs of the Norwegian Nobel committee and Nobel Institute were covered from Stockholm. The committee did not need to please anyone; it was free to choose whomever it wished without fear of economic consequences.

However, a new economic mind-set has been seeping in everywhere for decades. By the millennium, the ideology of the market economy and the push for growth had taken hold among those entrusted with awarding the Nobel Peace Prize. The three most visible aspects of this "growth" are the more pompous annual ceremonies, the annual Nobel Peace Concert, and the permanent Nobel Peace Center in Oslo.

The first change occurred in 1990, with a shift of venue for the ceremonies. The enormous interest generated by the prize to Gorbachev made it necessary to move the award ceremony from the Festive Hall of Oslo University to the much more spacious Oslo City Hall. Eight years later came the annual Nobel Peace Concerts, which soon developed into an American-style rock show that many find ill-tuned to the message. Then, in June 2005, after seven years of preparation, the Nobel Peace Center was opened in the old railway station at City Hall Square in Oslo. The center is filled with computer screens and cutting-edge electronic exhibition technology.

Lundestad was in charge of these innovations and procuring funding for establishment and annual operation costs. The Peace Center is one that can pride itself on delegations visiting to learn, including from the Museum of Modern Art (MoMA) in New York and the Tate Gallery in London, and it can boast of such a reputation for technological sophistication that even a delegation from the European Union came to study it as part of preparation for a new visitor center in Brussels.

These projects required between US$20 and US$28 million[1] of initial funding and around US$8 million in annual operating costs. The consequence was that a separate Norwegian Nobel economy had to be developed. Money from public and private sources proved to be available.

The five-member committee used to have responsibility for the annual awards, and that only, but now it has made the prize the material component for a business enterprise. Lundestad has moved from humble secretary to the Nobel committee to chair of an operation that seeks to compete in the international entertainment and adventure industry; the character, integrity, and independence of Nobel's prize being lost somewhere along the road.

Business gifts have strings attached

It is characteristic of the 21st century that industry, trade, and finance have penetrated new arenas and adopted roles that give political influence. Business knows the power of gifts. As long as contributions come from the state, paid by citizens in the form of taxes, people will have an influence on priorities through the democratic process. Private sponsorship means that decisions on what kind of cultural events people should be offered are taken outside popular influence. Either way people pay, through taxes or through purchase of goods and services. To reduce the state and let the market reign is to transfer decisions on what people should have to be made by the few behind closed doors in private board meetings.

According to the Norwegian Shareholders Act, gifts from a corporation must be in the interest of the corporation—and its shareholders. It is a matter of law that all such gifts must live up to the words of the German author Heinrich Böll: gifts from the prosperous always come with strings attached. The peace movement has long experience of such gifts—namely that, almost without exception, they are nonexistent. The 30 or more peace organizations in Norway that conduct peace work of the kind that Nobel wished to support have learned that there are no gifts to which to attach strings. From the public purse, they get the equivalent of US$400,000 a year in project funding—to share, with nothing from the business community. Only a handful of organizations have been able to rent office space and run a modest secretariat. The Norwegian Campaign for Nuclear Disarmament (NTA) and the Norwegian Peace Council are being supported financially by the trade unions.

Some would say I was proven wrong in 2006 and point to the Oslo Center for Peace and Human Rights that opened in that year. This was peace work in style, with generously salaried staff, first-class air travel, great hotels, and soon afterward elegant offices. The major Norwegian business corporations had bought a US$4 million mansion in Oslo's embassy district and committed themselves to cover operation costs for five years at US$2 million per year.

So, it is after all possible to get funding for peace work? Yes, if you have an amount of goodwill after a long political career and choose to convert it into charitable gifts. The Oslo Center for Peace and Human Rights was the solution that came up when Kjell Magne Bondevik pondered plans for his retirement. It opened only a few months after he resigned as prime minister of Norway. The plan was to employ the former premier and several long-time assistants to work for peace and human rights. Few of the popular peace organizations have a total budget that is more than a small fraction of the salaries paid to each individual staff member of the Oslo Center.

Many were surprised by the former premier's sudden interest in peace. He had led Norway into more wars than any other prime minister in the last two centuries. Only a few months before he made himself director of his own peace operation, the Bondevik cabinet decided to take all public funding away from the voluntary, popular peace organizations. In its last budget proposal, the modest total allowance to be shared among 30 organizations doing peace work in the Nobel tradition was reduced from about US$500,000 to zero.

In several newspaper articles in January 2006, I accused Bondevik and his center of low credibility, in terms both of peace work and democracy. My main grievance was the danger of corruption and of people losing trust that our political system is for them, if prime ministers, immediately after leaving office, could ask big corporations to finance a pet activity to busy themselves with in retirement.[2]

The case of the Oslo Peace Center has a lot to tell us about money and political freedom. In a long newspaper article I wrote the following on the chances of getting funds for "peace work":

> Popular peace work is on a collision course with the most profitable sectors of business. The experience of the peace movement is that the more the work is addressing the root causes of war, the more seriously it tries to end wars, the less the chance of getting financial support. Does the money from big business now pouring into Mr. Bondevik's peace work represent an exception to this rule? Hardly. Rather, the gifts tell us that the business community has experienced that Mr. Bondevik is a man they can trust.[3]

Dagens Næringsliv (*Business Today*, Oslo) deserves credit for printing the article. Not a single one of the readers protested against my views on the connection between financial contributions and political content. We may safely assume that if Bondevik had made disarmament and the abolition of war the main purpose of the Oslo Peace Center, he could not have hoped to attract generous financing from big business.

This leads to the next question: Is there any reason why the Nobel Peace Center and Concert are any different? Could they have the serious ambition of pursuing Nobel's purpose and still count on business corporations for funding? The answer seems obvious.

The main contributions for the Nobel Peace Center come from "Global Founding Sponsors," such as Telenor, Hydro and KPMG, Yara, Orkla, the Leif Høegh Foundation and other occasional sponsors of specific projects. The Oslo municipality contributes to a program for visits from schools.

Sponsors expect to be cultivated and pampered with great care. The Nobel system has had to learn some lessons on the degree of caution and delicacy that sponsors require. One embarrassing episode was a televised flare-up between the minister of culture and the Nobel director, who complained in harsh words of the ministry's reluctance to defray several million dollars more of the Nobel Center's operating costs.

The problem with the minister was sorted out quite soon, but the private sponsors were harder to tackle. Even though the director had not said anything negative about the Nobel sponsors, this confrontation led to adverse comment from professional public relations and sponsorship circles. They felt the Nobel Center had compromised its financial supporters. In an article entitled "Sponsors Slaughter Peace Center," experts on marketing and sponsorship had this to say:

> This is terrible. They have not kept their sponsors in mind at all. They have pursued their own needs. . . . They should have remembered that they also have sponsors who expect to be associated with something positive.[4]

When the Ministry of Foreign Affairs is among the important sponsors, it is likely to intensify speculations about alignment with Norwegian foreign policy. When the cultivation of sponsors becomes an important part of the work of the Nobel director, this is bound to affect the Peace Prize and its profile. The prize suddenly finds itself in a different environment. The mentality and the goals change with a new set of considerations to take into account. The guest lists change. The annual Nobel ceremony and banquet used to gather people from the cultural world, politics, and the peace movement, but increasingly those invited are financial sponsors.

At first glance, it may appear a good thing that bankers, industrialists, shipowners, and information directors show interest in the Nobel Peace Center, but how many of them would defend the idea behind the Peace Prize? These are circles that often express worry the authorities might listen to the organizations for peace and disarmament, and that actively oppose reductions in the production and export of arms and military material. In 1996, Director Bjarne Gravdahl told the Norwegian News Agency NTB that "[c]lose to one thousand jobs in the arms production at Raufoss AS may be lost as the indirect consequence of Norway's foreign aid and active role as a peace mediator."[5]

The development of a new and separate Norwegian Nobel economy has had dire consequences, placing the Nobel director on the horns of irreconcilable loyalties. On the one hand, he is the primary advisor to the Nobel committee; on the other, he is the Nobel director, depending on sponsorship from groups opposed to the purpose of the prize.

The deplorable result is that the prizes awarded will try to be as palatable as possible to business, government, and the municipalities. One example may be the 2006 prize shared between Muhammad Yunus and the Grameen Bank of Bangladesh, for engaging poor people in small-scale capitalism as a way out of their extreme poverty. The December 2006 peace celebration in Oslo became a sordid affair, where Yunus skillfully converted the enormous public attention on the Peace Prize into negotiating leverage in extremely tough business with the Norwegian company Telenor. The two parties were involved in a telecom operation in Bangladesh, Grameenphone, and Yunus wanted Telenor to sign over its shares in Grameenphone.

How many pondered the question whether Telenor as a main sponsor of the Nobel Peace Center could have played a role in the decision to award the prize to Yunus and Grameen? Whether it had helped him win or not, the award became a public relations nightmare for Telenor—and for the Nobel Peace Prize. Nobel would have been sorry to see what became of his prize.

It safely can be assumed that through the need for financial sponsors, the Nobel Peace Prize has forfeited two essential qualities of the prize that Nobel established: integrity and independence. The present custodians of the prize have found the perfect formula to ensure that the Peace Prize will be increasingly grandiose, pompous, and remote from its original purpose of supporting peace politics.

The business activities of the Nobel committee and the Nobel Institute appear to be a violation of the *Grundstadgar*, the fundamental rules, of the Nobel Foundation. Here the "Nobel institutes" are described in Section 11 as "scientific institutions and other establishments, that may be established to help in screening candidates for the prizes . . . and generally to promote the purpose of the Foundation." The financing by outside sponsors of the Peace Concert and the Peace Center cannot be legal, because these additions are closely connected with the Nobel Institute and under the same leadership, that is, the Nobel director. This arrangement seems hard to reconcile with the requirements of *Grundstadgarna* Section 12: "In their outside relations and financially the institutes shall have a free, independent status."

It is hard to see how the grand-scale sponsor programs can be reconciled with the prescribed financial independence. The business enterprises established by the Norwegian Nobel Institute will no doubt present an obstacle to correcting 60 years of betrayal of the obligations to Nobel. Yet it exacerbates the need for the committee to initiate a thorough rethinking of its obligations to Nobel and his expectations.

PEACE CONCERNS IN A BUSINESS CONCERN?

How far the Peace Prize has moved from the original idea is shown with great clarity in a comparison between the first secretary of the Nobel committee in 1901, Christian Lange, and the latest, Lundestad, who has been secretary since 1990. The two seem to be the strongest, most visible, of all the secretaries. Both have been pioneers, showing entrepreneurial spirit and the capacity to carry out plans. Both have left a personal imprint on the prize.

But the comparison ends there. The contrast between their achievements could hardly have been greater. Lange had an all-consuming practical and theoretical devotion to a world in peace, to law and order in international relations, to disarmament—all the ideas the will stands for. Lundestad is interested in historical research within the power and *realpolitik* tradition—his field is the Cold War and developments in U.S. relations with Europe. Lange, in parallel with Nobel's thought and work, was a central figure in the international struggle for peace. Lundestad doubles as a professor of modern history. While Lange wished to create a new world, Lundestad describes the old one.

Both have solid academic achievements, but while Lange related to the individuals and organizations struggling for peace and disarmament— they were the very air he breathed—Lundestad, both as historian and director of the Nobel Institute, is in a very different world.

With the main emphasis on mass communication, Lundestad must spend much of his time with public relations agencies, television companies, and sponsors of all kinds. He makes a valiant effort to communicate about the Peace Prize, but the "growth" that Lundestad strives for requires support from circles that do not have much understanding or sympathy for Nobel and the idea of the prize. They probably would shun him if he were to be true to Nobel and spread the true message. It is in line with this approach that Lundestad participated, in 2005, in the Bilderberger conference, a setting in which Western Hemisphere power elites meet in secret and develop policies outside democratic control.[6] He has yet to be seen when *champions of peace* organize meetings or *peace congresses*. He may perhaps claim that he has not been asked, but if so, why is that?

One hundred years ago Lange failed to realize his plans to make the Nobel Institute a "scientific" institution, a "peace laboratory, a breeding place of ideas and plans for the improvement and development of international relations."[7] This idea lay idle for many years until, to his credit, Lundestad developed a research program under the auspices of the Nobel Institute. The program chose nuclear disarmament as its theme for 2009, a subject clearly within the scope of Nobel's will.

All the same, how fundamentally different Lange and Lundestad are struck me when writing my first book on the Peace Prize. I was seeking answers to the question: Who are the people who might be fit to serve on the Nobel committee? This led me mentally to tour academics in peace-relevant institutions, first the PRIO, the International Peace Research Institute in Oslo; then NUPI, the Norwegian Institute of Foreign Affairs; and then, in a sudden flash, I moved on to a purely hypothetical idea: What about the Nobel Institute leader? Would Lundestad be a suitable committee member? My answer had to be "No."

True, the secrecy around the prizes makes it hard to tell what role Lundestad plays on the inside. But the Nobel Institute director has expressed publicly views on the will and the mandate of the committee that show him unsuitable. Lundestad is a prolific communicator: he writes books and articles and gives interviews. Opportunities abound for him to comment and teach on themes that interest him. It is therefore highly unfortunate that the idea of Nobel and the Peace Prize appear to have no appeal to him. What Lundestad has to say as a columnist in Norway's leading daily newspaper is so far from the Peace Prize and its idea that his routine use of the title "director of the Nobel Institute" is a travesty.[8]

One example will illustrate how remote Lundestad is from the idea of the will: five years after the 2003 attack on Iraq, Lundestad—in an interview on March 26, 2008, with *Aftenposten*—praised the Bondevik cabinet for having "handled the crisis in a very good way. Yes, this was almost a political masterpiece, says Lundestad, who is also the director of the Nobel Institute."[9]

The paper printed a furious rebuttal where Gunnar Garbo, the former leader of the Liberal party (Venstre), questioned the proclaimed mastership:

As long as Norway participated in the Security Council negotiations, the master stroke, according to Lundestad, consisted in working for a consensus, without flagging an opinion as to whether they wished a "yes" or a "no" to war. When later the US attacked without a UN mandate, Norway did the masterpiece of saying "no" to the war without any criticism of the USA. Immediately after Bush had prematurely triumphed that the illegal war allegedly had been won, the cabinet again showed its mastership by having the engineer corps in place, joining the occupiers only one month later.

The key to the Norwegian "success," Lundestad declared, was double communication. In that he may probably be right. Maybe such masterly weathervanes deserve a peace prize?[10]

"Norway's leading international brand"

In the press communiqué in which the minister of culture, Trond Giske, announced that the Peace Center would receive the equivalent of €3 million in funding from the state for 2008, he called the Peace Center important and went on to explain why: "For example, the Nobel peace prize is probably what Norway is best known for internationally."[11]

He was only echoing a main "selling point" in the Peace Center's efforts to obtain funding from public and private sponsors: that Norway indeed cannot afford to neglect her "leading international brand." The director of the Peace Center, Bente Erichsen, confirmed in a June 2008 interview that the argument works: being Norway's strongest brand internationally "of course has helped us in the hunt for sponsors."[12]

Could the prize be more completely off track? Was it really to promote Norwegian business interests abroad that Nobel entrusted Norway with the task of awarding his prize for world reform? The answer is obvious. The documentation in this book clearly shows that Nobel wished to promote the ideas of the peace movement, not to help Norwegian businesses become more competitive in the world economy.

We can safely assume that the goals of Nobel are impossible to reconcile with the new extracurricular activities of the Nobel Institute. Another statement by Erichsen during an interview illustrates this point. She saw sponsor agreements as an essential contribution to the operation of cultural institutions; however, she said,

> it is desirable to be strategic in the choice of partners and select sponsors on the basis of sympathies and values, *but in reality we cannot be choosy*. The battle for the crowns [Norwegian currency] is tough as granite. [Emphasis added.][13]

The consequences are inevitable: making the Peace Prize a leading international brand for Norway has removed it even further from Nobel's purpose. In this second metamorphosis, the co-option of the prize by the business community has reinforced the earlier co-option by the political parties.

Lundestad departs from Nobel's will

Geir Lundestad took over as Nobel Institute director and secretary to the Nobel committee on January 1, 1990. Eleven months later he was in charge of the Nobel ceremony for the first time, when the chair of the committee that year, Gidske Anderson, in her speech to honor Gorbachev, gave a precise and correct interpretation of the mandate of the committee and the content of the will. In particular she emphasized the obligation to follow Nobel's intentions:

> The Norwegian Nobel committee is an independent organization answerable neither to the government nor to the national assembly of our country. The five members of the committee are only answerable to their own consciences, and their decisions are based on the personal political judgment and sound common sense of each one. The guidelines *governing our work are* nevertheless clearly set out: these are to be *found in Alfred Nobel's testament*, written nearly a hundred years ago.
>
> The award this year is very much in line with Alfred Nobel's own wishes and desires. Nobel wanted the prize to be awarded to someone who had worked *to promote "brotherhood between nations." That was the expression generally used in his day to denote the substitution of international co-operation for conflict.* Nobel also wished his prize to be given to someone who had actively promoted a reduction in "standing armies" and worked for the "holding of peace congresses," what we *today would call disarmament and negotiation.*
>
> Seldom has our committee felt more *in tune with Alfred Nobel's wishes* than this year. [Emphasis added.]

The fundamentals of the committee's task can hardly be expressed more succinctly. Anderson mentioned both the personal responsibility of each member for a conscientious evaluation and the fact that the decisions had to be within the framework of the testament. She even mentioned, quite correctly, that the words must be read in accordance with the meaning they had at the time and correctly explained what Nobel himself wished to say when he used them.

When Anderson clarified the committee's work in this way in 1990, 30 years had passed since the last time a Nobel speech had mentioned in clear terms what Nobel intended to achieve by his will. The speech by Anderson was an exemplary description of the mandate, but the committee soon took leave of Nobel's intentions. Lundestad has shown little interest in the purpose of Nobel, he has worked to realize his own, rather than Nobel's vision.

The clarification in the 1990 Nobel speech could have signaled an era of renewed respect for Nobel and his prize. Instead we are left with a mystery of sorts: How could Lundestad possibly have overlooked or forgotten this precise description of his task—in his first year in the job?

DOES POLITICAL WILL TRUMP LEGAL WILL?

Knowledge and awareness fade over the years, and Parliament as well as the Nobel committee could easily be forgiven for a loss of memory over time regarding their responsibilities and what Nobel expected of them. But it is another story when gross neglect has happened in the face of recurring protests, incessantly reminding the custodians of the precise intention of Nobel, and complaints that they were ignoring the intention of Nobel. The objections have often been so loud and impossible to overlook that the disregard must have been a conscious choice.

The main example of disrespect in Parliament is 60 years old. In 1948, parliamentarians crossed a line when they started to place their own political and personal interests over loyalty to the mandate given by Nobel. Public protests on behalf of Nobel a few years earlier had no effect. An article printed in the December 1945 edition of *Fred og frihet* (Peace and freedom) published by the Norwegian section of the Women's International League for Peace and Freedom (WILPF), stated the following:

> In a great hurry this spring, *Stortinget* managed to establish a Nobel committee that gave us anxious forebodings. One had to fear the worst in the form of neglect of the will and instructions of testator, as so many times earlier, and regrettably this assumption proved to be correct. The prize has once again been awarded in violation of the meaning and condition of the testator. Will it be forever impossible to make Parliament grasp that it was to combat the very system of war itself, that and nothing else, that Nobel formulated his will? In the struggle against this system he stipulated three directives that the committee should respect, i.e. the work for [confraternization among nations, disarmament, peace congresses] . . . What then has the Red Cross done to abolish the war system?[14]

Written protests like this kept reaching the committee and the Women's League sent a letter of similar content to both Parliament and the committee. In the small country of Norway, people in politics and the media know each other and talk. But is it absolutely certain that the protests reached the Nobel committee? The answer is a clear "yes." One prominent figure in the Women's League since it started in 1915, and leader of the Norwegian section for 19 years, kept in close touch with the Nobel committee leader. Indeed, she was his wife, Martha Larsen Jahn (1875–1954).

A newspaper article in 1939 repeated once again the persistent demand from women's organizations for influence and complained that instead of Martha Larsen Jahn, her husband, Gunnar Jahn, had been offered a seat on the Nobel committee.[15] Gunnar Jahn was a member of the Nobel committee from 1938 and the longest-sitting chair from 1942 to 1966. When, in 1937, he received a phone call to inquire whether he would accept a seat on the committee, his very surprised answer was: "This must be wrong, you must mean my wife." The diaries of Mr. Jahn show that as chair during the first 20 postwar years he was fully familiar with peace work and peace organizations.[16]

Martha Larsen Jahn may have had an influence and helped to slow down the decay, I concluded in *Nobels vilje*. Jahn, and much of his family, including his parents as well as his parents-in-law, belonged to *Venstre*, the Liberal Party. He must have been close to the ideas that once must have inspired Nobel's trust in Norway and became a dedicated defender of the will almost to the end of his 25 years as committee chair.[17]

Has it been a conscious choice of Parliament to neglect the purpose of the Peace Prize? The question deserves a thorough study, but regrettably those in charge, in Parliament and on the committee, have ignored the protests and seem never to have wanted a clarifying study of the will and their mandate and whether they failed Nobel and broke the law. These are key issues on which all members of the two bodies had a legal obligation to acquire sufficient and relevant knowledge—not to know was not an option.

The determined will not to know was clearly demonstrated in the summer of 2008. On June 10, I sent an early draft of the Norwegian version of this book, in particular the legal part on interpretation of the will, both to Parliament and the committee, demanding that the intention of Nobel be respected. A fair and adequate response would have been to take the letter seriously, and either accept my arguments or initiate further study to see whether my objections were valid. However, both institutions rejected my plea with irrelevant or incorrect arguments.

The president of *Stortinget*, Thorbjørn Jagland, in a very short letter to me, dated June 24, 2008, wrote: "In addition, *Stortinget* has not passed acts that regulate the activity of the Nobel committee, and awards will therefore under no circumstances violate Norwegian law."

His answer left me in stupefied disbelief. Are general laws not applicable to the Nobel committee? The leader of Norway's legislative body was expressing a rather peculiar idea of the law.

Furthermore, Jagland added, "*Stortinget* has no authority to instruct the Nobel committee, neither in general nor in relation to specific cases." The remarks seem superfluous. No one ever doubted that Parliament cannot and should not give advance instructions to the committee as to who should win the individual prize. A general instruction may be another story. In fact, Parliament may discuss all issues regarding the Nobel committee and its policies and practices, past and future.

The remarks of Jagland further were contradicted by the parliamentary records; there was a comprehensive debate in Parliament in 1973–1974, in the agitation following the awards to Henry Kissinger and Le Duc Tho. The decision caused widespread consternation, and the Socialist Party (SV) proposed a change in the election system and was even prepared to elect foreigners to sit on the committee.

Before this debate there had been a widespread fear in *Stortinget* that if they discussed the work of the committee this might forfeit Norway's right to award the Peace Prize. But a letter from the director of the Nobel Foundation in Stockholm, Stig Ramel, brushed all such fears aside. Ramel took it for granted that Parliament was free to discuss any aspect of the prize it might find interesting, including the general principles for selection of prizewinners. Parliament also received an expert opinion from the professor of law Torstein Eckhoff, who confirmed that deputies could not censor or reverse individual prizes. Parliament was, however, free to discuss past prizes, he wrote, mentioning that the committee had been criticized several times earlier.

Professor Eckhoff noted one such example where a parliamentarian had voiced strong criticism of the Nobel committee for having failed to award the Peace Prize in 1932 and 1933; and further criticized the secret voting in the committee for making any form of effective control by Parliament impossible.

The professor went on to explain that the fear in several earlier debates in Parliament of even discussing the policy and prizes must result from a mistranslation, a linguistic "false friend." *Talan* (lawsuit) in Swedish is easy to confuse with *tale* in Norwegian (speech/to speak). The prohibition against *att före talan* (litigate) in Section 10 of the *Grundstadgarna* sought to avoid lawsuits, not to place the decisions above discussion, he wrote. Parliament, according to Eckhoff, is free to criticize the awards.

Still, the letter to Parliament from the Swedish Nobel Foundation's director did include a timely warning: even if Parliament has wide freedom to discuss questions regarding the Peace Prize, it should take care to avoid confusion about the independent status of the Nobel committee.

Eckhoff had not been asked to evaluate the purpose of the testament, but he examined the 1897 compromise agreement with Nobel's heirs, concluding that the only responsibility the Nobel committee had toward them was to respect three points: (1) all five prizes have to be awarded at least once in every five-year period; (2) the amounts of the prizes must never be less than 60 percent of the available share of the year's dividend; and (3) prizes must not be divided between more than three recipients. Eckhoff concluded, "As long as these conditions are respected, there will not be any basis for action from the Nobel heirs."[18]

As mentioned, the Nobel committee defended their policy by claiming that all Nobel committees, from the very beginning, had ignored Nobel. As if that would make the case any better! Not only is it incorrect, it is also both provoking and irrelevant.

Careful execution of an office demands that criticism is listened to and objections are taken seriously. Writing the Norwegian book, I had no basis for asserting that the Parliament of Norway and the Nobel committee had willfully ignored Nobel's purpose. What I could register, however, was that criticism had so far fallen on stony soil. At the very least, I had reason to question whether those in charge were seriously concerned to ensure that they executed their task correctly, within the will and applicable rules. I repeat: not to want to know is a choice—and to know is a responsibility.

The Labor party had been warned in 1948, both by the public and by the opposition, but it still used its absolute majority in *Stortinget* to roll over the protests against the new method for electing the committee. Since then the Nobel committee seems to have turned a deaf ear to all protests. The Peace Prize became an arena with its own rules, even beyond the particular bylaws and secrecy—a reality that only gradually would dawn on me as my attempts to restore respect for Nobel (and his will) proceeded.

Chapter 8

THE PEACE MOVEMENT: STARVING BUT PERSISTING

MEDIA DESCRIBE THE WORLD "AS IT IS"

Many will ask: What is this peace movement Nobel had in mind? What happened to it? Where is it today? Where do we see traces of it? Point one is to understand that because something is invisible in the media, it does not mean that it does not exist. Mainstream media tend to highlight the center of society, with dominant political and economic interests their main focus. When challengers are kept invisible, they also are kept away.

Grassroots efforts for peace are persistent, but as good as nonexistent in the media. The media portray the activities of states and powerful institutions, but rarely the oppositional movement struggling for a new and peaceful world order. Describing the world "as it is," the media sends a powerful signal that any effort to try to improve it will be wasted. The work of popular movements for peace is kept invisible and thereby constantly discouraged.

This is not a new situation. In 1971, the Swedish novelist and peace activist Per Anders Fogelström wrote a history of the peace movement called *Kampen för Fred* (*The Struggle for Peace*), subtitled "The Unknown Popular Movement." This description, unfortunately, continues to be just as true, making it necessary to portray the movements that continue their work today in the tradition of Bertha von Suttner, promoting the ideas Nobel wished to support with his 1895 will.

Suttner's spiritual successors do exist and their work is vital for global survival. They find both inspiration and guidance in Suttner's political goals and methods. She induced nations to meet at the great 1899 peace congress at The Hague, in the Netherlands. When this historic event opened, she was the only woman present and for its duration she kept a *salon* for diplomats and statesmen. This made her a pioneer in the "grassroots diplomacy" that increasingly has played a role in the initiation and conduct of major international conferences. But few can match the scope, impact, and style of the baroness at that first congress in 1899.

In her book in 1962, Jorfald explained the role of Suttner before and during the first Hague peace conference. In 1898, asked by a Vienna newspaper about her foremost wish for the near future, Suttner replied: "That some government would take the initiative to call a European peace conference."[1] Soon afterward the Russian czar initiated the great 1899 peace conference to achieve "a possible reduction of the excessive armaments which weigh upon all nations," and to revise existing principles on naval and land warfare. The time was "ripe to secure for all peoples a real and durable peace by getting together for international deliberations."

At her *salon* at the Central Hotel, The Hague, journalists and delegates swarmed around her. One author, Balduin Groller, explains: "The delegates sought her out to get information from the very source, *in a new science* where they felt novices. Bertha von Suttner is in fact a true encyclopedia in these matters and everything connected with them"[2] [Emphasis added]. An American delegate, Dr. White, wrote: "Not only did they seek her advice, but once she got a direct request for intervention—as the representative for a major power asked her, as representative of the pacifist world, to bring her influence to bear [on public opinion] to bring the crisis to a happy solution."[3]

In the modern age the grassroots input into global politics has been called the "third international superpower." Though their work most often involves invisible efforts behind the scenes, it often has decisive influence on the positions of nations. The media register and relate primarily to the state actors. If the media cared to give adequate attention to these civil society organizations (CSOs), and the hopes that their efforts and achievements offer, their role and influence would soon be much greater.

It seems fair to add that official foreign policy efforts for peace also fail to get much coverage in the media. At all times, some states are actively trying to minimize the use of power and the military; strengthen the United Nations; develop international law with treaties banning weapons, torture, and genocide; and punish war criminals. One may often feel uncertain as to how wholeheartedly states pursue these goals, but it would doubtless enhance their sincerity if the media showed more interest.

The popular peace movement—civil society—often has been a primary agent for progress on international law and order, and efforts to secure compliance with treaties when they come into force. "You are important in helping us keep the goal in sight," a state secretary in the Norwegian Ministry of Foreign Affairs once said during a meeting with people from the peace movement. Why then so little interest in the media?[4]

Two recent, concrete achievements are the international ban on landmines and the establishment of the International Criminal Court (ICC). When the ICC became operative at The Hague in 2004, it finally gave general application to the principles of justice administered by the victors in the Nuremberg and Tokyo tribunals to Axis war criminals after World War II. At the outset both the landmine and criminal court treaties were "impossible" ideas. The grassroots organizations were met with incredulous laughter from diplomats and politicians when they started in 1992. They were told it was no point in trying, such an idea would take 100 years to succeed."[5] Civil society, unwavering, went ahead, and in both cases, it took only around six years from the beginning of their struggle before the two treaties were approved and became operative.

When the Nobel Peace Prize of 1997 went to Jody Williams and the broad International Campaign to Ban Landmines (ICBL), rather than to those government ministers who had been instrumental in helping it through the final stages of negotiation, it was a laudable and well-deserved recognition of the role that peace organizations and civil society play in the development of international law through treaties.

A third example is the World Court Project, involving broad cooperation among key actors in the international peace movement, the International Peace Bureau (IPB), the International Association of Lawyers Against Nuclear Arms (IALANA), and the International Physicians for the Prevention of Nuclear War (IPPNW), who sought a legal verdict declaring nuclear weapons illegal. In its 1996 opinion, the World Court (the International Court of Justice [ICJ], at The Hague) gave an important clarification. In the opinion of the court, a strong majority of the 15 justices condemned the use and threat of nuclear weapons and unanimously declared that states were under an obligation to negotiate a treaty and achieve a concrete result: nuclear disarmament "in all its aspects." Millions of people around the globe had managed to take the world a huge step forward—in the face of staunch resistance from nuclear-armed countries. The media, however, showed practically no interest in the uphill struggle up to, during, and beyond this historic milestone in the campaign against nuclear weapons.

Success stories like these, known to but a few, are described in several articles in *Peace Is Possible* (Heffermehl, 2000).[6] The CSOs were not entitled to ask an opinion of the ICJ, as only nation-states, the United Nations, and its agencies can do so. A valiant lobbying effort was required to secure a sufficient number of countries first to vote in the UN General Assembly for a resolution asking the court for an opinion, to involve as many states as possible in the actual proceeding, and then to assist with written briefs and oral pleading. After the decision came moves to disseminate information and demand that states comply with their obligations.

During the final stages of the case, after four to five years of intensive lobbying by grassroots activists around the globe (with New York, Geneva, and The Hague as focal points), an unfortunate effect of the rules of procedure dawned on the core group of activists: in the oral pleading, the 20 or more countries would speak in alphabetical order. As a result, the United Kingdom and the United States would get the final word. The thought that the views of these two major nuclear powers should be the last input the judges received before they withdrew to decide the case was unwelcome news, but it gave these civil society groups a chance to show their strength and efficiency. Soon, at a meeting in Colombia between the heads of the nonaligned states movement, they convinced a prime minister that his country should appear for the oral pleading. In the last hour of the last day, before the court withdrew for deliberation, the advocate of *Zimbabwe* delivered an unforgettably forceful rebuttal of the arguments proposed by the United Kingdom and the United States.[7]

Media and diplomats that meet these activists tend to assume that they are employed and salaried by solid organizations. The reality is that peace organizations are suffocating and have to use far too much of their energy to supply the minimum funding they need to do the work. The military point of view is generously funded and defended by hordes of spokespersons salaried by the taxpayers. This is the situation: while peace activists desperately hunt for funding, the war sector is a huge operation with guaranteed funding from all citizens, thanks to constant lobbying by the military-industrial complex to shape political opinion and decisions. And, if criticized, the latter decline any responsibility: "We are just doing what we have been commissioned by the politicians to do!" Are they?

CSOs have also contributed to, influenced, and supported the work of various international commissions, including those named after German chancellor Willy Brandt, Tanzanian president Julius Nyerere, and Swedish prime minister Olof Palme. These concluded that real security could be obtained only through justice, "soft power," and "common security." In 1982, the Palme Commission stated: "International security must rest on a commitment to joint survival rather than on a threat of mutual destruction." This was a precise formulation of the idea behind the Peace Prize of Nobel, Palme's countryman. It is unlikely that Palme's work went undiscovered by the Nobel committee, but American sensitivities must have counted more than Nobel.

The Australian Canberra Commission on the Elimination of Nuclear Weapons, a broad international group of experts, said in 1996 that unless we succeed in abolishing nuclear weapons, sooner or later, they will put an end to us. Even former leading American generals and secretaries of defense have ended up supporting nuclear disarmament—a demand that has enjoyed overwhelming popular support throughout the nuclear age. Opinion polls indicate that when citizens in industrial countries with a high level of education were asked about nuclear weapons, around 90 percent favored their elimination. This figure was only 8 to 10 percent lower in nuclear-armed countries, such as France, Great Britain, and the United States. Democracy has failed so far to break the vicious circles in this crucial field of politics, but the massive antinuclear majorities of the world have received only sporadic help from the Nobel committee.

A pioneer in the British peace movement, Scilla Elworthy, organized an independent security think tank, the Oxford Research Group,[8] and developed innovative methods in the struggle against nuclear weapons. She mapped and targeted those responsible for the operation of nuclear weapon systems to make them see their wider personal, political, and legal responsibility for a potential nuclear Armageddon. She also organized discussions between delegations of high-level British and Chinese diplomatic, political, and military experts.

One of Elworthy's favorite stories is about an action group of British women who had homed in on a certain military officer and sent him a flow of informative letters and requests for a meeting. Year after year they continued, unperturbed by the total lack of reply. Never an answer, and one day it was too late—the man had left the military and moved on to become elected to Parliament. Yet the women were pleasantly surprised when, in his maiden speech in the House of Commons, the nuclear officer warmly championed the ideas that the women had striven so patiently for years to convey to him.[9]

A much-needed improvement would be for the media to move to the side of peace rather than, as now, the side of war. They cover wars and armaments without regard to existing international norms or treaties, such as the strict ban on war that is the central feature of the UN Charter. Reporting that neglects these important principles contributes to weakening them. The peace movement knows the standard response if they criticize the media: "We cover the things that happen. It is not our task to strengthen international law." Is not a violation of the international legal order an important aspect of "the things that happen"? The media have only two options: mention the law or treat it as nonexistent. A choice is unavoidable; the media become "participants," whether they like it or not. A world in peace is something that journalists refuse to see as realistic, with serious consequences for their perspective on the news and what they cover.[10]

GRASSROOTS INNOVATE DIPLOMACY

How many have learned through the media of the huge possibilities created by "new diplomacy"? This promising new drive in diplomatic processes grew out of civil society cooperation with states, and it has opened up a new dynamic in the development of international law. In earlier times, nothing could happen without consensus: every single state could drag its feet, slow down, commit itself to as little as possible, and in this way, bar all the others from making any progress. If a new treaty could not be stopped, opponents at least could ensure that nothing efficient would be done to implement it. This situation is changing now, with alliances formed by "like-minded states" that move forward and reach agreement even if the big powers do their best to sabotage it. Once these new rules are adopted, they gradually seep into the body of international law as binding for all, including those states that have not approved them (*ius cogens*). By taking an interest in the early phases of this process, the media could do a lot to enhance the speed, strength, and efficiency of these efforts to develop international law.[11]

Another concrete example of what grassroots diplomacy can achieve was experienced during the international negotiations in Rome in 1998 to establish a permanent ICC. The halls swarmed with grassroots lobby-ists, organized in a huge coalition for the ICC (now 2,500 organizations strong, see iccnow.org). Thanks to the efforts of women activists in Rome, sexual abuse in war was defined for the first time as a separate category of war crime.

The struggle for peace will be perceived as an impossible waste of energy as long as we fail to understand one key point: peace work is not about removing all conflict, but about learning to resolve our differences in a peaceful manner, without violence (and never make demands that transgress the limits of fairness and justice). There has been a tremen-dous development of insight, skills, and new methods for conflict resolu-tion. In the last 20 to 30 years, this field has flourished in academic research, teaching, practical training, and widespread use throughout society, including schools and prisons. Lawyers and courts of law have discovered mediation. In previous legal battles, in which one party lost everything, both parties would have been better served by attempting a dialogue. In the schoolyards and even kindergartens, bullies are being trained in a different language and are learning to solve conflicts by their mouths rather than their fists.

Thousands of young people have now had such training, and thou-sands have gone through advanced academic programs in international conflict resolution. These students of peace will want chances to exer-cise their skills in a relevant job—peace becomes a profession. The diplomats of the future will be better prepared and have more tools at their disposal, and thus they will be able to think differently about mili-tary power.[12]

The role that civil society plays in negotiations on peace and disarma-ment is hardly visible and little known. A feature of important interna-tional conferences is the presence of representatives of non-state organizations (including nongovernmental organizations [NGOs], also known as CSOs). These organizations keep watch over the diplomats of their own and other countries, launch ideas, pull and push the negotia-tors in the right direction, and find win-win alternatives. In conference rooms, corridors, and coffee shops at the UN headquarters, diplomats and peace activists mingle. The peace activists have access to most of the papers and the discussions, except when meetings are held behind closed doors. CSOs are asked for their advice or opinions, and quite often are given a separate session in which they can submit and argue their positions.

Consider the following example from the struggle against nuclear arms: before, during, and after conferences on nuclear disarmament, the Women's International League for Peace and Freedom makes competent and important contributions to the discussion (including through its Web site at www.reachingcriticalwill.org). Not least important is the League's efficient reporting of events as the conferences develop—from New York to activists around the world. The activists then lobby their foreign ministries to secure a counterbalance at home to the pressure their diplomats may face in New York.

The hope is to influence the way countries vote in the United Nations. Some of the most efficient spokespersons for CSOs, with a special chance of being heard, are those political and military experts who join the movements when they retire after long careers in government. These positions go all the way to the top, with the likes of Robert McNamara, the former U.S. secretary of defense; General Lee Butler, who was in charge of all U.S. nuclear forces; Douglas Roche, Canadian politician and diplomat; and hordes of administrators, ambassadors, and scientists committed to a better world.

Some visible spokespersons for civil society have little formal education, but have acquired impressive expertise in their special field. As a peace activist in Norway, I have for two decades had the privilege of being invited to the various events in celebration of the annual Peace Prize winner. Attending the 1996 Nobel banquet, accompanied by a well-known figure in the British antinuclear movement, Angie Zelter, I had the opportunity to introduce her to the chief justice of the supreme court of Norway, who got along well with a recidivist "criminal." Angie's *modus operandi* is to provoke trials by breaking into military bases, destroying equipment, and so on, and then using the subsequent criminal proceeding (and, one hopes, media spotlight) as a platform to argue that her petty crime was lawful as an attempt to stop a major crime. Citizens have a legal obligation, she says, to stop a crime of such enormous potential gravity and consequence as the nuclear policy of Britain. The (now-retired) chief justice of Norway, Carsten Smith, immediately, and with great enthusiasm, went into a detailed discussion of legal issues pertaining to war and peace. At the end of a long conversation, the chief justice asked Zelter about her university—where had she taken her exams? She answered, "I have no law degree, I am a potter!"

PEACE PEOPLE—A "CONFRATERNIZATION OF NATIONS"

The truth is that many of the grassroots activists, after decades of work in the field of disarmament, often know the themes and the political situation better than diplomats who keep changing their job. People in the peace movement monitor national positions, talk more freely, move more freely, and think more freely on possible solutions. In this way, they can be of invaluable assistance to the diplomats. Following is a selection of just some of those individuals who have taken the future on their shoulders and dedicated their lives to the struggle against nuclear weapons:

Tadatoshi Akiba, Colin Archer, Mary-Wynne Ashford, Peter Becker, Rosalie Bertell, Phon van den Biesen, John Burroughs, Martin Butcher, Jonathan Dean, Jackie Cabasso, Helen Caldicott, Michael Christ, Pol D'Huyvetter, Dieter Deiseroth, Bev Delong, Kate Dewes, Scilla Elworthy, Joseph Gerson, Jonathan Granoff, Robert Green, Regina Hagen, Xanthe Hall, Kate Hudson, Rebecca Johnson, Bruce Kent, Daryl Kimball, Sergey Kolesnikov, Karel Koster, David Krieger, Dominique Lalanne, Patricia Lewis, Hilda Lini, Yael Lotan, Ronald McCoy, Pamela Meidell, Saul Mendlowitz, Zia Mian, Ramu L. Ramdas, Ernie Regehr, Douglas Roche, Henrik Salander, Jürgen Scheffran, Alice Slater, Susi Snyder, Aaron Tovish, Rhianna Tyson, Hiro Umebayashi, Alyn Ware, Cora Weiss, and Peter Weiss, Christopher Weeramantry . . . and numerous others. (With my sincere apologies; picking some names that come to mind unavoidably does injustice to many who could just as well have deserved to be listed).

The American lawyers, the German physicists and lawyers, the British (a military officer, a priest, and a potter), the New Zealand kindergarten employee, the Pakistani political scientist, and the admiral from India—these names so vital to securing a future for our globe may appear foreign to most of us, but the fault is by no means theirs. The complaint belongs with any one of many editors and news desks.

The names on the list give us but an inkling of the diversity within a group of people from all around the world. They possess one essential advantage over the diplomats: they are above national borders. They view themselves as a community, play as a team, and stand together in their search for solutions in defense of a common interest in survival— they see all the people of the globe as one. These activists have realized a "confraternization" at the substate level and are working to achieve the same in relations among nations. *They are probably the only forces in the world in the 21st century that continue to pursue the concept of peace that Nobel formulated.*

Although Nobel committee members tend to be well versed in parliamentary politics within and among nations, they seem to know very little of, or at least they underestimate, this form of international cooperation for peace and disarmament. Had the members been qualified for their posts and loyal to Nobel, they would have been more familiar with civil society peace work and would know the importance of the closely knit ties among citizens across national borders. Furthermore, they would have recognized Suttner and her peace work as the historical antecedent of the 21st-century peace movement and would have seen its importance and understood how it embodies the ideas that Nobel had in mind.

For years, the Nobel committee could have worked to make this little-known movement and its "unrealistic dream" visible, afforded the protagonists respect and strength, and made the impossible a little more possible. It would have helped if the committee had heeded the precautionary words of Dwight D. Eisenhower, the famous World War II general who in 1946, as the U.S. Army chief of staff, formulated a policy of a close, continuing relationship between the Army and civilian scientists, industry, technologists, and the universities.

Only too late did Eisenhower understand what a political monster he had created. In 1961, in his farewell speech as president of the United States, he warned his successor presidents against the dangers inherent in a permanent military-industrial complex (close to the core of the will and the expression Nobel had used 66 years earlier, *standing armies*). This complex—"annually spending more than the net income of all United States corporations"—would be difficult to control and easily could endanger liberty and democracy, Eisenhower said. His historic speech contained the following passages:

> Disarmament, with mutual honor and confidence, is a continuing imperative. Together we must learn how to compose differences, not with arms, but with intellect and decent purpose. Because this need is so sharp and apparent I confess that I lay down my official responsibilities in this field with a definite sense of disappointment.
>
> Only an alert and knowledgeable citizenry can compel the proper meshing of the huge industrial and military machinery of defense with our peaceful methods and goals, so that security and liberty may prosper together.

To do their job properly, the trustees in the Nobel committee should look in the direction Eisenhower pointed.

Chapter 9

A MORE IMPORTANT AND MUCH MORE USEFUL PEACE PRIZE

POSSIBLE TO REVERSE MILITARISM?

It is not for a single person to make the Parliament of Norway pursue specific policies in security and military matters. Only the population of Norway can do that, along with our international partners and allies. But the incredibly ingenious Nobel managed to bind *Stortinget* to forever respect a specific approach to security policy in dealing with his prize. When, proudly accepting his wish, Parliament undertook to bestow his prize once a year, it also undertook to honor the struggle for general and complete disarmament—as a perpetual obligation. Even if the political attitudes of Parliament have changed since 1897, the core content of the will has not.

Stortinget gave its promise to the Nobel estate, and as with any other will, incurred a moral obligation to Nobel as well as a binding obligation toward the intended beneficiaries. In numerous foundations, trustees have to carry out the will of a testator even if, over time, they question its wisdom and purpose. At the least, lawmakers must feel bound by the laws they give, and there ought not to be a need for me to argue that respecting Nobel's testament is a wise and useful thing to do. Still, it cannot hurt for the Nobel committee to be reminded of this fact and for readers unfamiliar with peace politics to gain some idea what it is about.

Norwegian parliamentarians probably are no worse or better equipped than their colleagues in many other parliaments when it comes to understanding the Nobel approach to credible security. How can it be that the content of the Peace Prize and its enormous potential for good seem to be beyond their scope of attention and comprehension?

Numerous solid, official, national, and international reports have pointed out the urgent need for a serious response to the challenges emanating from arms races and military technology development.

Our Common Future, the 1987 report from a UN commission on the global environment and development, led by the prime minister of Norway, Gro Harlem Brundtland, contains a clear expression of realism about military security: "Among the dangers facing the environment, the possibility of nuclear war, or military conflict of a lesser scale involving weapons of mass destruction, is undoubtedly the gravest."[1]

The aforementioned Canberra Commission declared in its August 1996 report

> that immediate and determined efforts need to be made to rid the world of nuclear weapons. . . . Any use would be catastrophic.
>
> The proposition that nuclear weapons can be retained in perpetuity and never used—accidentally or by decision—defies credibility. The only complete defense is the elimination of nuclear weapons and assurance that they will never be produced again.[2]

Common Security, a report in 1982 by the commission led by Swedish premier Olof Palme, seems to repeat the idea his compatriot Nobel had in mind 90 years earlier when, in his will, he called for "*the confraternization of nations.*"

But years and decades pass without serious political action. Those reluctant to listen to "activists and troublemakers" should take note how often these invoke the many crucial, solid UN studies. How is it possible for those in political positions to move forward with eyes shut to these fundamental and pressing issues? Is that responsible political behavior?

Stortinget and the Nobel committee have had a surprising lack of courage to support the type of international reform that once inspired Nobel to entrust the Peace Prize to Norway.

LONG SHADOW OF THE TWO WORLD WARS

The 1985 article by Hovdhaugen (on the inner life in the committee, written by one of the two members who withdrew following the Kissinger/Tho debacle in 1973), is a useful illustration of how the general mind-set and the Peace Prize were transformed as a result of the Second World War. Hovdhaugen was in line with Nobel's thinking in his formative years, after World War I, but by the time he was elevated to membership of the Nobel committee, his ideas had changed in a way that many will recognize:

> All my life I have been occupied with peaceful co-existence between peoples. In my youth after World War I, I was close to being a pacifist. The establishment of the League of Nations and the considerable disarmament in all the Western countries during the first ten years after the war, nourished the dream that the world would once be able to avoid the terrible wars we had experienced, and manage to settle disputes between peoples by peaceful means. I was not alone in this dream.
>
> The rise of Nazism in Europe, and the dissolution of the League of Nations, made it necessary to rethink this pacifism. I saw our need to protect ourselves, also with tools of power, to be able to defend human dignity and democratic ideas.
>
> Following World War I, many, both the youth and other people, were naïve enough to believe that we had seen the last of the big wars. After the latest world war no one believed that. We got the Cold War, and the division of the world into two power blocs. In our situation today I have accepted both a strong defense and defense alliances.

Hovdhaugen shared this "realist" quest for a strong military with the majority of people in Norway after World War II. But how could a man who declared himself in favor of "both a strong defense and defense alliances" assume responsibility for awarding a prize whose purpose was to develop security with the opposite means and ideas?

Thinking within the confines of the nation state, Hovdhaugen's attitude is understandable. It reflects a long tradition that states have to safeguard themselves, but Nobel wished to elevate the states of the world to a level above the precivilized situation in which the law of the strongest ruled.

IS THE MILITARY UNDER DEMOCRATIC CONTROL?

Generally, sound politics requires a long-term perspective: one has to make plans and to evaluate potential consequences in advance and policy performance in retrospect.

There has never been a shortage of military projects and plans. The tools for military security have improved, and the capacity to defend has increased steadily since the age of clubs and stones. But one may ask whether overall security for citizens of the world has not moved just as steadily in the opposite direction. We are paying exorbitant sums for a system of security that, in fact, has developed into the gravest, most immediate threat facing mankind. Why are we unable to bring about the "confraternization among nations" that Nobel had in mind? It is not that people do not want it, but then why don't we get it? Obvious answers include, first, the defective international system, then a lack of insight and understanding, and, finally, all the vested interests that would be adversely affected by a solution, to mention only the most obvious obstacles.

The problem is extremely complex, of course, but paradoxically, a major component in this common global insecurity is the means used for security and the tangible political power of the military. In more states than we like to think, the military enjoys unacceptable political influence. Hidden behind thick curtains of secrecy and propaganda, military élites exercise a power that most people would abhor, if only they knew and saw it.

One who saw how much the military has political control in the United States was the economist and former U.S. ambassador to India, John Kenneth Galbraith. He noted that economists had developed neither interest in the military economy nor the professional tools to deal with it. For this huge and important sector of society, the questions of what to produce and in what quantities lay with the military itself. The military has the power to crush any member of Congress who might get in the way, Galbraith said, pointing to the enormous military budgets seen as necessary during the Cold War. This global confrontation between two superpowers ended, however, without significant reductions in military spending. To Galbraith, this was solid proof that in the United States the military had become an independent power. "The deeper truth as to its independent authority is now evident," he said in a 1996 lecture to the United Nations.[3]

The military is shrouded in pomp, honor and glory shielding it from questions and criticism. But is it really behaving in a manner loyal to society and fellow citizens? Myriad examples would lead to the reply: most certainly not. A system that lives from conflict is tempted to create conflicts to live. But when the military profits from successfully nurturing dangers and threats (and hiding the better alternatives), other sectors suffer. Less money is available for health services, education, communications, and culture. The reductions in public welfare and social security are not limited to each single nation. The whole world suffers, the environment suffers, and survival is put at increased risk.

Most people will see it as an overstatement to claim that the military-industrial complex is disloyal and defends its own narrow interests rather than the national interest. Have these critics considered the issue with an open mind? Are they aware what Eisenhower, after filling top positions in military and politics, had to say in his farewell speech as president in 1961:

> In the councils of government, we must guard against the acquisition of unwarranted influence, whether sought or unsought, by the military-industrial complex. The potential for the disastrous rise of misplaced power exists and will persist. We must never let the weight of this combination endanger our liberties or democratic processes. We should take nothing for granted.[4]

The Cold War had led to an insane arms race, but what happened when it ended? The prospect of a "peace dividend," wonderful music to most ears, was a grave threat to the military. But the top brass were quick to intercept any escape from their grip. In 1995 professor Michael Klare wrote a most instructive account of how U.S. generals Colin Powell and Lee Butler led a successful military campaign against the interests of their fellow citizens. He explains how, almost overnight, a new enemy was created to replace the Soviet Union, states in the developing world equipped with chemical and nuclear weapons. To guard against budget cuts resulting from the end of the Cold War, the U.S. military first calculated its needs on the premise that the United States had to be capable of waging a major regional war anywhere on the globe. But this was not enough; the U.S. military then recalculated its budget based on a need to wage *two* regional wars anywhere in the world, and at the same time.[5] This sufficed to prevent cuts in military spending.

Politicians are defenseless against servants who shy away from nothing in the pursuit of allocations. The killing of the "peace dividend" in 1990 was by no means the first time that Congress was deceived. According to Noam Chomsky, the U.S. military is the first to promote the interests of big industry and let the ordinary citizen foot the bill. Toward the end of the 1940s, airplane manufacturers had a production capacity far beyond civilian needs. Scaring the population with war and the Communist threat became an important means of keeping production high and saving the industry.[6]

In 1997, the world shared the joy of Jody Williams that, despite intense resistance from the United States, it had proved possible to achieve an international ban on landmines. One expert who had promoted the treaty made it clear that President Bill Clinton would not be able to run such a ban by the U.S. military. Isn't democratic control of military forces a basic requirement for a country to be admissible to the North Atlantic Treaty Organization (NATO), I once asked in a small opinion piece in the New *York Times*.[7]

Returning to events in Norway, the 1985 article in which Nobel committee member Einar Hovdhaugen explained how, after World War II, he had come to favor a strong military, has a noteworthy addition: "[on the condition that . . .] it is subject to free criticism and democratic control." This essential condition is hard to realize, and not only in Norway.

With the military determined to hold on to its entrenched power, enormous mobilization across societies and borders will be needed to roll back its position and role. It is essential to strengthen the international civil society that brought such progress as the landmines ban and the International Criminal Court and that, in 2009, encouraged President Obama to drop the missile shield in East Europe. It would help if Nobel Peace Prizes started to honor civil society efforts and "the new international superpower"—a term used by Jody Williams, in 1997, when she credited civil society with the treaty banning landmines.

Chapter 10

WHAT NOW FOR THE PEACE PRIZE?

AN APPEAL FOR POLITICAL DECENCY

My Norwegian book ended with an appeal to everyone involved with the Nobel Peace Prize to draw their conclusions from the fresh light I had thrown on Nobel and what he wished his Peace Prize to do for humankind. I said it was not just a matter of respect for the law, but a matter of political morality and decency as well. Into the bargain, respect for Nobel would result in a much better and more useful prize. My discoveries raised several uncomfortable questions for Norwegian politicians: What about a minimum of respect for the law? Were they as the trustees of Nobel taking money away from the purpose and the people it was intended for? Was Parliament using entrusted money to promote ideas they like better? Could their misconduct lead to legal trouble, potentially even involving the police?

Under the law, when trustees allocate money in violation of the purpose it must be returned. Summing up *Nobels vilje*, I emphasized that Nobel was courageous and innovative, and that the Peace Prize that carries his name was targeted precisely at the military as the heart and engine of the international war system. Even at the time when Nobel wrote the will, this was an audacious challenge, and he feared it would be too advanced and come too early to be understood and digested by contemporary European kings and politicians, not to speak of military officers. How right he was.

Since Nobel's peace idea is unfortunately beyond and ahead of Norwegian parliamentarians' understanding even in the 21st century,

I invited them to leave their committee seats, making room for those who believe in the political ideas behind Nobel's prize; they ought to stop using the prize to promote their own political ideas, along with the personal advantage of being on the prestigious committee.

I reminded the Norwegian political establishment how particularly sad it was that it had let Nobel's Peace Prize start to degenerate precisely around the time when it had the best chance in a long time to serve the world: In 1945, the United Nations was created precisely as a tool for the "confraternization of nations" that could end wars and military "solutions," just as Nobel had wished. The overriding purpose in creating the United Nations was "to save future generations from the scourge of war" and to commit nations to solving all differences by peaceful means—and never to resort to military remedies, except in response to aggression or by authorization of the UN Security Council.

Stressing that the issue of respecting the will was not a matter of political morality or taste, but rather an issue of the Norwegian lawmakers upholding the law, I again encouraged the Nobel committee to look into its obligations, moral and legal, toward Nobel.

This they apparently were not willing to do. Even having received a whole book exploring the legal issues, in October 2008, the committee refused to discuss it publicly or heed the content in the secluded committee room. The same happened with Parliament. The rather alarming conclusions of the book did not matter. The committee did not have the will to discuss or clarify the problems that had been raised; the committee paid no attention and neither did the parliamentarians.

It is indeed unique for a Parliament to assist a private person in the implementation of his will. But there can be no mistake: even if Parliament is a political body, the task of appointing the Nobel committee is not within Parliament's *political* functions under the Norwegian constitution.

The Nobel committee is not one of the committees of Parliament, but rather it is one of several thousands of Norwegian boards of foundations. Handling Nobel business, *even Parliament itself* must appoint, decide, and operate in accordance with the applicable, general laws of Norway to fulfill a role circumscribed by acts regulating private (not public) affairs.

Furthermore, in my book, I asked the Nobel committee members to reappraise their task and to begin conforming to Nobel's will, as a personal responsibility, and to do so every year—not every now and then. It would help the committee stay on the right course if it always, in announcing the prize, referred to the primary Nobel goal of a new and demilitarized international order and clarified in what way their award fulfilled the obligation toward Nobel. If this could become normal practice, it would remind the world what the prize is about and which candidates are qualified. Even the political peace movement entitled to receive the award long ago forgot for whom the prize was intended.

An adequate response to the complaints, from the Nobel committee, the committee secretary, and the Nobel Institute, would have been to read this new analysis and begin respecting Nobel and his great vision. In the Norwegian book, I adopted a mild approach, abstaining from conclusions that were too damning. Instead, I gave those concerned every opportunity to follow the general advice: when questions of wrongdoing are raised, and you are in the wrong, you should tell it all, reveal it at once, admit your mistake, apologize, and make amends. The Norwegian Nobel apparatus followed the opposite line, making it necessary to write this book and to put the matter much more bluntly. The committee's stonewalling invited further research to substantiate my conclusions, and in this process I came across new and much more serious evidence.

Committee must restore integrity and independence

In the Norwegian book, I appealed to committee members to reconsider their attitudes or resign. Those who did not find it natural and easy to realize a prize for disarmament ought to withdraw from the committee. Potential new members should weigh whether it would be correct for them to take a committee seat.

The committee was further asked to restore its integrity and independence, which had been forfeited by the new Norwegian Nobel "business" needing substantial funding from private and public sponsors. The effects of this questioning required thorough evaluation, including answering whether the committee secretary could have dual responsibilities—that is, can the person designated to give the committee disinterested advice be in charge also of programs requiring substantial income from sponsors? To ensure a secretary loyal to the intentions behind the Peace Prize, that person must not have other tasks and ties that could unduly influence or compromise his or her advice to the committee.

Selecting a qualified committee

Parliament was asked to scrap the system practiced since 1948, since the relative strength of parties in Parliament, with their widely divergent views, is irrelevant to serving Nobel properly. The 1948 system could permit even a party committed to the strongest possible military defense to take a seat on the committee. In fact, it is possible to maintain that this is exactly what has happened.

Having fewer politicians on the committee also would concur with the wish of the Norwegian authorities to stay at arm's length from the Peace Prize.

Who would be suited to serve on the committee? To help Parliament renew the committee in November 2008, I mentioned some examples, most of whom are not known internationally: Helge Ole Bergesen, Ingeborg Breines, Tove Bull, Inge Eidsvåg, Erik Dammann, Ingrid Fiskaa, Johan Galtung, Jostein Gaarder, Alexander Harang, Ivar Johansen, Bent Natvig, Mari Holmboe Ruge, and Erik Strøm. I also suggested some suitable names among retired parliamentarians: Gunnar Garbo, Theo Koritzinsky, Torild Skard, Reiulf Steen, and Berit Ås.

In view of the special Scandinavian background to the prize, I proposed one might even consider a Swedish member of the committee: for example, Tomas Magnusson, Maj Britt Theorin, or Jan Oberg.

The Foundations Act of June 15, 2001

In the autumn of 2008, both parliamentarians and the Nobel committee had been alerted to the implications of the Nobel committee serving as the board of a foundation and to the main rules regulating the tasks and responsibilities of such a board. Section Two of the 2001 Act on Foundations defines "foundation," and the Nobel Peace Prize does not seem to come directly under this definition. The Norwegian Nobel committee receives an amount "placed at its disposal for a definite purpose of an ideal nature," but the committee has no capital to manage. The prize money is transferred from Stockholm directly to the winner(s).

The seat of a foundation is where the capital is located and managed. In a normal situation, the Norwegian Nobel committee would be seen as an affiliate board of the Swedish Nobel Foundation, and Swedish law and jurisdiction would govern. The choice is probably of no consequence when it comes to the key issue of interpreting the will, since the rules of the two countries are similar. The potentially controversial issue is this: Which country's administrative authorities and courts have responsibility or authority to act in matters pertaining to the will? This question seems not to have an easy answer.

Sweden is the seat of the Nobel Foundation under the current legislation. At the time Nobel's will was executed, neither of the two countries had acts on foundations. From the very beginning, Norway insisted on full and exclusive authority over the Peace Prize and the Swedes acceded to this demand. Because Norwegian lawmakers never intended to change the original situation, the Norwegian Foundations Authority must have authority to take in hand all questions except those pertaining to financial management.

The historical background for my position here is explained by Ragnar Sohlman, Nobel's main trustee, who in a 1950 book gave an account of the negotiations in the winter of 1899 to lay down the *Grundstadgar* (bylaws) for the Nobel Foundation.[1] He clarifies the one controversy of importance, the only one for which the Norwegian delegation put its foot down: Nobel had placed the award of the Peace Prize in the hands of Norway, and the delegation would not accept a Swedish demand that the Swedish government should approve the separate bylaws for the Peace Prize. The Norwegian view prevailed and a set of rules called the "Separate statutes regarding the award of the Nobel peace prize" were adopted by the Nobel committee on April 10, 1905.

There was no question about which nation would take care of the money and be the seat of the Nobel Foundation, but the Norwegian position at the time was clearly that the Peace Prize task entrusted to the country came under Norwegian authority and sovereignty. Norway required a functional split and full authority over the bestowal of the Peace Prize, a position the Swedes accepted. When, where, and how has this understanding between the two nations been altered?

Section 7b of the Foundations Act empowers an official Norwegian agency, the *Stiftelsestilsynet*, with "supervising and controlling that the operation of foundations in Norway complies with the by-laws of the foundation and this act." The agency has a duty to act on its own initiative should it deem that Parliament or the Nobel committee are failing to respect the act and Nobel's will.

The Norwegian struggle for independence from Sweden is now remote history, and so far the agency in charge of Norwegian foundations seems more than happy to defer to the *Länsstyrelsen*, its Swedish equivalent. It took only two days after receiving my Norwegian book for a specialist lawyer in charge of foundations in the Swedish *Länsstyrelsen*, Michael Wiman, to decide that an investigation would be initiated into whether the purpose of the Peace Prize was being respected. After a promising start, and loud pronouncements in the media, the Swedish agency suddenly and inexplicably backed off. It considered itself competent, but it had decided not to take action. In my opinion, the agency is obliged to react to an obvious infraction of a will and I appealed to the *Länsrätten* (Stockholm County Court) against the decision. A decision is expected in the autumn of 2010.

TO TAKE NOBEL SERIOUSLY

Norway is bound by law to respect Nobel's intent. As a self-appointed "peace nation," the country should be able to understand the peace vision and the thinking about global security underlying the prize, and should be glad and honored to respect the promise it once gave to help Nobel realize his idea for the "peace work of the future."

It is time to heed the warning that Lee Butler, the four-star U.S. general, expressed when, in 1994, he stepped down as commander of all U.S. nuclear forces. He said that nobody—officers, analysts, or presidents—had understood the real risks and consequences, and how close the world (more than once) had been to total devastation:

> [The Cold War] had, indeed, been a period of crazy risks. I was convinced that deterrence could go wrong. We acted like a player of Russian roulette, who pulls the trigger ten times and then declares: look, it isn't dangerous at all! The roulette was excessively dangerous and arrogant. . . .
>   It is a wonder that we got out alive. . . .
>   The nuclear planning was so complex and the presentation so superficial that the presidents did not ask the right questions.[2]

In reality, the nuclear danger is just as ominous in 2010, if not more so, as it was during the Cold War. More countries, in more unstable regions, have acquired nuclear weapons or are about to do so. The situation has become so serious that retired military and political leaders in the United States, in articles in the *Wall Street Journal* in 2007 and 2008, urged the nations of the world to see the acute need for common action and to evolve a new policy to abolish nuclear weapons. The signatories included such heavyweights as Madeleine Albright, Richard V. Allen, James A. Baker III, Samuel R. Berger, Zbigniew Brzezinski, Frank Carlucci, Warren Christopher, William Cohen, Lawrence Eagleburger, Melvin Laird, Anthony Lake, Robert McFarlane, Robert McNamara, Colin Powell, Arnold Schwarzenegger, P. Schultz, William J. Perry, Henry A. Kissinger, and Sam Nunn. They quoted Gov. Arnold

Schwarzenegger, talking to the group in an October 2007 meeting: "Humans make mistakes. Why should mistakes with nuclear weapons be an exception?"[3]

It is not advisable to rely on eternal luck, in having nuclear weapons and never (again) exploding them. Norway has the chance to take a visionary initiative, seeking international support for the active peace intentions in Nobel's will. Some country must stop the world from sleepwalking its way toward certain extinction and be honest about the need for a new initiative to rescue humankind and the endlessly valuable gifts in our stewardship: life, nature, and culture. We are not entitled to gamble recklessly with the whole of history, present and future, on behalf of fellow humans today or of future generations.

Norwegian politicians could make a difference for posterity by taking the initiative and doing real justice to Nobel's idea of peace in practical politics. If Norway seriously wishes to be a "peace nation," the nation should urgently invite other nations to cooperate on the task of transforming the Nobel and Bertha von Suttner's shared vision into concrete policies. We may risk losing everything, or we can rescue the world, and in the bargain, free up huge funds for public benefit.

The situation is so critical that the normal procedure of negotiations may have to be reversed: nations should first commit to the goals, then to the timeline, and only then work out the details and practicalities.

My Norwegian book ended with this conclusion: it is high time for Norway to renew the promise that was given in 1897 and use the potential of Nobel's legacy in the conduct of Norwegian foreign policy. The Nobel Peace Prize ought to inspire change in Norwegian foreign policy, not the other way around.

Part II

War is peace.
—Barack Obama, 2009
(essence of Obama's Nobel lecture)

Chapter 11

NORWAY SHUTS ITS EYES
TO THE LAW

"A PROTRACTED CONTROVERSY CAN ONLY HURT NOBEL'S PRIZE"

As my work on a Norwegian book about Nobel's will progressed in the summer of 2008, my pulse was often set racing by exciting discoveries—in particular because it became ever clearer that Nobel had wished to support just the type of peace work I had been engaged in for years. This work for peace and disarmament has to a large degree been a minority pursuit on an access road, with little chance of getting onto the main highway because of heavy military traffic. Without a doubt, it was this specific work for peace and disarmament that Nobel had wished to reward. The conclusions about serious deviations from the will were so striking and elementary that it must be impossible for Parliament and Nobel committee not to take the consequences—at least so I thought.

Nobels vilje (*Nobel's Will*) arrived from the printer just in time to be launched three days before the mid-October announcement of the 2008 prize, and two months before a new Nobel committee was going to be appointed. It was well received. The book received excellent coverage in the major international newswires and in media around the world—on all continents, and in all countries. The finest coverage was in two main Danish newspapers (*Information* and *Politiken*).

The international media apparently had no problem understanding the legal points, and the importance of determining which activities Nobel himself had wanted the prize to benefit.[1] The Norwegian media were less able—or willing—to grasp the key themes. Thus, Norway's influential daily, *Aftenposten*, generally in favor of strong military defense, seemed hostile both to book and author. The paper withheld from the readers the essential keys to understanding the point of my criticism and singled out laureates Mother Teresa and Al Gore from my list of illegitimate prizes. These two examples then traveled the world media.

The elementary points on interpretation of wills mentioned in my first critical newspaper article, in August 2007, had been confirmed by everything I touched during the further research. Nobel must have had in mind a much more specific peace prize than the watered-down version of the Norwegian Nobel committee. In my view, I had discovered a major scandal.

But despite all my attempts, it was impossible to get a discussion going in Norway on the principles governing the interpretation of the will; or on the misuse of the prize for commercial purposes; or on the question of whether Parliament and lawmakers were breaking the law. The debates never took off; they never even started. There were exceptions. The Norwegian news agency NTB reported my view that the committee members were unqualified for the task and later showed interest in learning about the distinction between "friends of peace" and "friends of defense." The main national commercial television channel, TV2, lived up to journalistic principles by transmitting several interviews with me, while the news desk of the state-run Norwegian Broadcasting Corporation (NRK) showed little interest.

Since those responsible had not shown much interest in my original protest—that small newspaper article in August 2007—I wrote to the Nobel committee a week before the book came out, appealing for respect for the will and for a constructive and fair dialogue, since a protracted controversy could only hurt the prize. Modeling my approach on Gandhian peace norms, and not wishing to surprise an unprepared opponent, I had sent early drafts of the legal analysis nine months prior both to Parliament and the Nobel committee, allowing them ample time to prepare the necessary changes.

The response, however, was not exactly Gandhian, but appeared determined to subvert any discussion of my complaints. All the media could obtain from the Nobel committee chairperson and secretary, Geir Lundestad, was a few spurious replies or brief pronouncements that they would not participate in a discussion. Instead of the response expected from an institution devoted to peace, the committee's reaction smacked of the tricks used by business to neutralize opponents in public relations wars—where the worst, and most efficient, method is silence.

The general silence from politicians, the committee, Nobel historians, historians in general, Norwegian intellectuals, and book reviewers was as efficient as if there had been a command from on high to ignore this impudent critic of a national treasure.

THE MEANING AND VALUE OF DISSENT

Freedom of speech and dissent is meaningful or useful to society only if criticism results in efforts to put right what is wrong or unlawful. What is the use of criticism if those in positions of trust or power do not listen or pay attention—or bury dissent in evasions or nonsense? As a law student and business lawyer, I always believed that freedom of speech was so valuable an ideal that everyone must be taking it seriously. This belief lasted for years. It was only when I started really using this freedom that I got a more realistic impression. Things look very different, depending on whether you serve or challenge vested interests. The media become an efficient obstacle to new insights if newspapers require debaters to keep within accepted, conventional wisdom.

In all societies, you are not supposed to touch certain taboos and fundamental questions. Thought control has been horrible under Communism and Nazism, but even under Capitalism, voices of dissent are—not rarely and not unsuccessfully—met with repressive mechanisms. In Norway taboos protect our two chief industries. Do not ask whether it is wise to speed up production of oil to keep fuel prices down, how much sooner wells will be dry, or what will the oil prizes be 10 years from now. Why is there so little will to study what havoc the end of oil will cause to all societies on the globe? Nor should you question our second-largest export industry, the thousands of fish farms that produce one farmed fish out of every three or four they catch in the ocean. And you should not raise fundamental questions about the Nobel peace prize.

Stortinget and the Nobel committee pretended that the dispute was a matter of taste, but I had shown that they had no "interpretation." They were not researching what Nobel intended but making their own prize. The Norwegian lawmakers were violating the law, and if such infractions were to continue in the face of clear cautions, it would be a punishable crime. What those responsible actually did when told that they were mismanaging the peace prize can provide a case study of honesty in politics. But no matter how we view the law, we can evaluate how the system handled the challenge.

A study of these questions may tell us something about the level of Norwegian democracy. In a true democracy, political choices must be made on the basis of facts—and these must come into the open. Good decision-making requires that all relevant information is taken into account. The competitive nature of politics can make the facts a battle zone and it may be open to question what is relevant and what is true. But the very existence of facts must not become a matter of pragmatism and convenience; to maintain control by twisting the truth and keeping arguments hidden is unacceptable. Otherwise politics will become unprincipled, unpredictable, and autocratic.

In the early 1960s, owners of a factory accused of polluting the neighborhood would invoke the best arguments they could find, convincing or not. Then along came the public relations consultants, with their ability to deflect criticism through spin and—not least—silence. To our misfortune, these methods have invaded the political arena as well. No one expects politics to be a tea party, but can it do without a basic respect for truth, valid argument, or dissent? Feeding the public with disinformation, manipulative language, and other red herrings is not the way to build a thriving, healthy democracy with broad participation.

The questions whether the Norwegian political élite had betrayed Nobel touched on a national icon, an object of common pride and self-congratulation. If my conclusions were correct, the only acceptable follow-up in a democracy under the rule of law should be a solemn apology, combined with the desire to change and make amends. And I expected Norway to be a democracy under the rule of law.

The modern public relations methods to destroy fair discussion of complaints against the business sector are much more damaging if politicians yield to the temptation and let them permeate politics. Dissent and honest debate are the lifeblood of democracy. Of course, politicians cannot answer every complaint, but some questions deserve, even require, a serious response. And on the committee election issue Thorbjørn Jagland, the president of Parliament, should have been the first to condemn attempts to abort public debate by silence. Instead, he gave no response.

The real answer came in what happened next.

OCTOBER 2008—AHTISAARI WINS THE PEACE PRIZE

By the skin of our teeth, the Norwegian-language book *Nobels vilje* (*Nobel's Will*) was ready for release on October 6, less than one week before the announcement of the 2008 peace prize laureate. Fourteen months had passed since the newspaper article in which I had first urged the committee to reevaluate the will and its legal mandate. The committee had had an early chapter of my book in its possession for nine months. So there was reason to hope the 2008 prize would signal a new desire to respect Nobel and his wishes.

Instead, the name that chair Mjøs announced for 2008 was Martti Ahtisaari, the former president of Finland:

> [F]or his important efforts, on several continents and over more than three decades, to resolve international conflicts. These efforts have contributed to a more peaceful world and to "fraternity between nations" in Alfred Nobel's spirit.
>
> Throughout all his adult life, whether as a senior Finnish public servant and president or in an international capacity, often connected to the United Nations, Ahtisaari has worked for peace and reconciliation . . .
>
> Although the parties themselves have the main responsibility for avoiding war and conflict, the Norwegian Nobel Committee has on several occasions awarded the Nobel Peace Prize to mediators in international politics. Today Ahtisaari is an outstanding international mediator. Through his untiring efforts and good results, he has shown what role mediation of various kinds can play in the resolution of international conflicts.

Again the prize was being awarded mainly for resolution of conflicts rather than prevention through a changed international system. In several of the examples of Ahtisaari's work, in Namibia, Aceh, Kosovo, Iraq, Northern Ireland, Central Asia, and the Horn of Africa, the committee seemed to a considerable extent to confuse ending hostilities with "resolving international conflict." And Ahtisaari is far from *a champion of peace* in Nobel's sense, that is, someone seeking to end militarism. In interviews as a new laureate, he immediately urged Finland to join the North Atlantic Treaty Organization's (NATO) military alliance.[2] Ahtisaari also defended the 2003 attack on Iraq. With the award to Ahtisaari, the committee again demonstrated its preference for a fellow politician and showed total lack of insight into the specific peace work Nobel had in mind.[3]

One expert on the former Yugoslavia affairs, Jan Oberg of Sweden, wrote that the prize for Ahtisaari was another scandal, not respecting any of Nobel's three criteria: "Ahtisaari has repeatedly functioned as 'peace fixer' for Western power elites . . . a man who by his 'mediations' fully endorses the 'peace' brought about by militarist means and international law violations—rather than following the UN norm of 'peace by peaceful means.'"[4] The Oberg view seems to win full backing from the article "Getting to the table" in *Newsweek* on June 14, 1999.

Peace by coercion is not likely to last, a durable peace is a solution acceptable to both sides. The main example quoted by Oberg is the role Ahtisaari played in 1999 when, acting for presidents Clinton and Yeltsin, he forced an end to the illegal war against Serbia on NATO's terms. Several sources report that the discussion ended when Ahtisaari, in the decisive meeting on June 2, pointed to the table, moved aside the flower centerpiece and said "Belgrade will be like this table. We will immediately begin carpet-bombing Belgrade . . . There will be half a million dead within a week."[5]

When asked to comment on this account, Ahtisaari, in an e-mail to the author (February 16, 2010), denied having used such flourishing language, but confirmed that Milosevic had been given a 10-point plan, not open to discussion, for approval by next morning. Milosevic was told he had two options, either a yes or a no, but *"if you say no, then I can tell right away that you should have no illusion of what will follow. What will come is not going to be in our power. I would be misleading you if I'd say something else."* Not much of a rebuttal.

A qualified Nobel committee would have been cognizant of the development of modern forms of dialogue and *conflict resolution*. In the spirit of Nobel, it would have taken an innovative approach and honored the promotion of modern "peace technologies" instead of loyal service to NATO. The committee should have preferred another 2008 nominee, Steinar Bryn of Norway, and the Nansen Dialogue Network. Working in former Yugoslavia, this vast network has developed methods of dialog capable of healing recent, raw wounds of armed conflict. The network has demonstrated that deadly hate and hurt on both sides can be transformed into a fraternal experience of shared history and fate.

NOBEL COMMITTEE: TWO NEW MEMBERS, NO CHANGE

Since Parliament was to elect new members of the Nobel committee in late November 2008, it too had been kept informed of my legal conclusions, by letters to President Thorbjørn Jagland, first in January and again in June. A short, rather peculiar, response in June made it necessary to explain thoroughly to Jagland the law, the peace prize, and the seriousness of continuing to break the law. A two-page letter outlining the situation was sent to him on July 10, 2008, in his two capacities. As president of Parliament, he must rectify the election process, and as chair of the elections committee, he would have to search widely—outside Parliament—for qualified members.

Then silence set in. A few calls to parliamentary staff produced evasive answers. No response was offered. When a response finally came, it was alarming. In a late October interview, President Jagland, ignoring the book that had laid out the legal situation to him, stated that the parties were entitled to their seats on the Nobel committee and there was nothing to be done about it.[6] This was wrong—of course Parliament was free to reintroduce the pre-1948 election procedure. Politicians should not fool the public with false information about the law.

But worse was to come.

In early November, the media reported that Jagland would become the Labor Party's new member of the Nobel committee.[7] Now, *there* was one good reason for him not to respond, not even acknowledge receipt of my letter and book. They had disturbed his plans.

Since the prime lawmaker in Norway made no indications that such encumbrances as the law would stop him, I made a last attempt in an article—"Defend the dignity of the *Storting,* Jagland"—printed in *Dagsavisen,* a major Oslo newspaper.[8] First I questioned whether it could look credible that the Nobel prize was independent of Norwegian politics if one chose to elect a former prime minister, foreign minister, and president of Parliament to the Nobel committee. Then I asked whether Jagland, or any Norwegian mainstream politician, legally could be qualified for a seat on the committee. Were they not all unsuitable through long political lives in the service of ideas on security very different from those Nobel wished to reward? The article finished with these words:

> I do not expect Jagland to agree with me, but . . . he has to show my criticism unfounded or take the practical consequences of it. Should Jagland

place himself on the Nobel committee without first having explained where the book *Nobels vilje* is erroneous, it will give honor neither to Stortinget nor to himself.

A week before the election of new Nobel committee members, I wrote an e-mail (November 27, 2008) outlining the problem to all members of Parliament, an extraordinary step intending to clarify that this time the situation would be different: "*Stortinget* will be acting in bad faith—each single representative will be accomplice to a violation of Norwegian law."

The effort was in vain. The discussion in Parliament on December 3, 2008, was perfunctory. Without mentioning my book—but potentially as a response to it—two representatives declared their support for the proportionality system. A move to stop the two new committee members from meeting in the Nobel committee while they were still in Parliament (until the mid-September 2009 election) was not approved.

The leader of the *Stortinget* election committee was elected to the Nobel committee, as the choice of the Labor Party. One committee member, Berge Furre of the Socialist Left Party, had resigned and was replaced by Agot Valle from the same party. Both these new members may now sit for six years. Kaci Kullmann Five (Conservative) was reelected, and Inger Marie Ytterhorn (Progress Party) and Sissel Rønbeck (Labor Party) have three years to serve before their six-year terms expire.

In Norway gender equality is strictly observed, but the four women committee members elected the sole male among the five to be the chair.

To show the seriousness of this decision, it is necessary to demonstrate through direct quotations how explicit my letter of July 10 to Jagland had been on the legal constraints. Recalling that in 1897 *Stortinget* had pledged loyalty to Nobel and its task in the "peace work of the future," the letter opened by saying it was now time to investigate whether Parliament was still keeping its obligation to respect the law. In this matter,

> both *Stortinget* and the Nobel committee *in their roles as executors of a testament* are subject to the laws, on inheritance, foundations etc., like any other board of a foundation in Norway charged with the implementation of an endowment. The Nobel committee has no mandate to

formulate its own concept of peace, which is what it actually has done. Under Section 19 of the Foundations Act, all awards must be in conformity with the statutory purpose.

Calling for a changed committee and warning against a serious and punishable infraction under Section Eight of the Foundations Act, I wrote:

> In keeping with his intention, Nobel must also have had notions of the type of people who would sit on the committee, and this must be binding on the election of Nobel committees and require *Stortinget* to ensure that it is composed of members who understand and will support the purpose of the prize. . . .
>
> In my opinion it must be an obvious responsibility for you, as president of *Stortinget* and at the same time leader of the election committee, to . . . re-examine the established routine in relation to the purpose of the testament and to take suitable measures to ensure that those elected to the Nobel committee have both knowledge of, and sympathy for, active work for peace and disarmament. The committee must have a composition that fulfills the moral and legal responsibility of *Stortinget* towards Nobel and the testament.

Another principle was also infringed upon. That people in executive or active political positions may not sit on the Nobel committee has been the established norm for decades. For cabinet members this has been the rule for seven decades, although for parliamentarians the ban came later. Jagland had shown bad judgment in combining roles, when in 2006 he helped former Prime Minister Bondevik, a political opponent, establish the Oslo Center for Peace and Human Rights. By inviting a cross-party group of politicians to sit on the board, Bondevik managed to protect his center from criticism against this novelty in Norwegian politics. As president of Parliament, Jagland—rather than becoming president of the board of the Oslo Center—should have defended Norwegian democracy against a development that permits a prime minister to pass the hat to big business immediately after leaving office. This unavoidably creates uncertainty among voters about their allegiance and integrity, and whether those elected serve the nation or special interests. In addition, foreign policy is the prerogative of the cabinet, and as president of Parliament, Jagland should have stayed away from this position.

The rule that a seat on the Nobel committee may not be combined with active political positions has applied to offices inside Norway, but must be the same at the European level. Jagland ignored all protests against combining a seat on the Nobel committee with a leading position in Europe. One who protested was the professor of law Ståle Eskeland, who declared himself in total agreement with criticism of this unfortunate combination of roles voiced by his colleague at Oslo University's Institute of Public and International Law, Professor Eivind Smith. Eskeland recommended that Jagland's successor as president of *Stortinget* should drop a hint to Jagland, since he himself seemed not to understand how the combined roles could impair international esteem of the peace prize. Eskeland added:

> *Stortinget* can and should release Jagland from his post as a member of the Nobel committee. If this happens against Jagland's wishes it will weaken him in his position as the Secretary General of the Council of Europe. Out of concern both for the Nobel prize and the Council of Europe, Jagland ought to reconsider the situation.

There was no sign that Jagland was so inclined. The Norwegian parliamentarians have managed to establish the Nobel committee as a personal privilege, and they show a determination to keep it that way.

The political working style I watched in operation was a profound disappointment. The Nobel committee and Parliament were clearly breaking the law. Ignoring all protests, the pro-NATO political majority had for years misused funds belonging to their political opponents.

A system in which even the most convincing arguments and facts have no influence on those elected as representatives of the people is not my ideal of a democracy under the rule of law. When all my calls for respect for law and democracy fell on deaf ears, it felt totalitarian in both nature and effect. It had a particularly distressing effect on me, I discovered, because in Norway we tend to define our political culture as very different from what I had experienced.

Chapter 12

PEACE PRIZE 2009:
THE OBAMA GASP

2009: A RECORD NUMBER OF NOMINATIONS

In a press release in September 2009 the Nobel committee announced that nominations for the Peace Prize had reached a new high, a total of 205, of which 33 were organizations. The committee keeps the names and nomination letters secret and appeals to nominators to do the same. But not all respect this. To some, a little publicity may seem the most they can gain from the nomination, while others may hope to improve the prospects of their candidate.

In the week preceding the announcement of the winner for 2009 I tried to make a list of all the nominees and was able to find more than 50 likely nominations, 25 percent of the total. Most of them were found by Internet search and I also had private knowledge of some nominations. The list gives an idea of how far the prize has lost contact with its purpose as defined in Nobel's will. When the committee itself does not know what Nobel understood by *champions of peace*, how could one blame nominators around the world for believing that any good, laudable activity can qualify?

The list includes a number of unusual people, with much to their credit, but many have little or nothing to do with the struggle for a fundamental change of the militarized world order. I evaluated those I was able to find placing them in two categories: qualified or not qualified.

Considering what Nobel wished to support, many are way off the mark or would be directly hurtful to the purpose of the prize. A main group of those not justified included the many humanitarian and human rights campaigners; three Chinese dissidents Hu Jia, Wei Jingsheng, and Rebya

Kadeer; the two Irish musicians, Bono and Bob Geldof; Ezzeldeen Abu al-Aish of Palestine; Nigerian chief Gani Fawehinimi; Greg Mortenson, United States; Denis Mukwege, Democratic Republic of Congo; Leonard Peltier, United States; Irena Sendler, Poland; SOS-Kinderdorf International, Austria; Lidia Yusupova, Chechen Russian; founders of Twitter, United States, for their role in postelection Iran; Morgan Tsvangirai, Zimbabwe; Zivko Popovski-Cvetin, Macedonia; Sima Samar, Afghanistan; Illinois governor George Ryan for opposition to the death penalty, United States; Stanley Tookie, antigang activist, later executed, United States; and for the environmental protection movement Greenpeace, and Inuit activist Sheila Watt-Cloutier of Canada.

A good many of the nominees seem irrelevant to the Nobel criteria. With the greatest sympathy for what she has been through, and delight over her release, French-Colombian hostage Ingrid Betancourt ends up outside the criteria, as does Piedad Córdoba, the Colombian senator who negotiated with the FARC (the Revolutionary Armed Forces of Columbia) guerillas. Same with former U.S. President Bill Clinton's role in the release of hostages in North Korea: Clinton was never in the front-line working to reform the world and throw off the yoke of militarism.

Two former national leaders who took their nations to war, Prime Minister Tony Blair of the United Kingdom, and U.S. President George W. Bush, are clearly not Nobel material. In February 2010, Blair had to answer to a government-sponsored inquiry into possible war crimes and war of aggression against Iraq in 2003. Among the things that became public in the hearing was how the government lawyers, including (until immediately before the attack) the chief legal adviser of the British Foreign Office, considered the war illegal. One of them, deputy legal adviser Elizabeth Wilmshurst, resigned in protest against what she saw as a grave violation of international law.[1]

Motives are unclear for nominating the following people: Abdelaziz Bouteflika, Algeria; John Endicott, the Republic of Korea; Mustafa Jemilev, Crimean Tatar; Nursultan Nazarba Rajasekhara Reddy, Andhra Pradesh, India (died September 2009).

Disqualified is also the late artist Michael Jackson, but another American singer, Pete Seeger has lived a life of musical mobilization against arms and wars. A prize to symbolize the contribution that art can make to combat militarism and war cannot be automatically excluded.

The 2009 nominees most critical of the military power establishment are probably David Ray Griffin, United States, and the 9/11 Truth

Movement, but are they *champions of peace* in the sense that Nobel used the expression? U.S. senators Richard Lugar and Sam Nunn have made important efforts to reduce the nuclear threat, but what are their views on abolishing the military altogether? The same applies to nominated politicians, such as Nicolas Sarkozy, president of France, for the European Union's role in the Russia-Georgia conflict; and (in my advance evaluation) President Barack Obama.

Based on the information available, in my evaluation, among the nominations for 2009, only 11 of the 54 names were qualified under Nobel's will. The following, it seems to me, are doing great work in the direction of disarmament and international reforms of the type Nobel had in mind:

- Steinar Bryhn, Norway, new methods of dialogue to heal fresh and very raw wounds from recent war
- The Cluster Munition Coalition, for the treaty banning cluster bombs
- Professor Emeritus Richard Falk, United States, international law and organization
- Professor Johan Galtung, peace research pioneer, organizer of Transcend University and Network
- Gunnar Garbo, Norway, proponent of international law, United Nations, nonviolent conflict resolution
- Federico Mayor, Spain, ex-director-general of the United Nations Education, Scientific and Cultural Organization (UNESCO), culture of peace
- Mayors for Peace, international mobilization of antinuclear cities
- Jan Oberg, Sweden, peace academic, practitioner, networker
- Gene Sharp, United States, leading authority on alternative, nonmilitary defense
- UNESCO, Paris, for Culture of Peace initiative[2]
- Mordechai Vanunu, Israel, nuclear whistleblower

2009 prize announced: Barack Obama

U.S. President Barack Obama was included on my list of unqualified candidates. Still, my immediate reaction on hearing Nobel chairperson Thorbjørn Jagland announce Obama as winner the 2009 Nobel Peace Prize was spontaneous delight. History was audible in the Nobel Hall where journalists from around the world filled the room with an audible gasp, a special mixture of shock and joy.

In this gasp I heard the resonance of a long period of sad decline in American values. The presidency of George Bush had been a trying period for all types of people working for a better world, for peace, for respect for the U.S. Constitution. When Obama carried the 2008 election, it had kindled new hopes. Obama seemed to represent an antiestablishment political counterculture and people around the world saw the potential return of the American values they respect and believe in, those opposed to big finance and the games of military power elites.

This time the Nobel committee used language that placed the 2009 prize in relevant terrain; it had been

> awarded to President Barack Obama for his extraordinary efforts to strengthen international diplomacy and cooperation between peoples. The committee has attached special importance to Obama's vision of and work for a world without nuclear weapons. . . .
>
> Obama has as President created a new climate in international politics. Multilateral diplomacy has regained a central position, with emphasis on the role that the United Nations and other international institutions can play. Dialogue and negotiations are preferred as instruments for resolving even the most difficult international conflicts. The vision of a world free from nuclear arms has powerfully stimulated disarmament and arms control negotiations. . . .
>
> His diplomacy is founded in the concept that those who are to lead the world must do so on the basis of values and attitudes that are shared by the majority of the world's population.[3]

The Nobel committee did not repeat specific language from the will; in broad terms, it described Obama as a man who promised cooperation, change, and great hope to the world. My spontaneous enthusiasm lasted long enough to be picked up on by a couple of nearby journalists, but the Nobel chair had hardly read to the end of his announcement before my cell phone rang and I had an indignant Professor Johan Galtung, a founder of peace research on the line: "This is terrible, a new scandal from the committee. Obama is a belligerent president who continues the policies of Bush, only with much more energy." Apparently I had to recheck the Obama track record. And of course the award of Nobel's Peace Prize, any peace prize, to a commander-in-chief engaged in two wars is strange, to say the least. Many shared the Galtung position in the days that followed

Quite a few commentators felt the committee had made a pitiful figure. A proud Nobel committee should bestow luster on others, not borrow light from shining stars. How much had it counted that the prize machinery could profit from increased visibility and more interest from sponsors? And why was the mayor of Oslo, together with staff, this time present at the announcement? This struck me as unusual. Could the mayor have received a discreet hint? A well-informed source later claimed that promotion of Oslo as a tourist destination had been a motivating factor in the selection of the 2009 winner.

In the days that followed, many discussed the judgment and motives of the committee chair—and of the secretary. The 2009 prize meant that in the course of seven years Geir Lundestad, the professor of modern U.S. history, would have managed to host three American leaders: Jimmy Carter in 2003, Al Gore in 2007, and now Barack Obama in 2009.

A common reaction was that this was too early. From serious commentators to "people in the streets" and stand-up comedians, many ridiculed the prize for a president "who had done nothing yet, no result to show . . . nothing more than words so far." Many in the media and the general public rightly observed that Obama had been president for only 12 days at the cutoff date for nominations for 2009.

It ran against the established interpretation when the committee chair, Thorbjørn Jagland, again and again in the autumn of 2009 maintained that it was normal practice to give the 2009 prize for work during 2009. In his speech in honor of Obama on December 10, 2009, Jagland said the prize was given for Obama's work in "the preceding year," meaning in this case since the previous award in December 2008.

What Nobel wrote was "*under det förlupna året*," which means a year that is expired or has been completed. This expression was always understood as "the full year before this year." One would believe that after 20 years as Nobel Secretary Lundestad would know and have been able to help Jagland get this right. In English, Jagland's mistake is less striking, since—on looking into it more closely—I have discovered that the official translation of the will into English makes use of "preceding year" where "expired year" would have been more precise.

As to the accusations of Obama not having achieved anything, I tend to disagree. Obama has done more than words, for example, by dropping the antiballistic system in East Europe.[4] In addition, words *are* deeds in international affairs. In diplomatic discourse fine nuances send subtle signals that are watched and interpreted with the utmost care. Words change the world and the language on the urgency of nuclear disarmament in Obama's Prague speech in April 2009 did change the political landscape. Only weeks before the Nobel announcement, Obama had chaired a meeting of the UN Security Council that agreed unanimously to a resolution committing nations to address nuclear disarmament. The United States, which had snubbed the United Nations for eight years, seemed to have returned to the world organization, and Obama had achieved a shift in several important fields of international diplomacy.

Obama's words on nuclear disarmament came at a particularly opportune time, when a full year of preparations remained before the April 2010 nuclear review conference in New York. Under the 1968 Treaty on the Non-proliferation of Nuclear Weapons (NPT) reviews must take place every five years. These conferences have always been the scene of endless foot-dragging. The five nuclear-armed states have been unwilling to disarm, which was their part of the 1986 mutual commitment to a nuclear weapons–free world. Instead, they keep requiring that the rest of the world must abide by the treaty and abstain from acquiring nuclear weapons.

But how could the committee select the leader of the most powerful military the world has ever seen, currently involved in two wars, for Nobel's disarmament prize? The U.S. president could make embarrassing decisions during the two short months remaining before the award ceremony. A fairly common reaction was that a clumsy and badly informed committee had complicated things for Obama, adding to his heavy burden and diverting attention when he had endless foreign and domestic problems to tackle. Media reactions were mixed, to say the least, but the award met with the usual friendly comments from prime ministers and political colleagues around the world. Most earlier Nobel laureates joined in the praise. Others were furious, however, and pointed to unfortunate Obama decisions, an increase in U.S. bases around the world, a refusal to relinquish U.S. landmines, and slow progress in closing the illegal Guantánamo Bay interrogation camp.

As for me, maybe a slow learner, I still kept my hopes that something good would come out of this. Since at this stage, the committee had had ample time to study the will and its obligations, I presumed it must have reason to believe that Obama was longing for a golden opportunity to launch plans for great reforms of the world order in a visible way and in a receptive setting. But not many shared this optimism.

In his Nobel lecture Obama would have to admit that in the immediate future he was restrained by two inherited wars, but he also would have the chance to use his unique rhetorical skills to focus on a new future for the United States, the United Nations, and the world. He could, if the

United States really had returned to the United Nations, weigh in on reports by and to UN secretary-generals on violence and war, including the latest 2004 report to Kofi Annan "A More Secure World: Our Shared Responsibility" from Annan's high-level panel on collective security.[5] Obama could have given generous recognition to the report of the Hans Blix–led Weapons of Mass Destruction Commission, "Weapons of Terror" (2006). Seeing the need to rein in the military-industrial complex at home and abroad, Obama would, so I hoped, take inspiration from the voices of reason in speeches of earlier Nobel laureates—all posted on the Nobel Foundation's Web site (www.nobelprize.org). He would find many inspiring words on dialogue, understanding and cooperation, justice, and combating poverty in the speeches.

The speech of Kofi Annan (2001) and those of many other laureates are about ending or resolving violent battles more than their prevention (which was Nobel's concern). There are fine words on nuclear disarmament in the speech of Mohamed El Baradei (2005). In 1997, the American Jody Williams closed her Nobel lecture calling the ban on landmines "historic because, for the first time, the leaders of states have come together to answer the will of civil society."

In 1990, in a rare case of respect for Nobel, the chairperson, Giske Anderson, correctly restated the idea of Nobel's will in her speech, including disarmament. And Soviet leader Mikhail Gorbachev, in his acceptance speech, included a relevant passage:

> Immanuel Kant prophesied that mankind would one day be faced with a dilemma: either to be joined in a true union of nations or to perish in a war of annihilation ending in the extinction of the human race. Now, as we move from the second to the third millennium, the clock has struck the moment of truth.[6]

But true Nobel thinking is rare in later decades; to find expressions of his vision of peace through drastic reductions in armaments, Obama would have to go back one and a half decades. In 1995, Joseph Rotblat, United Kingdom, after crushing many myths and much wishful thinking about nuclear weapons, drew the unavoidable conclusion:

> The only way to prevent [the ultimate catastrophe] is to abolish war alto-gether. War must cease to be an admissible social institution. We must learn to resolve our disputes by means other than military confrontation.[7]

To find a laureate with broad devotion to Nobel's core idea would have taken him back 35 years, to 1974, when the prize went to Sean MacBride, who had served as leader of the International Peace Bureau since 1968 and was a former Irish foreign minister (1948–1951). MacBride also invoked nuclear weapons as an urgent reason to appeal for international law and order. His Nobel lecture was exemplary for the type of attitude, reasoning, and language that Nobel wished to reward:

> The practical imperatives for peace are many and far-reaching. But there is no shortcut and each must be tackled energetically. They are:
>
> 1. General and Complete Disarmament, including nuclear weapons.
> 2. The glorification of peace and not of war.
> 3. The effective protection of human rights and minorities at national and international levels.
> 4. Automatic and de-politicized mechanism for the settlement of international and non-international disputes that may endanger peace or that are causing injustices.
> 5. An international order that will ensure a fair distribution of all essential products.
> 6. An International Court of Justice and legal system with full automatic jurisdiction to rectify injustice or abuse of power.
> 7. An international peacekeeping force and police force with limited function.
> 8. Ultimately, a world parliament and government.
>
> I can already hear many say, "Utopia," "impossible of achievement." Of course, it will be difficult, but what is the alternative? The nearly certain destruction of the human race.[8]

MacBride, in 1974, even mentioned *General and complete disarmament*, once modern diplomatic language for a goal once so ambitious that Nobel hesitated for a couple of years before daring to express it in his will. But in his lecture, MacBride regretted that this goal, central to Nobel's purpose, had long ceased to be a theme of international diplomacy:

> This was the accepted aim of all governments and of the United Nations up to the end of 1961. Why has this objective been dropped? Why is it never even mentioned now? The extent to which agreement had been

reached in 1961 may be gauged from the two opening paragraphs of the joint Soviet-United States statement of September 20, 1961:

1. "The goal of negotiations is to achieve agreement on a program which will ensure

    (a) that disarmament is general and complete and war is no longer an instrument for settling international problems, and

    (b) that such disarmament is accompanied by the establishment of reliable procedures for the peaceful settlement of disputes and effective arrangements for the maintenance of peace in accordance with the principles of the Charter of the United Nations.

2. The program for general and complete disarmament shall ensure that states will have at their disposal *only such non-nuclear armaments*, forces, facilities and establishments as are agreed to be necessary to maintain internal order and protect the personal security of citizens; and that states shall support and provide agreed manpower for a United Nations peace force.

The Soviet and American draft treaties prepared at that period represented an extremely wide measure of agreement, and few points of controversy remained. Yet in a matter of a very few years these objectives were dropped and replaced by the "cold war." Is it not time that we got back to General and Complete Disarmament?

Far from considering General and Complete Disarmament, the major powers are engaged in the greatest arms race that has existed in the world. Negotiations are only aimed at limiting *the increase* of defensive weapons and the *increase* of ballistic nuclear weapons. And this, only because the arms race is so costly that it is bankrupting their economies; they can no longer afford further escalation. The present negotiations do not relate to disarmament—they relate to phased armament. [Emphasis in original.]

Considering the present economic crisis, the final words of MacBride on arms races (and wars) "bankrupting their economies" ought to have had an alluring appeal to Obama as he explored what to include in his own Nobel lecture.

OBAMA SPEECH: WAR IS PEACE

On December 10, 2009, 113 years after Alfred Nobel died, Obama held his Nobel lecture in the Oslo City Hall, in front of 1,000 guests, including royalty, cabinet members, diplomats, parliamentarians, and the Norwegian élite. The speech was transmitted to the world by direct television broadcast and by hosts of reporters and photographers, a setting that invited great thoughts and language. Those who hoped Obama would use this unique chance to launch bold and innovative ideas were discouraged at an early point in his speech. Where Bertha von Suttner 104 years earlier had hoped a new world order would be in place within a few years, Obama called for patience:

> I do not bring with me today a definitive solution to the problems of war. . . .
> We must begin by acknowledging the hard truth that we will not eradicate violent conflict in our lifetimes.[9]

Not only did Obama's speech presume a permanent military institution, he seemed to defend permanent war through his elaboration of "just war" and the need "to think in new ways about the notions of just war and the imperatives of a just peace." The reception was enthusiastic, the audience was fascinated by the eloquence of Obama; the media praised his speech as the best ever held on Norwegian ground and the smartest. Here was a leading politician with exceptional historical and philosophical insights, sufficient to tackle the difficult contradiction of waging war while speaking peace.

They were right; in terms of form, this was a truly brilliant show attracting enormous support and sympathy. But critical analysis was rare. Upon closer examination, I agreed with a friend who said: "What if it had been George Bush saying the same—it would have released worldwide outrage!" In their admiration of Obama's oral dexterity, many seemed led to condone the wars they were against. For me it was different: Hardly ever had I looked forward to a speech with greater hope, and never had I listened with greater disappointment.

How was it possible not to notice the glaring discrepancy between his speech and the points mentioned by chairperson Thorbjørn Jagland in Obama's honor? Many saw Jagland speaking in defense of the committee's decision. Then Obama, in his acceptance speech, did his best to prove the critics right without being found out. His speech was, indeed, such a masterpiece—of deception and seduction—that only a thorough analysis can reveal the rhetorical tricks that this great illusionist played on his audience. This analysis has a lot to tell us on what the prize is *not* about.

The Nobel committee had emphasized Obama's "extraordinary efforts to strengthen international diplomacy and cooperation between peoples. . . .

Dialogue and negotiations are preferred as instruments for resolving even the most difficult international conflicts." But Obama spoke little of diplomacy, cooperation, or alternative instruments to solve conflicts. He seemed to claim a U.S. right to resort to war whenever it saw the need. Some examples are as follows:

> War, in one form or another, appeared with the first man. . . . There will be times when nations—acting individually or in concert—will find the use of force not only necessary but morally justified. . . . I face the world as it is, and cannot stand idle in the face of threats to the American people. . . . So yes, the instruments of war do have a role to play in preserving the peace. . . . I understand why war is not popular. But I also know this: the belief that peace is desirable is rarely enough to achieve it.

A passage in the citation welcomed by many was that the committee attached special importance to Obama's vision of and work for a world without nuclear weapons, which "has powerfully stimulated disarmament and arms control negotiations." This is about a deadly emergency in which the United States may hold the key to the world's rescue from extinction. Even if Obama mentioned nuclear disarmament, he had little to offer. No bold promise to lead by example, not even that the United States would comply with its own legal obligations:

> One urgent example is the effort to prevent the spread of nuclear weapons, and to seek a world without them. In the middle of the last century, nations agreed to be bound by a treaty whose bargain is clear: all will have access to peaceful nuclear power; those without nuclear weapons will forsake them; and those with nuclear weapons will work toward disarmament. I am committed to upholding this treaty. It is a centerpiece of my foreign policy. And I am working with President Medvedev to reduce America and Russia's nuclear stockpiles.
>
> But it is also incumbent upon all of us to insist that nations like Iran and North Korea do not game the system. Those who claim to respect international law cannot avert their eyes when those laws are flouted. Those who care for their own security cannot ignore the danger of an arms race in the Middle East or East Asia. Those who seek peace cannot stand idly by as nations arm themselves for nuclear war.

Obama deserves credit for a rare honesty as to the reciprocal nature of the 1968 NPT. It is not often that heads of a state with nuclear weapons mention their own obligations under that treaty. Obama, however, did little to pave the way for results at the April 2010 NPT Review Conference. He made no offer to institute negotiations on a treaty for the abolition of nuclear arms; no recognition of the high-quality blueprint for nuclear abolition proposed as a UN document by the peace movement; and no acceptance of international inspection also of U.S. nuclear installations. Obama talked of the danger of an arms race in the Middle East, but he had no proposals for the Israeli nuclear weapons that drive other nations in the region to desire their own. He said nothing bold or helpful to change the diplomatic deadlock and follow up his promising initiative in September 2009 in the UN Security Council.

The Nobel committee citation says, "Obama has as president created a new climate in international politics. Multilateral diplomacy has regained a central position, with emphasis on the role that the United Nations and other international institutions can play." Yet the Obama speech was surprisingly thin in support for the United Nations, referring to

> the destruction of World War II and the advent of the nuclear age, which made it clear to victor and vanquished alike that the world needed institutions to prevent another World War. . . . America led the world in constructing an architecture to keep the peace: a Marshall plan and a United Nations, mechanisms to govern the waging of war, treaties to protect human rights, prevent genocide, and restrict the most dangerous weapons.

This form of combined mention, putting the United Nations on a level with the Marshall Plan, denigrated the world organization. The worst omission in his speech is the missing affirmation of the primary purpose of the United Nations—that all states, big and small, are banned from use of military force except in two situations: (1) if authorized by the Security Council or (2) in self-defense. The latter is permitted when, and only when, a state must respond at once to stop an attack in progress and cannot wait until the Security Council has had a chance to discuss the situation.

Obama's speech has a fundamental defect: he is like a man lecturing in 2009 on modern transportation who fails to mention airplanes. Since 1945 a president speaking on the preservation of peace should not be praised for expounding theories on "just war"; he should be confirming his respect for the existing rules of international law and the need for all states to respect the ban on aggression. Under the UN pact, the Security Council cannot authorize the use of force without first considering alternatives. Far from being at the cutting-edge of common security thinking, and evoking a "right to peace," Obama seemed to consider, for the United States, war as a legitimate tool in international affairs:

> To say that force is sometimes necessary is not a call to cynicism—it is a recognition of history; the imperfections of man and the limits of reason. I raise this point because in many countries there is a deep ambivalence about military action today, no matter the cause. At times, this is joined by a reflexive suspicion of America, the world's sole military superpower.

Similarly, Obama said toward the end of his speech: "I have spoken to the questions that must weigh on our minds and our hearts as we choose to wage war." Treating war as an option he negated the most fundamental of all principles. Hardly anything Obama said was more disappointing than his neglect of the laws of war and his effective rebuff to the United Nations.

While professing respect for the legacy of Martin Luther King and Gandhi, Obama immediately went on to deny the practical value of their teaching. Even his few references to earlier Nobel laureates were turned into arguments for constant war and eternal militarism. Obama admitted he would not have received the prize if it had not been for Martin Luther King:

> I am living testimony to the moral force of non-violence. I know there is nothing weak—nothing passive—nothing naïve—in the creed and lives of Gandhi and King.
>
> But as a head of state sworn to protect and defend my nation, I cannot be guided by their examples alone. I face the world as it is, and cannot stand idle in the face of threats to the American people.

The wish to defend his nation appears highly respectable, a reasonable justification of the need for military strength. But it is also a confusing argument, and it is misleading. Obama backed it with a reference to the praiseworthy war against Hitler. It was easy for the audience to forget that the war against Hitler was a fully legitimate defense against an aggressor. Much, or most, of the U.S. use of military force is not legitimate self-defense. The wars against Afghanistan, Iraq, and Serbia were all cases of aggression, which is the supreme crime in international law. The crime of aggression is so serious because "it contains within itself the accumulated evil of the whole," according to the judgment against German Nazi leaders at Nuremberg in 1945.[10]

What about the use of military force in defense of U.S. business and economic interests? It has been admitted openly again and again by high U.S. officials that its military power is not only about defending the homeland and American lives, but also about protecting "the American way of life." This was the explicit reason President George Bush, Sr. used to justify the 1990 military buildup toward war with Iraq. Defense Secretary William Cohen said the same to workers at Microsoft, Seattle, in February 1999.[11] Arguing the case for "securing American military pre-eminence in the 21st century," he said:

> I will point out that the prosperity that companies like Microsoft now enjoy could not occur without the strong military we have . . . conflicts in far-away lands such as Bosnia, Korea and Iraq have a direct effect on the U.S. economy. The billions it costs to keep 100,000 American troops in South Korea and Japan, for example, makes Asia more stable—and thus better markets for U.S. goods. The military's success in holding Iraq in check ensures a continued flow of oil from the Persian Gulf.[12]

But this was not the picture of U.S. intentions that Obama gave in his speech:

> Yet the world must remember that it was not simply international institutions—not just treaties and declarations—that brought stability to a post–World War II world. Whatever mistakes we have made, the plain fact is this: the United States of America has helped underwrite global security for more than six decades with the blood of our citizens and the strength of our arms. The service and sacrifice of our men and women in uniform has promoted peace and prosperity from Germany to Korea, and enabled democracy to take hold in places like the Balkans. We have borne this burden not because we seek to impose our will. We have done so out of enlightened self-interest—because we seek a better future for our children and grandchildren, and we believe that their lives will be better if other peoples' children and grandchildren can live in freedom and prosperity.

The citizens of a long list of nations tend to see this differently, including Chile, Cuba, Grenada, Indonesia, Iraq, Nicaragua, Palestine, Panama, Serbia, Venezuela, and Vietnam, to mention just a few. Most media reports are short on historic context and leave out the significant role that U.S. overt and undercover operations in the past have played in creating the difficulties and antagonism that later will be used as rationale for involving the United States and its allies in violent conflicts. When Iran got a democratic leader in 1953, Mohammad Mossadeq, the United States ousted him and installed the terror regime of the Shah. The United States was friendly with Saddam Hussein and supported his despotic regime for more than a decade. The United States was happy for the Soviet invasion of Afghanistan and strengthened Osama bin Laden, al-Qaida, and fundamentalist Islam as tools to hurt the Soviet Union. Many are the peoples in the world who have seen the United States comfortably cooperating with their despotic rulers; many would have gladly gone without the U.S. concern for the "freedom and prosperity of other people's grandchildren" that Obama referenced.

The mixture of despair and hatred resulting from U.S. foreign policy is visibly demonstrated in all the security measures to protect U.S. embassies; everywhere surrounded by high fences and armed guards. Only a changed foreign policy, with more equitable distribution of wealth in the world and less reliance on superior military force, can end terrorism. The course presently pursued only makes matters worse.

Immediately after the perfunctory respect Obama paid to Gandhi and Martin Luther King, he went on to deal a blow to nonviolence. Rather than showing sense of multilateral diplomacy and cooperation, Obama spoke as if the only alternatives are nonviolence or brutal military force:

> I cannot stand idle in the face of threats to the American people. For make no mistake: evil does exist in the world. A non-violent movement could not have halted Hitler's armies. Negotiations cannot convince Al-Qaeda's leaders to lay down their arms. To say that force is sometimes necessary is not a call to cynicism—it is a recognition of history; the imperfections of man and the limits of reason.

Obama would not have been unaware of how the powerful British forces were driven out of India in 1947, through a successful nonviolent campaign led by Gandhi if the Nobel committee had given Gandhi the award he deserved. Obama's miss could also have been avoided if the committee had shown loyalty to Nobel and decades ago preferred another of the nominees for the 2009 prize, Gene Sharp. This American professor, the world's preeminent scholar on the history of nonviolent defense, could have taught Obama a lot about the potential of nonviolence. And so could earlier president Franklin D. Roosevelt whose "Look to Norway" praised the Norwegian war effort—a historic example of civil society in nonviolent resistance to occupation. Sharp once lived in Norway to study this history, the very type of cultural innovation for peace that Nobel wished for the world to benefit from.

But the Obama remark on Hitler raised the recurring question from militarists: "What will you do against the Hitlers?" The first, simple answer is this: do not create them. The international trade in arms helps unsavory regimes and dictators come to power and stay. When, in the year before World War II the British export to Germany of rare nickel—a strategic commodity—increased steeply, the defense minister said: "Such exports do help Germany to rearm, but it is a commercial matter, not within the province of the Government to interfere."[13] Again and again military forces have ended up fighting against arms produced by factories back home. Western Hemisphere nations, including Britain, France, Germany, and the United States, supplied Iraq and Saddam Hussein with vast deliveries of the most advanced and tailor-made military equipment that money could buy during the decade leading up to the first Iraq War in 1990.[14]

Avoiding humiliation of other countries can help avoid war. The Women's International League for Peace and Freedom fought valiantly to prevent the peace treaty after World War I from humiliating defeated Germany. The humiliating terms of the Versailles Treaty gave Hitler plenty of material for his rise to power, playing on revenge. Obama (and his State Department and presidential advisors) should read the groundbreaking studies of Dr. Evelin Lindner (another obvious Nobel candidate) on humiliation and how to make the world more stable and peaceful.

Obama, with every reason condemning Hitler's aggression, seemed to imply that U.S. wars are legitimate:

> The world rallied around America after the 9/11 attacks, and continues to support our efforts in Afghanistan, because of the horror of those senseless attacks and the recognized principle of self-defense. Likewise, the world recognized the need to confront Saddam Hussein when he invaded Kuwait—a consensus that sent a clear message to all about the cost of aggression.

Even if this is the common version in mainstream Western politics and media, it is not necessarily correct. The two attacks on Iraq, as well as those on Afghanistan and Serbia, violated the ban against aggression and were war crimes. However often North Atlantic Treaty Organization

(NATO) leaders repeat it, the attack on Afghanistan was not a case of legitimate self-defense in response to 9/11. An action by a group of people is not aggression in international law; there was no military attack, not on the United States, and not by Afghanistan. The Bush administration rejected a Taliban offer to extradite Osama bin Laden to be tried in an international court.[15] In actual fact the 9/11 events were used as pretext for an attack that had been planned two years earlier.

In his speech, Obama repeated a claim that the attack was self-defense authorized by the UN Security Council. But self-defense needs no authorization—and the Security Council never gave it. The operative part of UN Security Council Resolution No. 1368 (2001), passed three days after September 11, 2001, did mention cooperation on intelligence and sequestering funds, but did not mention military action, a measure so serious it would have required express authorization.

In fact, the claim of "UN-authorized self-defense" is a good example of untruth as a political tool. A few words—a superfluous and innocuous truism in the preamble—have been misused systematically to create the impression that the attack on Afghanistan had "UN authorization." To point out the obvious: (1) legitimate self-defense applies in situations in which there is no time to seek UN authorization, and (2) military action not expressly mentioned in the operative part of a resolution is not authorized by the United Nations.

The U.S.-U.K. "shock-and-awe" attack on Iraq on March 19, 2003, was claimed to be a legitimate action against a bandit state with weapons of mass destruction (WMDs). A year before the attack, U.S. Secretary of State Colin Powell and Security Advisor Condoleezza Rice had both declared on public television that the weapons inspections in Iraq had been effective and that the regime of Saddam Hussein no longer posed any military threat. The leaked Downing Street memo from a secret meeting on July 23, 2002, with intelligence staff at the British prime minister's London residence, revealed that U.S. President Bush and U.K. Prime Minister Tony Blair were determined to go to war whether Iraq had WMDs or not and knowing full well that an attack on Iraq would violate international law.[16]

Obama's warm defense of humanitarian intervention might serve to justify the attack on Serbia in March 1999. That attack was approved by NATO, but not by the UN. The Security Council—argued NATO countries—was entrusted with the authority to secure international peace and security,and deadlock in the Security Council authorized NATO to act on its own. This line of justification of war conveniently forgets a deliberate compromise made when the UN Treaty was negotiated to

ensure that military action could not be taken unless the five countries
with veto powers agreed. Security Council member states must not risk
ending up on different sides in a major conflict.[17] Unfortunately, this principle of international relations was not respected in the case of Serbia.[18]

Fabulous—and disappointing

Obama could not qualify for the Nobel Peace Prize, because he was
no *champion of peace* as Nobel understood the term, he was not in
favor of a total reform of the international system with abolition of the
military, and he had not made his achievements in the *expired year*.

It is difficult to comply with all aspects of the will in minute detail,
every time, but this does not justify ignoring Nobel's will completely,
as the committee has done increasingly often. In my view, irregularities
with details are easy to forgive if only the core obligation is respected—
that is, to show the best possible loyalty to Nobel's specific, antimilitaristic
purpose. The first step is to understand what moved Nobel to establish
the prize and to respect his intentions. When it has been established that
the words of Nobel's will refer to the program of the peace movement
and that his will resulted from discussion with, and prodding by, Suttner,
then the preconditions for the award are defined.

When the committee announced the 2009 prize, it had for more than a
year had reason to acquaint itself with Nobel's purpose. If the committee
had done this, it would have been possible to formulate reasons that
could have made even the prize for Obama appear to be an act of loyalty
to Nobel. The committee could have used the 2009 prize to shake the
world to wake up to the intolerable problem of nuclear weapons. The
committee could have signaled to the whole world the need for a major
turnabout at the April 2010 Nuclear Review Conference. With *Stortinget*
misusing appointments to reward retired party hacks, however, there is little chance that the prize will challenge NATO orthodoxies in such a way.

I could only agree with all those who thought President Obama had given
a fantastic speech after receiving the Nobel Peace Prize. But he gave no
promise of change. Obama dealt with war and armaments as an unavoidable part of the relations between states, now and forever.

The Nobel committee should have avoided giving the U.S. president
a platform for an all-out assault on the very idea of Nobel's Peace
Prize. Both committee and laureate must take blame for the fact that
this went terribly wrong.

Obama's affront to Nobel cannot be put down to an excusable lack of information on his part. The president was aware of the true purpose of the Peace Prize. To ensure that he was fully informed, I spoke with a senior official at the U.S. Embassy in Oslo who promised to do her best to communicate my views to the president, his speechwriters, and other assistants. To this end, she received the full English-language manuscript of part I of this book.[19]

Furthermore, when Obama announced his intention to give the prize money to an unidentified charity, I sent a suggestion both to the U.S. Embassy official and directly to the president over the White House Webmail. In addition I sent an opinion peace (probably unsuccessfully) to several U.S. newspapers:

> Obama money for Nobel cause?
>
> A book I published last year on Nobel and his peace prize showed that Nobel's purpose was to challenge the military. Nobel wished to secure future funding for those intrepid, but poor, "champions of peace" who advocate a profound change of international relations, a so solid international "brotherhood" that it would permit reduction of national military forces. President Obama's anti-nuclear initiative was a prime factor in the committee citation and hardly anything would have pleased Nobel more than to see him passing the money on to the anti-nuclear movement—at home the Lawyers Committee or Nuclear Age Peace Foundation, internationally the doctors' or lawyers' campaigns (IPPNW, IALANA), Middle Powers Initiative or the Parliamentarians or Mayors for Peace.

As of February 2009, no information suggested that the president had followed the recommendation of giving a modest lift to the citizens' movements against nuclear weapons.

It's not Just War, it's just war

The committee that made its first grave mistake giving the prize to an incumbent U.S. president had now come full circle. While Theodore Roosevelt delivered a first strike in 1906 defending a healthy will to wage war, Obama managed a worst strike in 2009. His address was a long, wall-to-wall, articulate affront to everything Nobel wished to achieve through the prize.

Many, like me, had hoped, even believed, that Obama stood for deep change and harbored latent ideals of rewriting the U.S. tradition as an often imperialist, warrior nation. That hope was forcefully crushed by his Nobel speech.

As to the Nobel committee, in 2009 it pretended a strong awareness of the testament of Nobel and repeatedly declared loyalty to his will. It quoted specific words that Nobel used, and claimed to be following the wishes of Nobel. Unfortunately, the committee and its secretary could not have gone to the trouble of acquainting themselves with the pivotal elements in the criticism; they had neither understood the significance of finding out what Nobel must have thought and wished nor had they studied my evidence of his intention, nor my analysis of the changing policy of the Nobel committees. The citation for Obama contained a statement clearly intended to counter the criticism: "For 108 years, the Norwegian Nobel Committee has sought to stimulate precisely that international policy and those attitudes for which Obama is now the world's leading spokesman."

This was a rather sweeping, bold, and clearly untenable statement, even before the Obama speech. After the speech, it would seem impossible to repeat. But Obama's attitudes should not have come as a surprise. Had the committee studied properly his attitudes and his books, such as *The Audacity of Hope*, it could not have given Obama the award.

An unusual leak from the internal discussion in the committee suggests opinion was split and that Chairperson Thorbjørn Jagland, a man far from having a reputation for infallible judgment, had to push hard to get a majority for Obama. Sources close to the prize—the three historians Stenersen, Sveen, and Libæk, who wrote the centenary history—questioned the motives and wisdom of the 2009 prize in an article in the Stockholm newspaper *Dagens Nyheter*.[20] The three felt sure that the main architect behind the prize for Obama was Lundestad, whose use of the prize for the promotion of Norwegian interests is widely seen as a service to Norway of national importance.

In the *Dagens Nyheter* article, the three Nobel historians describe Secretary Lundestad as Norway's leading expert on the U.S. and an admirer of the president. Even though he is not a committee member and has no voting rights, they describe him as an active secretary, who, with his long experience, knowledge, and convincing rhetoric, has a strong influence on the decisions of the committee. The three see Lundestad as most likely the chief architect behind the 2009 prize.[21]

Their opinion is in sharp contrast to earlier descriptions of secretaries playing no role in the deliberations, but many signs make probable that they are right. A major shift in the balance of power between committee and secretary seems to have occurred in the last decade. Lundestad has to a large degree become the face and voice of the prize. He explains how

---

The Norwegian Nobel Committee 2010

Thorbjørn Jagland (Chairman)
President of the Storting

Geir Lundestad (Secretary)
Professor, Director of the Nobel Institute

Kaci Kullmann Five (Deputy Chairman)
Adviser Public Affairs

Sissel Rønbeck (Member)
Deputy Director, Directorate for Cultural Heritage

Inger-Marie Ytterhorn (Member)
Senior political adviser to the Progress Party's Parliamentary Group

Ågot Valle (Member)
Member of Parliament

From Nobelprize.org (May 2010).

Figure 12.1 Norwegian Nobel committee 2009–2012 as presented on nobelprize.org as of June 4, 2010.

"we" think and gives the main interview on the award posted each year on the Nobel Foundation Web site. Lundestad's consistent use of "we," lays no distance between the committee and the secretary. The same blurred role is illustrated on the Web site, where the committee seems to have six members—the secretary appears as one of the committee, placed between the chairperson and vice chairperson in the list of members.

This would not have been such a disaster if the secretary had been a devoted supporter of Nobel and the purpose of the will. He seems to be the opposite, with an attitude toward Nobel's intended recipients somewhere between indifference and aversion. Increasingly guided by commercial thinking, his powerful position is annihilating the intention of Nobel and a disaster for the peace work that Nobel wished the prize to support.

The secrecy surrounding the committee deliberations makes it hard to offer reliable judgments of Lundestad's influence. Based on my personal contacts with the committee chairs and members during the last 20 years,

I venture the following hypothesis: During Lundestad's first 10 years in the job, a strong committee chair confined him to the role of loyal secretary. Francis Sejersted may well have been the most competent Nobel chair ever, and he was respected with good reason (though he, too, did not understand how to interpret a will and the need to respect the specific purpose of Nobel[22]). In the last decade, the position of Lundestad has been strengthened by a combination of weaker leaders in the chair and the substantial extracurricular commercial activity developed by the secretary.

The pomp and circumstance has taken precedence over substance. The result is a more and more popular prize, increasingly coveted by the world, but at the same time ruinously corrupted by commercial thinking. The world's military-industrial sector is probably happy that the Nobel Peace Prize is no longer the challenge it was intended to be. Two safe conclusions can be drawn as a result of the 2009 prize: (1) the vast commercial activities of the Nobel Foundation are damaging to the independence and integrity of the prize and (2) the combination of the roles of committee secretary and commercial director must end immediately.

Chapter 13

IN SEARCH OF THE LOST NOBEL

TO FOLLOW OR NOT TO FOLLOW THE WILL?

There was little will to respond to my Norwegian book, both from the committee and the Nobel secretary, until suddenly after six months, over almost a full-page article in *Aftenposten*, Geir Lundestad delivered a massive attack, "Om å tolke Nobel" ("Interpreting Nobel").[1] The label was deceptive and the whole article just showed that the committee did not interpret Nobel at all. It has been confirmed again and again, not least by Lundestad, that the committee had formulated its own idea of a "peace prize." Giving, in the little space allowed for response, a specified list of the key points in my analysis, I challenged Lundestad to explain where I could be wrong. Again, silence set in.

Lundestad had not made relevant arguments in his article and had provided little basis for a discussion. But I found two sentences particularly puzzling: "None of the many authors who have written on the peace prize agree with Heffermehl's interpretation of Nobel's will. Committees have since 1901 applied a different interpretation." The first sentence spurred me on to make a survey of some of the many people who have put the same criticism to the committee. Lundestad's second sentence is untenable, both because my interpretation generally was followed during the first four decades and, regardless, long tradition is no excuse for continuing a wrong. But months later a thought, a question, snuck up on me: Was the committee ever *very* loyal to Nobel?

In 2008 the Nobel chair, Ole Danbolt Mjøs, used his speech in honor of Martti Ahtisaari to deliver a discreet, but unmistakable, slap to my book two months after its publication. Mentioning the rule on the "preceding year," he drew sympathizing snickers when he called this an example that "it is not easy to read every sentence in the will of Nobel in a strictly literal way." But there are sentences and sentences; difficulties over points of minor importance do not justify gross disrespect for the very idea of the will.

One year later, the public relations strategy had changed somewhat, and the committee had started to insist it was following the will, its wording, content, and Nobel's intention and spirit, now, as always. This took the form, for example, of the following bold sentence in the committee's press release to announce the prize for Obama: "For 108 years, the Norwegian Nobel Committee has sought to stimulate precisely that international policy and those attitudes for which Obama is now the world's leading spokesman."[2]

But in making statements, one has to be consistent; if this was the truth, what then with statements Thorbjørn Jagland had given half a year earlier, when he had just been elected chair of the Nobel committee? Then *Aftenposten* had carried an interview with a direct quote in the headline: "No award possible with a literal interpretation of Nobel." Once more with a misunderstood, but discreet and unmistakable, address to my criticism (and neglecting the disarmament purpose of the prize) Jagland stated that none of the laureates since year 2000 could have been appointed if the committee had followed the words of the will strictly, since "the concept of peace has changed considerably since Alfred Nobel wrote the will."[3]

Jagland, in the Nobel speech in honor of Obama called the will "its *frame of reference*" (emphasis added), and then he quoted the three criteria and said, "The question was actually quite simple. Who has done most for *peace* in the past year?" (emphasis added). But Nobel gave his prize for "*champions of peace*." Unfazed by numerous reminders of what Nobel actually meant, the committee failed to ask the correct question: Are there still people that pursue the political work that Nobel wished to reward with the prize? Why is it so hard to get this right?

The committee always had ample resources at its disposal to enable it to give the best possible answer to this question. First of all, the Nobel Institute was established primarily to support the committee in observing the will and selecting the winners. The committee has a well-educated secretary and Institute director on call, with a team of learned consultants in addition to general staff. A comprehensive, well-staffed library is available to keep the committee informed of relevant developments in research and literature. The library collects media reactions, good and bad, including claims that the committee has failed to respect Nobel's will. If valid and relevant research into the purpose of the prize and interpretation of the will has not reached the committee, it can only blame itself.

At any point during more than 100 years, the committee could have chosen to commission a professional, legal analysis of the possible limits of its mandate. Apparently it has not done so, despite the continual protests. Such an analysis would have been kept secret, but nothing in what the committee has done or said indicates any such analysis was commissioned.

Also, information, research, and arguments from the outside apparently have been of little interest; protest and criticism from the public have had little impact.

A long history of criticism and comment contradicts the line of the committee. These protests have shown the historical background that motivated Nobel to write the will, as well as the intimate connection—indeed, cooperation—with Bertha von Suttner that resulted in the will. My impression was that in every decade the committee has faced pressure to understand and respect Nobel and his intention, but that the committee has been unbelievably resistant to complying.

A literature search to check whether "None of the many authors who have written on the peace prize agree with Heffermehl's interpretation of Nobel's will" proved this claim by Lundestad to be very far from the truth. The following is by no means an exhaustive list.

2005: CENTENARY COMMEMORATION OF SUTTNER'S AWARD

A number of events were organized to celebrate Suttner. Conferences in Vienna and Prague highlighted her role in making Nobel include a Peace Prize in his will. This resulted in books and reports that all found their way to the Nobel library, not least because the head librarian, Anne Kjelling, participated and gave lectures at some of these events. Through her, the committee and secretary had every chance to be updated and obtain the most recent results of the research on Suttner—and what it revealed about the peace work Nobel had in mind.

One volume that celebrated the Suttner centenary was edited by Laurie R. Cohen, *"Gerade weil Sie eine Frau sind. . . ."* The Nobel secretary and committee could for instance have gotten valuable insight from an article by Regina Braker on Nobel's intention in establishing the Peace Prize. Braker refers to the last letters between Nobel and Suttner written only weeks before he died and quotes a line from Nobel's last letter to Suttner in praise of the peace movement,

I am pleased to see that the pacifist movement is making progress. This is the civilization of the masses, above all those who fight prejudice and darkness where you are in high rank. It is these titles that constitute your real nobility.[4] . . .

Braker then observes that the Nobel committee does not follow this will (she is unaware that the committee does not "interpret Nobel" but follows its own wishes):

So far, however, the Norwegian peace prize committee has interpreted the wish of Nobel, that he also maintained in his will, in a different way.[5]

Another book in 2005, *Friede—Fortschritt—Frauen* (*Peace, Progress, Women*) was published by the Bertha-von-Suttner Association in Austria. It contains a lovely account by Irwin Abrams of his lifelong study of the Peace Prize and mentions the last letter in which Suttner lists for Nobel "all her accomplishments which his financial support had made possible, saving the Rome Congress, establishing peace societies in Vienna, Berlin and Budapest, and getting the International Peace Bureau started" and she implores him to "[g]ive a lever to Archimedes" and "never withdraw your support from us—never, not even from beyond the grave, which awaits us all." And Abrams is clear: "Without Bertha von Suttner, no Nobel Peace Prize!"[6]

A scholar on Nobel and Suttner history, Professor Peter van den Dungen of Bradford University (United Kingdom), offered enthusiastic praise for Abrams in his article "Irwin Abrams—Historian and Champion of the Nobel Peace Prize."[7] Based on writings by Abrams in 1962, 1972, and 1992, Professor Dungen included the following passage:

Abrams writes that [the Biedermann volume on the correspondence between Suttner and Nobel] represents a revisit of the correspondence he first analyzed thirty years before. He concludes, as before, "What does seem clear from these letters is that without Nobel's 'Chère Baronne et Amie,' [Suttner] there would have been no Nobel peace prize."[8]

1991: KENNE FANT—EARLIER WILLS

The history of preparation, the road pursued to reach a final will, can offer valuable help in the interpretation. Earlier drafts or revoked wills may contain slightly different expressions, words may be dropped, modified, or replaced. To trace the development of the thinking may help readers understand the final result.

Nobel's relation to the Austrian Peace Society is a case in point, demonstrating how much history can do to clarify what the testator intended. The society, founded by Suttner in 1891, got 2000 members in three weeks on a program based on the simple principle that human society "has to seek the foundation of its true welfare in unity, not separation; in mutual cooperation, not in mutual enmity."[9] Taking the full consequence of this, the society concluded, meant disarmament. Nobel joined this society as a member and gave generous financial support. Two years later Nobel, in his 1893 will, singled out the Austrian Peace Society as a beneficiary to receive an annual share of the proceeds from his fortune. In his final will, in 1895, we find the support for peace work repeated in a widened form. Nobel had dropped the specific mention of the Austrian society in favor of the "champions of peace" in general, describing these by three criteria. It is striking how closely these three criteria replacing the Austrian Peace Society match the political platform of the society, and this provides a significant clue to what was on Nobel's mind when he wrote the peace criteria into his will. This is the type of connection that would greatly impress any judge seeking to determine the true content of Nobel's will.

Swedish filmmaker Kenne Fant, in his written biography *Alfred Nobel*, first published in 1991 in Swedish, shows a keen awareness of how important the prehistory of a will can be.

According to Fant, Nobel's interest in peace was clearly influenced by the passionate appeals of Suttner, but it started earlier. He became more and more philosophical. Nobel wrote to a Belgian peace worker as early as 1885: "The more I hear the cannons dispute, the more blood I see flow, looting legalized and the handgun sanctioned."

Noting the warm acclaim Nobel had expressed for Suttner's book *Lay Down Your Arms*, Fant writes, "Their continued exchange of letters reveals that Bertha had not succeeded in convincing Alfred that her peace strategy was the best."[10]

In a letter to Suttner, as the peace congress in Bern was approaching in 1892, Nobel expressed doubt that the main problem for peace organizations was money:

Good intentions alone will not assure peace, nor, one might say, will great banquets and long speeches. You must have an acceptable plan to place before the governments. To demand disarmament is ridiculous and will gain nothing. By calling for the immediate establishment of a court of arbitration, you hurl yourself against a thousand prejudices.

But Fant concludes that even though Nobel disagreed with some of the details, he sympathized with the central message of Suttner in *Lay Down Your Arms,* and, Fant notes, the Bern conference made an impact on Nobel.

As a result of the conference, Nobel retained former Turkish diplomat, Aristarchi Bey, with the main task of keeping him *au courant* with the activities of the peace movements. Nobel soon fired Bey as he was dissatisfied with his reports. In a letter in 1892 to Bey, Nobel entertained ideas on a binding agreement between states and mandatory arbitration of disputes: "Let us admit that anything is better than war." A binding agreement to defend collectively any attacked country would make partial disarmament possible, but still "there has to be an armed force to maintain order."

Similarly, in a letter dated January 7, 1893, Nobel warned Suttner against impatience: disarmament, as well as compulsory arbitration "is an ideal we can only reach slowly and with caution." The real significance of this letter is the introduction, where, after wishing his dear friend a happy new year, Nobel mentions the idea of a *peace prize*—it seems for the first time:

> I would like to bequeath part of my fortune for the establishment of peace prizes to be awarded every fifth year (let us say six times, for if at the end of thirty years we have not succeeded in reforming society, we shall inevitably revert to barbarism) to the man or woman who has contributed most effectively to the realization of peace in Europe.

Suttner voiced dissatisfaction with the idea. In her view, the movement needed money rather than prizes. It may be a sign of her influence that Nobel, drawing up his second will two months later on March 14, 1893, stipulated that 1 percent of his fortune would go to the Austrian peace association and that the Peace Prize should go to someone who had made pioneering contributions in "the wide field of knowledge and progress." In an addendum, he specified the struggle for a "European peace tribunal" as particularly worthy of consideration.[11]

Even if he mentions Nobel's reservations, Fant understood *that it was the final decision, the will, that counted.* His book enjoyed wide distribution by respected publishers, both in Swedish and English. In his chapter on the Peace Prize, Fant stressed the exchanges and cooperation with Suttner that had led Nobel to formulate his last will as he did. Fant is not in doubt when he concludes:

> That Alfred had Bertha in mind when he composed this [the three criteria of the 1895 will] is *evident from the fact that he immediately informed her* of his final version. She was overjoyed: "Whether or not I am still alive by then does not matter; what you and I have given will live on." [Emphasis added.]

1962: URSULA JORFALD—HARD TALK ON DEAF EARS

Ursula Jorfald was a teacher, Norwegian feminist, and champion of peace, a prominent activist in the Women's League for Peace and Freedom.

In the opening words of her 1962 book on Suttner and the Peace Prize, Jorfald recalls a comment in 1905, when Suttner received the Peace Prize: "As the apostle of the cause of peace, she stands as one of mankind's greatest benefactors," but then noted that people forget fast and mercilessly. Following the "Great War" Suttner's pioneering role was soon forgotten.

A special value of the Jorfald book is her thorough description of the contemporary mental landscape at the time of Nobel, essential to understanding what Nobel had in mind. Jorfald further depicts the peace movement in the 1890s, its thinking, the supporters, the frequent meetings, and the annual peace congresses that followed the first such conference in 1889 in Paris, as well as the optimistic belief that the curse of armaments and wars could quite soon be eliminated.

After describing the two main organizational pillars of the work—the International Peace Bureau (IPB) and the Interparliamentary Union—Jorfald places Suttner at the center of all this flourishing activity and, most important, describes her correspondence with Nobel, his strong ties to the peace movement, his membership and financial support, and the fact that in 1892 Nobel came to see Suttner at the Bern Peace Conference.

Jorfald had good reasons for writing this book. It seems to have been the finale of a long, thankless struggle, since the late 1930s, to make the Nobel committee respect Nobel and his purpose.

Jorfald's excellent book is in two main parts, first the life story of Suttner and next the story of the corruption of the Peace Prize. It is a thoroughly substantiated and convincing criticism of how the Norwegian Parliament and Nobel committee have mismanaged the prize. The difficulties she faced getting her book published were the same as I watched at close range a few years ago, with a book on the North Atlantic Treaty Organization (NATO) written by Gunnar Garbo, who is a leading Norwegian thinker on matters of peace, disarmament, international law, nonviolence, and nonaggression. Garbo was leader of the Liberal Party (Venstre), a former parliamentarian and ambassador, and has been nominated for the Nobel Peace Prize at least twice. He studied the history of NATO and produced an excellent critical analysis, but he found it difficult to get criticism of the military into print. Having combed the publishers of Norway, he ended up being his own publisher—exactly as Ursula Jorfald had had to be 40 years earlier.

It is hard to tell how well Jorfald's book was distributed and received. We may, however, take for granted that this seasoned peace activist and her colleagues in the Women's League prodded parliamentarians and Nobel committee members, as well as the Nobel secretary, to read it. Jorfald may have led August Schou to change his earlier doubts regarding Suttner in 1964, when—two years after the Jorfald book—he wrote about the Peace Prize in a volume on the history of the Norwegian Parliament over 150 years.[12] Jorfald inspired others, too. A significant portrait of Suttner, referring in part to Jorfald, was included in *Educating for Peace*, a pioneering work published in 1985 by Norwegian peace researcher Birgit Brock-Utne.

Jorfald's book must have been an important achievement of the Women's League when it came out, and it was a guaranteed "home run" as the chair of the league was married to the chair of the Nobel committee. Gradually, helped by critics from outside, the historians close to the Nobel Institute have stopped denigrating the role of Suttner. They cautiously have acknowledged her influence on Nobel. But every time awareness was achieved, it seems soon to have died again; 30 years later, it was Harald Bjørke in a small pamplet (1989) and Gerd Grønvold Saue in a major biographical novel (1992) who tried to resuscitate Suttner. Jorfald's book seems to have had limited success at home, but the book made it to France, where a translation was published.[13]

All of these efforts clearly did not reach their most important goal, but fell victim to what looks like a pattern: no matter how well the true meaning of the Peace Prize has been explained to the committee, it does not change anything—nothing and nobody can influence the Nobel committee to comply, over time, with its mandatory obligations to Nobel and to the *"champions of peace."*

Having experienced the Nobel committee stonewalling my own book, I got a distinct feeling of *déjà vu* when I saw the fate of Jorfald's book. This proves that I am not the first to be dealing with a committee that moves in a world of its own, outside common norms of response to respectful social debate. My case was by no means the first time the committee has fought the obvious truth by ignoring it. The way the Jorfald book failed to have any effect makes it an essential part of the history of the prize: the history of gross neglect of Nobel's wishes was discernible as early as 1962.

"Gross neglect" is a strong accusation. But rereading the Jorfald book, I became aware that the accusation of disrespect for Nobel was not new. I discovered that the Nobel Library had added a hard cover and that I had overlooked the short text on the back of the paperback that Jorfald managed to produce. There Jorfald had stated the purpose of the book—to show how the Nobel Peace Prize was connected with Suttner:

> Bertha von Suttner also achieved such a strong influence on Alfred Nobel that he established the peace prize. In later years there have been attempts to explain away this fact. The purpose of this book is then—following extensive research—to document that this view is not correct.

"Attempts to explain away" is how Jorfald, in 1962, perceived the situation. She wished to see the truth prevail, but her energetic and competent criticism for more than 30 years fell on deaf ears.

NEW YORK 1942: HERTA E. PAULI

In the course of four years, two solid volumes on the Peace Prize were published in New York. First, in 1938, a professor of Scandinavian History at NYU, Oscar J. Falnes, in his book *Norway and the Nobel Peace Prize*, described the line taken by the committee, but failed to address the limits of its power to redefine the prize. Only four years later, a study by Herta E. Pauli, on the dynamite king as architect of peace, went to the core of the matter. In convincing detail Pauli described the development of thought that led Nobel to establish the peace prize and how the three criteria of the final will were "fully in line with the pacifist doctrine of the period. It fitted Bertha's work so well that it seemed to have been written with her in mind."[14]

As proof of Nobel's intent, Pauli quotes from Nobel's letter to Aristarchi Bey, the Turkish diplomat retained for a year as his special secretary in peace matters. Here Nobel wrote that Bey had not carried the cause forward and had "not converted to the cause sponsored by Mme de Suttner a single person of any importance." He also scoffed at Bey's proposal to start a "special organ of publicity . . . If I had had the slightest belief in this method of propaganda, I should have gone to Mme de Suttner, who already edits a paper of this kind . . ."[15]

It is surprising how Schou, the Nobel secretary who took over four years after the Pauli book was published, and after him Sverdrup, managed to introduce uncertainty about the role of Suttner. Pauli's book ended up as one more of the many examples to show that the committee has been unwilling to listen and learn, and is impervious to outside critics.

Bad as that is, I was surprised to find—when I managed to get behind the façade—that critics on the inside did not fare much better.

REVEALING DIARIES—THE SECRETS
BEHIND THE FAÇADE

The bylaws of the Nobel Foundation contain a strict prohibition: divergent opinions may not be included in the record "or otherwise divulged." Compliance with this rule has been nearly perfect. Only in a few instances, notably Kissinger and Arafat, has the façade cracked and given limited glimpses of life inside the committee. An intimate insight was always missing. In this situation, it was a sensation to discover two diaries. Politicians often write diaries, and a couple of committee members proved to have shared some reflections in private moments with their diaries. Fortunately, two such diaries have been deposited with the National Library of Norway. First is the diary of Halvdan Koht, committee member from 1919 to 1944, who made short notes from several meetings up to 1930.

Second is the diary of Gunnar Jahn, member from 1938 to 1966 and chair from 1942; his notes are comprehensive and revealing. They lay bare the atmosphere, content, and form of the internal discussions in a transformative period for the prize. The notes show Jahn as a valiant, but lonesome, defender of the peace purpose of Nobel against a majority that did not seem to care much. His diaries are so relevant as proof of my central claims that substantial excerpts have been included as appendix 2.

Reading the diaries I sense great drama and a spectacular new light on the history of the prize; the committee chair spent 25 years in a constant, most often losing, battle with his colleagues to have them respect the intention of testator. I imagine that this must be just the kind of material professional historians would love to discover. One cannot but wonder how or why the Nobel historians, Stenersen, Sveen, and Libæk, and Lundestad, himself a historian, could avoid finding them interesting.

Gunnar Jahn—staunch defender of Nobel

In his notes from a committee meeting in 1946, Jahn recorded that he had listened with impatience to lavish praise for John Mott (United States, international scout leader, Christian missionary). He felt that Mott had contributed to a better world, but he had heard

> not a word on his work for the cause of peace . . . I would have to go for Emily Balch as the only one who fulfilled the terms of Nobel's will, by her work in the International Women's League for Peace and Freedom. I could not see how Mott's work was qualified for the peace prize, his work was in the purely religious field.

Noting that Mott had not done anything to speak up for peace in the critical years before the war, Jahn concluded: "There is no way that I can go for Mott." Jahn finally caved in, but he refused to give the speech for a person he considered clearly unqualified—he left "the sermon for Mott" to the members who had pushed his cause.

In 1948, Jahn drew sympathy from several committee members when he expressed dislike for the new proportionality system used by Parliament to elect committee members. He puts most of the blame on scheming by Olav Oksvik, a Labor Party member of Parliament.

Again, in 1949, Jahn spoke up for Nobel, unable to see that the committee could be "permitted" to award the prize to the International Labor Office (ILO)—"an institution established by the governments." The ILO had to wait until 1969, three years after Jahn left the committee.

Likewise, in 1950, Jahn protested against Ralph Bunche. Much good could be said about him, but "I could not find that strictly speaking he has instituted any peace action on his own initiative . . . it was first and foremost as a functionary of the UN he had been active." Bunche got the prize.

Next, in 1951, Jahn protested against labor leader Léon Jouhaux whose work "did not touch directly the cause of peace," and who Jahn thought had done little after the war to earn the Peace Prize. Jouhaux got the prize.

In 1952, Jahn felt Albert Schweitzer was the "only candidate ranking high enough. . . . But it is hard to find him compatible with the statutes in the will of Nobel." Next year he gave in. Schweitzer got the 1953 prize.

This is but one example of how group pressure to conform seems so heavy that Jahn, at times, even having declared that a result was against the will, deferred to committee members who apparently showed no interest in what Nobel had had in mind.

The thinking of the group, Jahn clearly included, was ruled by Norway's official policy during the Cold War, and as a member of NATO. In 1953, Jahn agreed to award the Peace Prize to George Marshall, but only with considerable reluctance, and making clear that he could accept Marshall only since his original postwar European recovery plan proposed "that aid should be given both to east and west, there was a great idea and a real effort for peace." Marshall got the prize.

The diaries further show a discrepancy between the easy support for conspicuously unqualified candidates such as Mott (1946) and the difficulty that "*champions of peace*" had in being considered for, not to speak of winning, the Peace Prize. The 1947 discussion of Gandhi is a case in point. Another illustration is found in the discussions in 1958 that secured a prize for Georges Pire (Belgian priest, mainly social work), whereas Norman Cousins (U.S. antinuclear protagonist) never got it. While Jahn understood that Cousins was an early champion in the most urgent disarmament struggle ever, he got no support in this; the other members felt he "was too thin," only 46, and none of them believed "that his activity in America had made any difference." Why did the committee not help Cousins to "make a difference" at an early stage of the antinuclear struggle? A case of pure sabotage against Nobel?

In 1958, Jahn was, he noted, "rather aghast that several of the committee members were fixed on Helen Keller as their candidate this year. I cannot really understand that she could possibly get the prize, despite being the special and valuable human being she no doubt is." Jahn noted a peculiar response: "Hambro said: Schweitzer had not done anything for peace either, when he received the prize." To justify an unqualified candidate, Hambro argued that the committee had done wrong before.

In 1962, having vigorously defended a prize for the U.S. antinuclear activist Linus Pauling, Jahn ends his entry regretting that the members do not respect the legal limits of their mandate: "I underlined as strongly as I could that the committee should not take political considerations into account, but exclusively point out the person who recently had done the most in the struggle against war. If this is the question, I concluded, I cannot find any other than Linus Pauling." Clear language from the chair, clear result: no prize for 1962.

In other instances, the committee was reluctant to award the prize to politicians when it was impossible to tell what those politicians might later do. Even the hypothetical possibility that Canadian Lester Pearson might return to active politics was seen as a sufficient obstacle—no prize awarded in 1957. A similar attitude was expressed to Nehru in 1960. As a *potential* political officeholder Pearson was not considered eligible—definitely different from the standard that permitted Obama to win in 2009.

According to his diaries, Jahn spoke up against disrespect for the will on numerous occasions, but his protests generally fell on deaf ears. Even in cases in which Jahn disagreed, the pressure to conform seems to have been so heavy that at times—despite having clearly declared that a result was against the will—he went along with the majority, which appears to have shown no interest whatsoever in his protests. In 1963, discussing the Red Cross as a potential winner, Jahn had had enough. The committee chair said to his colleagues:

> If we continue to give the prize to institutions I shall have to ask *Stortinget* to free me from the task as member of the committee. The prize, I said, must first and foremost be awarded to individuals who have struggled for peace and here we have two men who have in particular excelled: Bertrand Russell and Linus Pauling.

Jahn repeated the same clear language when the committee met a second time to decide on the 1963 prize, saying he did not oppose "institutions" *per se,* but "we really cannot constantly give the prize to those who have healed the wounds of war. What is correct and also in keeping with the will of Nobel is to seek out individuals who have struggled for peace." He again pointed to the "two persons who could be possible to consider, Russell and Pauling." Result: the 1963 prize went to the Red Cross.

The diary shatters any image of a qualified and conscientious committee. Again and again the members with responsibility for the implementation of a will have been told, by Jahn, that "this we are not permitted to do," "this is against the will," "this person is not qualified," "this is not what Nobel had in mind." The continuous struggle to have the will respected must have been costing Jahn a lot. When, in 1963, he threatened to leave the committee if the prize went to the Red Cross, a footnote to his entry on the ultimatum disturbs the image of the indefatigable hero:

> Before the meeting adjourned I said I could reluctantly be prepared to give one of the prizes for the Red Cross, but that I felt it ought to be sufficient that they had received the peace prize twice. I also added that I would appreciate it if someone else could be found.

As I understand it, Jahn, the Nobel chair, clearly aware that it would be a violation of the will, agrees to go along with a prize to the Red Cross. With open eyes he decides to drop Nobel. Even Jahn gave up. In his last year on the committee, 1966, he appears to have considered half-heartedly a prize for birth control even if "that is a long-term project that does not bear directly on peace."

The Jahn diaries provide more than a ray of light on the secret committee: they floodlight persistent neglect of the law. They show that Jahn often raised the key question: Who are the intended or legitimate beneficiaries? In a couple of instances, the committee did submit controversies over minor technical questions to the Foundation in Stockholm, showing that the committee was aware of this possibility. But it never sought guidance on the issue that really mattered: Who are the intended beneficiaries? How can it have been possible not to understand the legal nature of the question and address the recurring controversy over the content of the will in a serious and professional way? Was the committee's freedom of choice preferable to a legal clarification?

Apparently the majority of members did not care much. Whenever Jahn mentioned the will and the statutes, his arguments seem to have been politely ignored, and hardly ever contradicted. This is perhaps not surprising. Silence is what often happens in politics when truth is on one side and power on the other. But, again, this was not a "political" situation. As trustees, the members of the Nobel committee were legally bound by other standards, requirements, and responsibilities.

Writing the Norwegian book in 2008 I mentioned in passing that two private diaries written by committee members had, upon their death, been deposited at the National Library of Norway. I knew that Øivind Stenersen and his two fellow centenary historians had read the diaries but their text gave me the impression that these diaries could not contain much of interest. The three historians mention the Jahn diaries just twice and only to share competing views on which laureate to award the Peace Prize.[16] When I looked for myself, at a late stage in the preparation of this book, I was deeply shocked. The historians had benignly overlooked the fact that Jahn, during his 25 years in the chair, had protested constantly that his fellow members were violating the will, the very kind of information that would have interested many, not least historians.

It is a paradox that despite the energy Jahn mustered in defense of the will, he never seems to have used his trump card: the law. Why did he fail to raise the question as a legal issue? Jahn was not only an economist—he got his law degree in 1907. It is hard to think that Jahn could avoid seeing the legal limits to the committee's mandate. It is tempting to speculate: Was there an atmosphere of exceptionalism within the Nobel committee that apparently placed its deliberations beyond and above the law?

In a sense, the members must have felt like masters of the universe. The secrecy gave them license to say and do as they wished, and at the same time, to respond to criticism or not. Moreover, they had the comfort of being in line with a promilitary majority in Norway. After World War II, public opinion had turned against the fundamental idea of Nobel's will, and the committee members must have felt they were managing the prize in a useful way.

Koht—violations as early as 1922

The Jahn diaries show strong protestations on behalf of Nobel as early as 1946, but similar internal protests can be traced back even further. The notes by committee member Halvdan Koht reveal a committee lacking commitment to Nobel and his intentions. Koht's notes for 1928 and 1929 mention that several prominent and typical *champions of peace* were discussed—Jane Addams, Carl Lindhagen, and Elsa Brändström—but no prize was awarded in those years.[17]

Most important, as early as 1922, there was a heated discussion as to whether the Norwegian polar explorer and humanitarian Fridthjof Nansen was qualified. Several spoke out against a prize for humanitarian work. Koht records a protest by Hans Jacob Horst, who felt that

the achievements of Nansen [Nansen passport, humanitarian relief for refugees] were far from what Nobel had intended. I showed that the committee had often given the prize for work of the same kind and warmly defended Nansen. . . . Horst developed at length [his argument] that it had been wrong to give the peace prize to Dunant and the Red Cross.

Again we see that, as Hambro would later do, Koht defended an unqualified winner by the (wrong) earlier decisions of the committee, rather than by Nobel's intention in 1895.

At least this shows a real discussion. There is no reason to believe that Horst changed his view that the humanitarian prizes violated the will. Still, unanimously, Nansen received the 1922 prize.

In 1925, the chair, professor of law Fredrik Stang, proposed the League of Nations. Koht spoke strongly against this, "holding that it would run against the statutes of the prize." A long discussion ensued, and Koht felt so strongly about it, he records, that he said he would leave the committee if a majority voted to award the prize to the League. At an adjourned meeting there was heated debate, during which Koht maintained his firm opposition, and Stang was unable to get a majority. Stang then insisted that no prize be given, and so it was decided.

This seems to be a rare example of a discussion in the committee where those ostensibly defending Nobel's will won a majority, in my view regrettably, because I find them wrong. The row was over the word *institution* and Koht disliked the way Stang "extended it to include all possible things, but in my view nations and associations of nations could not in any sensible way be included here." Koht's entry here is a revealing, early indication of a basic error in approach. The members discuss how *they* understand words, rather than what *Nobel* meant. The fact that the chairperson, Stang, a law professor, discussed the word "institution" (not taken from the will's description of beneficiaries) in this way, is an indication that he too related to the will in a superficial manner. A deep interpretation should have led him to the role of Suttner and its significance for a proper reading of the words in the testament.

I believe that Koht, with his restrictive understanding, and Stang, accepting every kind of "institution," were both wrong and that in this case Koht would have had a strong case and been respectful of Nobel's will if he had pointed out that the prize was intended for individuals, not for organizations. That being said, Stang's defense of institutions in this particular case, if successful, would have given a result in line with the spirit and the letter of Nobel. The League was a typical "confraternization of nations" to avoid war, exactly the type of effort that the will of Nobel envisaged.

The Koht diaries do not always show the two representatives of the peace movement on the committee in the first three decades, Bernard Hanssen and Hans Jacob Horst, as strong or principled defenders of the will and its purpose.

Unfortunately even Moe, who in his 1932 book explained that Nobel had had the program of the peace movement in mind, failed to understand the legal obligation to respect his intention. But, how could the chair, professor of law, Fredrik Stang miss this obvious point?

It is tempting to ask: Were the limitations and obligations of the committee mentioned as a legal issue at any point before the discrepancy with the will became so glaring that I reacted with articles in 2007 and a Norwegian book in 2008?

DID NOBEL EVER GET THE COMMITTEE HE WANTED?

My study of the Jahn and Koht diaries revealed that as early as 1922 a committee member was passionately convinced that the humanitarian prizes were not in keeping with the will—but even so he voted for a humanitarian prize. Koht's defense for the illegal prize was that it had often happened before, that is, he did not care to argue or show that this was correct, but justified a new error by referring to past mistakes.

This is the same style of argument that was repeated by the committee and Lundestad in 2008, responding to my criticism by claiming that "the Nobel committee has always had a broad understanding" and that "[i]f this is wrong, it is original sin—since it first happened in 1901." As a defense, these claims are just as invalid now as they were nearly nine decades ago. When it is discovered that a will has been misinterpreted, the obvious consequence is to get the things right as soon as possible. One cannot by custom establish a right to embezzle or steal money.

After a considerable period of further study, I started to wonder whether the secretary might nevertheless have a point. It struck me that the Nobel committee never became the ingenious and wholehearted, innovative, inventive warm defender of disarmament and fundamental reform of international relations that Nobel must have hoped for. I started to seriously doubt Nobel's choice of trustees.

Norwegian politicians in the decade leading up to the dissolution of the union with Sweden in 1905 spoke warmly of arbitration, the great conflict resolution idea of the period, but they also prepared for war. The first Nobel committee included a leading voice in Scandinavian and European peace activism, Bjørnstjerne Bjørnson, a national poet in Norway, who had since 1880 been promoting the peace movement's ideas at the time. Evidence suggests that he did research on the intentions of Nobel, talking to Emanuel Nobel among other people, to find out what his uncle had intended with the Peace Prize. In a foreword to an 1890 book by the to-be-named Swedish Nobel laureate Klas Arnoldson (1908), Bjørnson spoke up for complete mutual disarmament between Norway and Sweden, feeling certain that this would act as an example to be copied.

Bjørnson is often mentioned as an important reason for Nobel to entrust the Peace Prize to Norway. But Bjørnson, too, would be drawn into the military mind-set: as the nation moved toward a showdown with its union partner, Sweden, support for military preparedness became a strong national sentiment.

My original belief—that at least in the first decades pacifists on the committee ensured loyalty to Nobel's intentions—began to crumble as I read the diaries of Koht. Even the peace people on the committee seem not to have seen abolition of the military as an urgent matter. Several of the committee members in the first two or three decades came from the Norwegian Peace Association, which called for a look into the early history of this group. It is one of several peace associations founded in the 1890s, still alive and active even in the 21st century, like the Swedish equivalent, the Swedish Peace and Arbitration Society (SPAS), and the IPB, founded at the same time.

When, in *Nobels vilje*, I pointed to Bjørnson as an example of the strong peace profile of the early committees, I was unaware of what historians had to say about the divisiveness and belligerence within the Norwegian movement at that time. Bjørnson, one of many high-profile members of the peace group, used the expression "peace sheep" (*fredsfaar*) of those fellow members who opposed the military. In return, the true pacifists said of Bjørnson that anyone who wished "to end the fear of wars by military spending" was more of a warrior than a friend of peace.[18] The strong language is not surprising, since in Norway at that time there was strong backing for the need for military force if the dissolution of the union with Sweden should turn violent.

Within the peace association, Bjørnson was in line with another prominent member, Halvdan Koht, the later foreign minister, who was strongly against the views of the "dreaming idealists." To end internal strife and make the association more attractive to those who accepted the need for military defense, he sought a showdown by proposing a change in the bylaws' definition of purpose for the 1902 congress of the association: "In its work to end war, it is not the program of the association to impede the defense of the fatherland."

The hard-line pacifists won the vote, but would soon find themselves marginalized in a country fearing imminent war. Koht, Bjørnson, and Horst, peace people closer to practical politics and more tolerant of— even warmly defending—military defense, moved on to political influence and soon found a new playing field—the Nobel committee.

Bjørnson and Horst were Nobel committee members from the beginning. The latter, with 30 years of committee service, became one of the two longest-serving members. Koht was first a consultant to the committee from 1904 to 1907, then an active member from 1919 to 1937. Without doubt, the three shared the goals of peace and had a genuine wish to break the militarist tradition. But even the peace movement members of the Nobel committee seem to have dropped Nobel's visionary goals in favor of a pragmatic approach. Nobel left the Norwegians a Peace Prize intended as a lighthouse to direct the struggle for disarmament, but the stingy trustees never turned up the full light. This was signaled with the first prize in 1901 that both disappointed Suttner and let Frédéric Passy share with Henry Dunant.

Prizes in the early decades went largely to deserving winners, but warm and wholehearted backing for Suttner and her total rejection of war failed to materialize, even if that must have been what Nobel had hoped—and was entitled to hope—of the committee. According to the law, the main obligation of trustees is to be faithful to the testator's wishes. If the parliamentarians were lukewarm to the promise that Parliament gave in 1897, their legal obligation was still to honor the task entrusted to them by Nobel. They should not have forgotten what the task actually was—and not have filled the seats on the committee from their own ranks, but have looked elsewhere seeking people loyal to the task.

Official Norway, even if pleased with the honor, balked at the utopian ambition of the Peace Prize, and did not at the time—and even less since—embark on a brave foreign policy governed by the peace and justice ideas. Instead Norway let down Nobel and Suttner from the start.

But the challenge of human development is not to choose between realism and idealism; it is to realize the ideals.[19]

DEMOCRACY, TRANSPARENCY, AND ABUSE OF MAJORITY

Jahn's diaries show that, despite numerous protests from those entitled to the prize, and even from the committee chair, his fellows on the committee preferred other people and other political ideas than those described by the testator. It is disappointing and harrowing to see Norwegian lawmakers caring so little about their own legal obligations—and the rights of others. The prize was conceived in another period; in the 21st century one may ask—even if the committee deliberations must be secret—would the Peace Prize be more serviceable with transparency and a possibility of public discussion of the candidates and their relation to the will?

In addition to the law, the Jahn diaries raise a question of political propriety: Is a parliamentary majority badly overstepping political boundaries, too, when it uses a legacy meant for political opponents to favor its own political ideas? The question is this: Who can control elected politicians when they benefit from joining together rather than controlling each other? Similar problems in other parliaments seem to confirm that power has its temptations; the 2009 scandal of British parliamentarians using public funds for private purposes is but one recent example.[20]

Safeguarding democracy and the rule of law in Europe are the primary tasks of the new secretary-general of the Council of Europe, Thorbjørn Jagland, who is now also the chair of the Nobel committee.

Stortinget took swift action when an independent investigation found that Norway's Parliament had taken liberties in the management of its own pensions. Bending the rules, former parliamentarians had been permitted to take parliamentary pensions even if they were still young, able to work, and in well-paid jobs. In a matter of weeks after the report was published, the management of parliamentary pensions was transferred to an independent, professional administration. I suggest that, as in the case of parliamentary pensions, a group of experts should be commissioned to evaluate the content of the will; how the Nobel committees have related to the "champions of peace" and the specific peace work Nobel wished to support; and whether *Stortinget* has respected Nobel's intention in its selection of Nobel committee members.

Chapter 14

AN URGENT ABOUT-TURN

Oslo, January 2010

The meeting hall at the Nobel Peace Center was packed with people, listening to ForUM (Forum for Environment and Development) launching a political report on moral dilemmas in Norwegian foreign policy, not least between arms exports and peacemaking. When one of the four panelists, in a senior military position, defended the burgeoning arms exports of Norway—the "Peace Nation"—I felt I had to confront him, saying that the military was selling an illusion of security at an exorbitant price, placing the continuation of life on earth in constant jeopardy. Given the unceasing research and development into new weaponry and continuous military planning, did he ever spend time thinking how to break the pattern? His stuttering reply was, "Er, that would presuppose a wholly different approach, such as strengthening the UN, developing international treaties, and a new international order with enforcement of laws . . . much like we have within each single nation." I replied, "Exactly—and since we are gathered here at the Nobel Peace Center, I would like to remind you that that is precisely the idea behind the Peace Prize that Nobel established 115 years ago." But it was clear that he had never spent much time brooding over how to make his job superfluous.

THE MILITARY, DEFENDING ITSELF OR THE NATION?

What has happened to Nobel's prize is not unique. It seems to be a law of nature that anything and anyone who has the temerity to challenge the military is heading for defeat. Even institutions have survival instincts and vested interests will vigorously resist any attempt to free the world from the yoke of militarism. The decay of the Peace Prize seems to be just one of many examples.

Daniel Ellsberg is the man who helped to end the Vietnam War and the Nixon presidency by publishing secret Pentagon papers. His important contribution, for example, in the book *Secrets* (2003), is to show how defenseless American democracy is when a much too powerful military sector, shielded by secrecy, is not loyal to the interests of the American people.

Having been informed of my Nobel discoveries, Ellsberg mentioned that a parallel development might have happened to the Carnegie Endowment for International Peace, established at the same time and having an original statement of purpose similar to that of the Nobel Peace Prize.[1] Much the same can be said of peace research, which in its infancy had ambitious plans to discover ways to undo militarism and create a better world. Now it is often trapped by the need for funding sponsors such as the ministries of defense and of foreign affairs, and chooses its topics accordingly. The development of the International Peace Research Institute of Oslo (PRIO) is a case in point. The PRIO which turned 50 in 2009 is quite far from making the difference that Johan Galtung and fellow founders once dreamed of. A PRIO insider, not wishing to be named, had this to say: "Everyone talks about funding possibilities, more than about what they wish to achieve with their research—and it is not just Norway, but much the same everywhere."

An indication of PRIO's decline was that one of the many who publicly praised the Obama Nobel speech was the head of the politics and ethics program at PRIO, Henrik Syse. In a full-page newspaper article, "War is defensible," he discussed the Christian Just War tradition—completely ignoring two centuries of development of international law and the ban on war in Article 2.4 of the UN Charter.[2]

For 50 years Norway had a political party trying to get the country out of NATO and to find ways to create a more just, peaceful, and less armed world. Since 2005 this party in its present form, the Socialist Left Party (SV), is part of a coalition cabinet dominated by the Labor Party. In February 2010, a party spokesperson defended Norway's record levels of arms exports. The party's road to power required dropping the original purpose.[3] Today, it has been broken in through bullying in the media every time it shows the slightest hesitation in allegiance to NATO and a strong military defense. In earlier times this party was probably the only one in Parliament that could have been counted on to stand up to defend Nobel and the intention of the Peace Prize. Now there was not one word of support from the former "peace party" or any other party in the *Storting* at any stage in my work to restore Nobel's prize for the *champions of peace*.

When finally there was a sign of visible interest in the Peace Prize from people in *Stortinget*, it was for not being invited to the December 10, 2009, banquet in celebration of Obama: "I note that this has become a dinner for sponsors where information directors in private corporations are preferred to the presidents of parliament," Per-Kristian Foss, one vice president of *Stortinget* said to Norway's main business journal, *Dagens Næringsliv*.[4]

I remember a friendship in the 1980s with Jiri Dienstbier and other Czechs in Charter 77 [dissidents invoking Helsinki accords on political rights]. As the first post-Communism foreign minister, Dienstbier voiced big plans for reducing arms production . . . and we know where those hopes ended. The same goes for Nelson Mandela—in the early days after he came to power in South Africa, I read a news story in which he declared that the country's military production must be cut and the social needs of his people met. Other interests soon proved too strong for even so forceful a politician as he.

I am sure many people will fear that if the committee embarks on a new policy, with less well-known peace laureates at the center of attention, Nobel's Peace Prize will lose some of its glamour. Yet, I believe the prize will gain in significance and content—and, after all, it was Nobel who chose to what and to whom he wished to give his prize. In addition, it should be cause for reflection if a prize challenging the military proves to be of less interest to the world's political elites and media.

The whole field of military "defense" is in deep conflict with democratic governance. Consider two Norwegian examples of a universal problem. In 1998, Defense Minister Dag Jostein Fjærevoll addressed Parliament on Norway's future role in the March 1999 attack on Serbia. The minister said Norway would follow standard official policy not to take any part in any operation lacking UN authorization. In fact, the cabinet—in a secret resolution two months earlier—had committed Norwegian air forces to the attack, a decision that violated Norway's constitution.[5] Similarly, for lack of UN authorization, Norway did not take part in the attack on Iraq in March 2003—officially. In a clandestine move, Defense Minister Kristin Krohn Devold supplied essential radar equipment (the "Arthur" missile tracer) to the British for the illegal attack.[6]

In *Peace Is Possible* (2000), I mentioned the response of the German Kaiser Wilhelm II when he was invited to the 1899 Hague Peace Conference: "Imagine a monarch, holding personal command of his army, disbanding his regiments, sacred with a hundred years of history—and handing his towns over to anarchists and democrats!"[7]

The secret services operate as a "state within the state," violating laws at home and abroad—in striking contradiction to the elegance and respect on the surface of diplomatic relations. The military often controls parliaments, presidents, and prime ministers, instead of being controlled by them. Secrecy serves to obstruct legitimate debate and criticism, the quintessential core of democracy. That power unexposed to public scrutiny runs a high risk of being misused applies everywhere, whether it is military leaders or the Nobel committee. A question appears warranted: "The Kaiser is dead, long ago, but has democracy ever gained control of the military sector?"[8]

The nations and citizens of the world are kept in thrall to an irrational, asocial, dysfunctional tradition. Too many make their living from continuing the pattern and will strike back at any threat—as the U.S. military did when the prospect of a peace dividend appealed to many at the end of the Cold War. The enemy is within, and there are innumerable accounts of the military as an antisocial agent. The way the military aborted the Gorbachev-Reagan deal on nuclear disarmament that almost resulted from their Reykjavik Summit in 1986 is probably the most searing example ever. Seymour Melman, in his book *Pentagon Capitalism* (1970), explains how efforts to end the Vietnam War by a negotiated settlement again and again were frustrated by the actions of a military wishing to show the value of military operations applied with skill. According to Melman, "It is difficult to discover the limits beyond which these men are not prepared to go."[9]

COUNTERING THE MILITARY AS A THREAT TO US ALL

If it is true that the military is unable to deliver anything but an extremely deceptive, costly and risky illusion of security, where are the media and the academic researchers that relentlessly, systematically, over time, lay bare the political role of the military as a menace to the real security of the nation and the well-being of its citizens? How many investigators are digging into the costs, the risks, and the deceptiveness of military activity—and pushing the need for a better-organized world? The problem goes beyond broadcast news depending on commercials;

it is about deep attitudes. Are not the print media—ambitious to show "the world as it is" but rarely mentioning voices for change as part of that reality—a solid obstacle to change? In his Nobel speech for Frank Kellogg, in 1929, Johan Ludwig Mowinckel formulated a most urgent moral and practical challenge:

> We must bring people to understand that it is not enough to proclaim war to be a crime, but that it is necessary for all to recognize with every sense and emotion that the murder of hundreds of thousands of human beings to settle an international dispute is no more justifiable, no more pardonable than the murder of a single individual to settle some personal quarrel.

Princeton professor Richard Falk has pointed out the absurd incongruity between our absolute moral and human rejection of the use of torture against individuals, on the one hand, and the wide acceptance of torture of whole nations in war, on the other.

Unfortunately, the Nobel committees have lacked the innovative and visionary mindset that Nobel must have hoped for. Where, for instance, are the Nobel Peace Prizes for William Hartung and his Arms Trade Resource Center, or other campaigns against the arms industry and trade such as the British or European campaigns against arms trade (CAAT and ENAAT)? Or, what about the Campaign for Nuclear Disarmament? The International Association of Lawyers against Nuclear Arms? The Citizens Action for Nuclear Disarmament (ACDN)? Movement for the Abolition of War? The Women's League and their www.reaching criticalwill.org Web site? The School of Nonkilling Studies? The Cluster Munitions Coalition? The International Peace Bureau (in 2010, 100 years have passed since its first Nobel)? The Middle Powers Initiative? The Coalition for the International Criminal Court? The Human Dignity and Humiliation Studies? The Peace Ministries campaigns? The Peace Alliance? The actions for disarmament? The 2020 Vision Campaign? Peace Education campaigners? Peace researchers (those who have not lost direction)? Www.betterworldlinks.org? Transcend? The Transnational Foundation? The conflict resolution networks, and others in the vanguard of nonviolence and conflict resolution? All the women and women's organizations for peace? The grandmothers, in black and in white? CODEPINK? Abolition 2000? The Fourth Freedom Forum? World Without War? The World Order Models Project? The Global Marshall Plan? The military bases campaigns? The Peace Tax campaigns? PeaceJam? The British American Security Information Council? Scilla Elworthy and the Oxford Research Group? The small arms campaigns? The parliamentarians, the mayors, the physicians, the lawyers, the engineers and scientists, and the Hiroshima victims for nuclear disarmament? The Bulletin of the Atomic Scientists? The Nuclear Age Peace Foundation? The Kuala Lumpur Initiative and Perdana Global Peace? Bruce Gagnon and his Web site space4 peace.org?

And what about the people working for government intelligence, in cabinets and the diplomatic service, who try to throw sand in the war machine as it gears up for new adventures, such as Americans Scott Ritter, Dan Ellsberg, and John Brady Kiesling; in Denmark, Frank Grevil; in Britain, Clare Short and Katharine Gun; in the UN service, Frank Halliday and Hans von Sponeck; and in Israel, Mordechai Vanunu? Even if not all these whistleblowers are supporters of the disarmed world that Nobel had in mind, they would have been much more relevant than most of those who have won the Peace Prize in recent years.

The Austrian peace educator Werner Wintersteiner raised a timely question in an article on Bertha von Suttner and her emphasis on educating young people for peace: "How can high school students get to know about peaceful organization of the world, if teachers do not enlighten them on the topic? Not in a single subject is there mention of the idea of peace."[10] Maybe, in a world thoroughly bred in the militaristic mind-set, some of the first new prizes true to Nobel's purpose should go to those people on all continents who have championed for decades the cause of peace education, including the Global Campaign for Peace Education, Educators for Peace, Peace Boat, Elise Boulding, Federico Mayor, Betty Reardon, Cora Weiss, Ghassan Abdullah, Adina Shapiro, Amada Benavides, Alicia Cabezudo, Catherine Hoppers, and Lalita Ramdas.

I could go on for days. It would take years to make a comprehensive list and describe all those forces for change whose cause has been wronged by the Nobel committee.[11] In one way or another, they are all working in opposition to the military tradition, the power and violence approach to security. Not that all of them are qualified for the Peace Prize—several of those struggling to abolish particular weapons (nuclear, landmines, and cluster munitions) do not actively seek the *general and complete disarmament* that Nobel's prize presupposes. The fact remains, however, that this is the political landscape the committee members must move in to find Nobel's change-makers, the *champions of peace,* in the 21st century.

Furthermore, the rule reserving the right to nominate only to groups of people well established in society has been unfortunate. This provision—which was not part of Nobel's directions—has limited the influx of nominations of the most relevant candidates. The people Nobel wished to support early stopped considering this prize as theirs.

The Nobel committee and secretary have met my criticism by simply repressing it, their response bearing resemblance more to the business world than to that of peace. First, my reminder of the clear wording of the will and the centrality of disarmament had no effect. Second, a whole book proving that the words Nobel used must fit his intention precisely had no impact. Third, when I told the committee that they had given the prize "for peace" instead of "for the *champions of peace*" mentioned in Nobel's will, they kept silent. Fourth, when shown numerous examples that for generations the committee has openly been formulating its own concept of peace, it made the claim to "always" have followed Nobel's will. Paradoxically, such undignified methods of discussion become possible only by the secrecy rules originally meant to preserve dignity and respect for the prize.

The committee pretends to be meeting 21st-century peace issues better than if it had shown respect to Nobel. If that is what it does, it should stop denying that it is formulating its own prize. Furthermore, this assertion reveals that the committee does not understand that the deep reform of international relations that Nobel wished to support is much more urgent, relevant, and vital today than in 1895.

It was only when I made my own check of the Gunnar Jahn diaries that I understood the level of disregard for Nobel and how long it had been that way. In our time it is hard to find anyone in the Norwegian Parliament who has the insight or sympathies required by law to sit on the Nobel committee. It makes me both sad and mad to think of all the valuable peace work that is offered to a world trapped in tradition and unable to listen—and how the Nobel committee fails to promote the deep change it was asked to nurture with Alfred Nobel's money.

The devastating problems ahead—overpopulation, pollution, exhaustion of natural resources, and the destruction of nature's own productive capacity—will confront us in the not too distant future with a crisis that can be met only through a common emergency response. Money spent on national military forces can only aggravate the damage, and the dangers, and does so without resolving any of the problems.

Even more than in 1895, we need a *confraternization of nations*, based on justice, law, and democracy.[12] The industrial world has prospered economically from its military and commercial bargaining power, at the same time attracting an influx of people from countries deprived of those same fundamentals for their own prosperity. When immigrants see their new countries hitting and maiming relatives in the villages they came from—an aunt, a parent, a nephew, a mullah—with air strikes, their loyalty to the new country is tested.

The intermingling in western capitals of people from around the world limits what nations can do; a bad foreign policy can backfire at home. For a host of good, mandatory, reasons a fair, nonviolent foreign policy has become indispensable. For more than half a century, however, the Nobel committee has favored the existing military-based international system instead of defending the directly opposite approach that Nobel wished to support. It is now high time the Nobel committee (as well as the secretary) stops cultivating a vague and diluted concept of "peace" and starts to support the *champions of peace*, respecting what Nobel meant using that precise expression. If the committee members cannot be true to Nobel's intentions with enthusiasm, they must leave their seats to the many others who can.

Appendix 1

HOW TO EARN THE NOBEL PEACE PRIZE

1. SHOW THE RIGHT MERITS

As long as the Norwegian Nobel committee continues to ignore what Nobel had in mind, almost any great deed can win the award. But the expression Nobel used in the 1895 will was not "peace," but rather "*champions of peace*," clearly a reference to the political movement challenging the military and violence as a tool in international politics.

Two fundamental and diametrically opposed roads can be taken to achieve national security. The *champions of peace* Nobel wished to support financially are those who seek to end the vicious circle of armaments and war by a deep reform of the international system and the way nations relate to each other; that is, by developing international law, cooperation, and justice, creating sufficient mutual trust to make general and complete disarmament possible.

The Nobel will of 1895 contains six criteria to help us understand who Nobel had in mind as the most deserving and legitimate recipients. First, Nobel used two general expressions that apply to all five Nobel prizes:

during the *expired year*
has *conferred the greatest benefit on mankind.*

Then, he used four particular expressions regarding the Peace Prize:

the *champions of peace*
the *confraternization of nations*
the *abolition or reduction of standing armies*
the *holding and promotion of peace congresses*

Nobel wished the prize to benefit further work for the cause of peace and the winner should be able to make practical use of the prize money in the political work for peace and disarmament. The purpose of the Nobel Peace Prize in the 21st century may be expressed as giving support to and honoring *proactive efforts* to prevent war. Here are some examples of relevant efforts:

- Abolishing or reducing military forces, both equipment and troops, military research and development; banning types of weapons, ways of using them, or particular military strategies.

- Promoting a new and peaceful international order based on law, global order, and democracy in the form of treaties and law enforcement at the international level; spreading global justice, respect, and solidarity among nations.

- Promoting alternatives to the use of military power and threats, such as mandatory arbitration, systematic prevention, and early discovery of conflicts, and their nonviolent resolution.

- Organizing peace congresses and other initiatives to win broad international support for treaties on peace and disarmament.

- Developing a peace culture, creating a new understanding and consciousness through upbringing and education for peace within all parts of the education system and media.

The Nobel Peace Prize was not designed for the following:

- Ending hostilities and caring for the victims, reparative measures. Nobel wanted deep change of the war system and wished to reward work to prevent wars from breaking out.

- Resolving local or national problems or conflicts. Nobel's perspective was global, and winners should have worked actively and with determination—thinking, writing, organizing, or similar—for peace through disarmament in the political, educational, and cultural arenas.

2. RECEIVE A NOMINATION

The bylaws restrict those entitled to nominate. Any one of the following people—from any country in the world—may submit proposals:

- Members of national assemblies and governments
- Members of international courts of law

- University chancellors; university professors of social science, history, philosophy, law, and theology
- Leaders of peace research institutes and institutes of foreign affairs
- Former Nobel Peace Prize laureates
- Board members of organizations that have received the Nobel Peace Prize
- Present and past members of the Norwegian Nobel committee
- Former advisers at the Norwegian Nobel Institute

People cannot nominate themselves. This is practiced as a (questionable) prohibition against (board) members nominating organizations to which they belong.

A valid nomination normally will be confirmed by the committee secretariat within April. If a valid nomination has not been acknowledged, check with the Nobel committee.

3. ENSURE THE NOMINATION IS SUBMITTED IN TIME

The deadline for nominations is February 1. Nominations after this deadline will be considered as nominations for next year—unless adopted by someone in the committee. (Members of the Nobel committee are entitled to submit their own nominations as late as at the first meeting of the committee after the expiry of the deadline.)

Nomination letters, with curriculum vitae and relevant documentation, should be addressed to the Norwegian Nobel committee, Henrik Ibsens gt. 51, N-0255 Oslo, Norway (letters must be postmarked no later than February 1), or submitted by e-mail to postmaster@nobel.no.

Appendix 2

EXCERPTS FROM GUNNAR JAHN'S DIARIES

REVEALING THE SECRETS OF THE NOBEL PEACE PRIZE COMMITTEE ROOM

Gunnar Jahn, who was Nobel committee chair 1942–1966, wrote comprehensive private diaries. The following summary notes of his records regarding Nobel matters have been taken down by the author in English (from the Norwegian original text). They are being published here for the first time by permission of Jahn's daughter, Nanny Jahn Hayes.

Gunnar Jahn, with his 26 years in the chair and 29 years on the committee, became the longest-serving chairperson, and the 15 years from 1949 to 1963 was the longest period without any changes to the committee.

The names of other committee members serving with Jahn and mentioned in the diaries are: From the Conservative Party, Carl Joachim Hambro, and John Lyng; from the Labor Party, Martin Tranmæl, Halvard Lange, Gustav Natvig-Pedersen, Aase Lionæs, and Nils Langhelle; from the Agrarian Party, Birger Braadland; from the Liberal Party, Anders Vassbotten, and Christian Oftedal; and from the Christian Democratic Party, Erling Wikborg.

From 1920, Jahn had been director of Norway's Central Bureau of Statistics. From 1934–1935 and in the first cabinet after the war he was minister of finance. From 1946, he was director of the National Bank of Norway. Jahn dictated the diaries, showing his prolific political activity, to his secretary, who then typed them.

Almost all of the transcript below is Jahn's private minutes from the formal Nobel committee meetings. A few of his other short diary reflections on the Peace Prize and the committee work have been included in parentheses. The author's additions are included in square brackets.

1946

[Decision: prize shared between Emily Greene Balch and John R. Mott.]

Spring

("Saturday and Sunday I was busy with the Nobel prize. My opinion is that Emily Balch is the only [choice] among those nominated.")

(Later, at a private party, Jahn had "a long conversation with Christian Oftedal on the Nobel. He has Mott in mind, not for what the man has done, but because he wishes to honor the ecumenical movement. After all, he is more and more hooked on the religious. The death sentence [during the war] and prison have brought him there.")

November 14:

(I was two minutes late, they were all there: Smitt Ingebretsen, Martin Tranmæl, Kristian Oftedal, Mr. Braadland and August Schou. . . .) "To avoid putting pressure on the Committee, I started the meeting hearing the opinions of the others. [In this way Jahn set a democratic pattern, which, according to a reliable source, has been followed since.] Smitt Ingebretsen began with John Mott [world mission conference (1910) and international boy scouts leader] and praised him endlessly. He mentioned the valuable work he had done—no doubt about that—but not a word on his work for the cause of peace." Tranmæl for [Russian socialist Alexandra] Kollontai. "Oftedal supported [committee colleague] Smitt Ingebretsen, but elaborated it further, quoting Worm-Müller's panegyric of Mott when he was nominated in 1934. Braadland felt it was difficult to decide, but he was inclined not to award a prize. "Now I took the word: I said I would have to go for Emily Balch as the only one who fulfilled the terms of Nobel's will, by her work in the International Women's League for Peace and Freedom. I could not see how Mott's work was qualified for the peace prize, his work was in the purely religious field and even if his organization had helped prisoners during the last war, I could not find anything that had been said after 1934 that would justify a prize to him, and this in a period when one had every reason to make an effort for the cause of peace. I felt repulsed by what Worm-Müller had written, poetic outbursts of profuse praise from many corners without actually being founded on reliable information. To me this defeated its purpose. I could also not vote for Mrs. Kollontai! In the first place there is no indication that peace in the understanding of Nobel, and in mine, has played any central role in her life. . . . But nothing came out of it. Then I took a new round of opinions. Smitt Ingebretsen again spoke at length about Mott. Tranmæl said that if he could not have Kollontai he would as an alternative vote for Emily Balch, and then he said some words to the effect that the people Mott had co-operated with were now old people and that we had to keep in contact with the times and I have not seen, he said, that he has done anything about the questions that are now current and positive work for peace. Should the prize go to any Christian organization, it would have to be the Quakers. If they had been proposed he would immediately have voted for them. Oftedal was still for Mott, but also spoke well of Emily Balch, but it was a problem that Jane Addams [United States, laureate 1931] had got it and in this way they had got theirs. True, Emily Balch had organized many congresses, but Mott had organized even more. Braadland was still unable to decide. I took the floor and spoke a little of Emily Balch and then I mentioned how important it was in this way to pay recognition to the work of women for that which, to me, was most important—if one in that way could mobilize women in the struggle against war. But, I said, I understand that you are menfolk and that that has an effect; that this is women, whose work has such difficulties in gaining recognition, and that constantly is smiled at because you think it so impractical, a little 'peace-sheepish.' But this is not at all the case when it comes to Emily Balch and her organization. I have taken the trouble, which probably none of you has, to go a little outside what the consultants have written, both with regard to Emily Balch and Madame Kollontai, and I think I have a good basis for asserting what I say. There we were. So, I took a trial vote. I nodded to Braadland and said: 'Vote for Balch.' But he voted for Mott. He looked over to Smitt Ingebretsen and I could see his fear of not being in the company of that which was the most conservative. This was the trial vote. We now had three for Mott, one for Kollontai and one for Balch in the first round. Then I said: 'There is no way that I can go for a prize for Mott.' Then Oftedal proposed sharing the prize, saying it should not be understood as a compromise, but he felt it was right what I had said about Emily Balch, even if he still could not give up Mott. But he said he would feel it was an excellent solution if they got half each. This was eagerly welcomed by Braadland and Smitt Ingebretsen was fully in favor. Tranmæl and I were against. Both of us now were in favor of Emily Balch. The discussion went on for a while and it was entirely deadlock. Braadland again raised the possibility of not awarding a prize, but won no support, and in order to achieve anything at all the decision was to divide the prize, against the votes of me and Tranmæl. As the result was clear, I said: Yes, then one of you gentlemen will have to hold the speech for Mott. Oftedal said: Can't Hambro do that when he returns home? No, I said, you who have insisted on him will have to do it. They were very reluctant, since they felt it was my obligation. I said: It is not a given that the Chair must always give these speeches. It may well be left to others. And it will be in Norwegian, so now I assume the sermon [!] for Mott will be held by Smitt Ingebretsen."

1947

[Decision: prize for 1947 shared between Friends Service Council and American Friends Service Committee.]

March 14:

(Not much to speak of among the candidates but we managed to select some. I think the only that can come into question this time are the aid organizations of the Quakers.)

October 30:

"Smitt Ingebretsen promoted Gandhi in a long and rather superfluous lecture. Tranmæl felt obliged, I understood, to raise Mme Kollontai, but did so in a very feeble way. He had a number of objections to Gandhi, first and foremost that his latest statement, even with his retraction, was not clarified. Then he mentioned the purely political aspect, in opining that the conflict between Pakistan and India would have to be cleared up first before one could give the prize to Gandhi, who was also most strongly attached to one party. Then came Oftedal, who also pleaded the case for Gandhi. And then I was apprehensive about Braadland, but [he . . .] agreed with Tranmæl—he was willing to vote for the Quakers as well. I did not say much. About Gandhi I said: 'True, he is the greatest character who has been nominated, but we should remember that he is not only an apostle of peace, he is also a nationalist, and I am not sure whether his humanitarian attitude in South Africa—where he started his work—would have had such effect if it had been about defending negroes as [well as] Indians who worked in the mines there. In addition, we should remember that Gandhi is not naïve. He is an excellent jurist and lawyer. And in addition I cannot overlook that some of that is present in his latest statement. Even if he probably denied it, this is not a satisfactory retraction. He should have quoted exactly what he said and not circumvented it."

1948

[Decision: reserved (for possible decision next year).]

November 18:

"We were all there and all, except Oftedal, agreed that a peace prize could not be awarded this year. Oftedal was for Gandhi and would not bow to the rule in the will on awarding prizes post mortem. [Author's note: not said in will.] I cannot see other than that it would have run against the purpose of testator to award the prize post mortem. As we know, there was rather different information from Sweden now than when we last discussed the question. No one in the committee was actually happy about the Storting's new election of [Nobel committee] members—not to stick to our seats, but because the Storting had based the election on the proportionality method [distributing the seats to parties]. In this way they had managed to get Kirsten Hansteen in as first deputy [committee member]. Tranmæl said: She is the least harmful from that quarter [Norwegian Communist Party] because in my view she is not ill-natured. Braadland said that he had declined to be elected as second deputy member and I find this quite reasonable. Even August Schou reacted strongly against the election. I cannot grasp why they threw [Halvard] Lange out. They probably must reckon he will keep his post as foreign minister for another five years. This is possible, but not certain, and he is at least one of the few in this country who is a given as member of the committee. But Oksvik [Labor whip] is out hunting scalps, and one of those he would most like to have at his belt is that of Lange. I then said, so Tranmæl could hear it, how I considered the games of Oksvik. He probably knows already, but it is good at times to be able to sow some seeds that can grow."

1949

[Decision: prize for 1949 awarded to Boyd Orr.]

February 23:

(". . . the first meeting with the new ones: Lionæs and Natvig Pedersen. They again elected me as chair and threw out Hambro [as vice chair]. It was, as Hambro said, a vote guided by politics.")

October 12:

"First a long debate on the International Labor Office and it was primarily Natvig-Pedersen who pleaded its cause. He would not understand that this is an institution established by governments with a given purpose, and that under the statutes we cannot award the prize to institutions of this kind. He was very insistent and as serious as only descendants of people from the Stavanger district can be. Hambro was entirely negative. He promoted [Salvadoran jurist José Gustavo] Guerrero, but he did not win, mainly because we are going to have a case before the court [International Court of Justice] at The Hague next year, and it is difficult to award the prize to a man who will pronounce judgment in a case where Norway is a party. Eli [US First Lady Eleanor] Roosevelt was defeated immediately, in spite of the defense of her presented by Mrs. Lionæs, which was very weak. Now we were left with a choice between [World War II Italian partisan Riccardo] Cassin and [Scottish nutritionist Sir John] Boyd Orr. The latter was Tranmæl's candidate, and in the end it became him,—Hambro would have wished to reserve the prize for next year. Hambro knows these people better than we do, but he destroys his case by his strong negativism towards those he does not like and his weak argument in defense of those he wishes to promote. My impression is that when he has supported Guerrero so strongly, it is not only because of the letter from Klæstad that has influenced him but also his son's opinion—his son who is an employee of the Hague court [Edvard Hambro, the International Court of Justice (ICJ) Registrar]."

1950

[Decision: prize for 1950 awarded to Ralph Bunche.]

September 22:

"Natvig-Pedersen was as a principle for [Indian prime minister Jawaharlal] Nehru, alternatively [UN mediator on Palestine] Bunche,

Tranmæl was for Bunche, Hambro same. Mrs. Lionæs was minded not to award a prize this year. Despite all the good things that can be said about Bunche, I could not find that strictly speaking he has instituted any peace action on his own initiative. However fortunate and important the result in Palestine may be, it was first and foremost as a functionary of the UN he had been active.

But Bunche was elected, and to general satisfaction from what I read in the papers."

1951

[Decision: prize for 1951 awarded to Léon Jouhaux.]

February 23:

([On a discussion of politics, outside the committee] "I said how dangerous it is that so much is being written by the Communists on the imperialism of the US, while no one in honesty explains to people that Russia is probably the European country that has conquered most other peoples. All their history has been dictated by the expansion toward East and South-West, apart from what they have conquered in Europe. Someone should take this up, try to find someone knowledgeable about Russian history who could soberly and calmly describe what has occurred.")

November 1:

("Afterwards I had August Schou [Nobel secretary] here, and we perused the agenda for Monday 5. Heaven knows whether the Labor party folks will promote Jouhaux. In my personal opinion this would be fairly distant from what was intended with the Nobel prize.")

November 5:

"We had strange voting. Natvig-Pedersen had made this list: Nehru as number 1, The Institute of International Law and the Interparliamentary Union as number 2, and then as number 3 [French trade union leader Léon] Jouhaux. . . . I emphasized that the essential work of Jouhaux did not directly touch the cause of peace and that I could not find that any of the things he had done in the period after the war could make him entitled to the peace prize. I further said that I had met Jouhaux and heard him many times, and that I was not impressed, but I added that it of course speaks to his credit that he has stuck to one line throughout his life, both in the question of war and peace and as far as the position and progress of the working class is concerned."

1952

[Decision: prize for 1952 reserved.]

August 16:

"Natvig-Pedersen was for [governor of the Reserve Bank of India] Sir Benegal Rau [discussed even if the name cannot be found in the Nobel peace nominations register—http://nobelprize.org/nomination/peace/], Tranmæl for [British campaigner for disarmament Philip] Noel-Baker, Hambro for [U.S. founder of Moral Rearmament Frank] Buchmann and Aase Lionæs, who was in doubt as to whether any prize should be awarded this year, was alternatively for Noel-Baker. I felt that [French missionary surgeon] Albert Schweitzer was the only candidate ranking high enough among those nominated this year that he could be a possibility. But it is hard to find him compatible with the statutes in the will of Nobel."

1953

[Decision: prize for 1952 awarded to Albert Schweitzer; prize for 1953 awarded to George Marshall.]

October 30:

"It was not a very simple matter to gather all in favor of a peace prize this time. Natvig-Pedersen started, proposing Schweitzer for 1952 and Nehru for 1953. Tranmæl had three proposals for 1952: Noel-Baker, [U.S. proponent of post-war European recovery plan George] Marshall and Schweitzer, and among these he preferred Marshall. For 1953 he wished to propose Nehru. Hambro's proposal for 1952 was Nehru, Schweitzer and Marshall and for 1953: Moral Rearmament. Aase Lionæs suggested Marshall, Nehru and Schweitzer. She meant that the choice must be between these three. I said: Under no circumstances can I accept Nehru, and I explained my attitude further by referring to Kashmir and because I was not sure about the statement by Natvig-Pedersen that India's foreign policy strictly endeavors to safe-keep peace. They probably—now as before—aimed at becoming the leading power in Asian politics, and even if this were not the case, one should wait and see whether Nehru could contribute to solving some of the most difficult problems facing us today: peace in Korea and peace in Indochina. Should he succeed there, and also be able to solve the Kashmir conflict, then I will be prepared to award him the peace prize. To give it to him today, with the reasoning that it would be desirable to award it to a non-European, does not count much to me. If we were to give it to him today, the Moslem world may be right to a degree that we have taken a stand in the conflict between India and Pakistan. Both Tranmæl, Hambro and Lionæs agreed, after hearing what I had to say, that Nehru should not be considered this time. I then asked the others to comment on Moral Rearmament and emphasized what I find good about this movement, saying that much of what I had read and seen had made a certain impression on me, in particular their work in countries outside Europe in Africa and Asia. Tranmæl was strongly opposed to Moral Rearmament and he first and foremost tied this view to Buchmann as a person. Mrs. Lionæs was fairly sympathetic towards the movement, but she was not happy about their way of working, in particular the advertising [on?] American coloreds they are undoubtedly conducting. A similar view was expressed by Natvig-Pedersen. Some debate ensued, ending with Moral Rearmament being put aside. I further said that I was not very much in favor of Marshall, but that I could admit that behind his original plan that the aid should be given both to east and west, there was a great idea and a real effort for peace, and that it was not his fault that Russia declined to join. I emphasized that if I accepted Marshall it would be because of his original plan. I made this rather clear, since Mrs. Lionæs had said that his greatest contribution was the indirect fight against Communism in Europe. The end result was that the prize for 1952 went to Albert Schweitzer and the prize for 1953 to George Marshall. The committee has enjoyed favorable press coverage. The only sour ones are the social democratic papers in Sweden."

December 10:

"Finally came the day for the award of the prize. People everywhere, and from what I hear my speech for Schweitzer [not present] went well. The speech of Hambro had the form of a biography of Marshall, which took most of his time. Only a few words were spoken of the Marshall plan, and he did not make clear what it signified. Also not clear was that the Marshall plan was meant as help to all of Europe, east as well as west. As I was about to hand over the prize to Marshall, flyers were thrown from the gallery and white sheets of cloth were displayed with the inscription: "Go home Marshall" on the one, and on the other "Hiroshima, Nagasaki. And then something was shouted from the gallery. (On the flyer see attachment protocol). It all lasted only a few seconds and then everything was calm again. [We did not notice much], but it made a strong impression on people in the rear of the room. The ceremony was not stopped, it continued as if nothing had happened. The result of it all, anyway, was that Marshall received a much larger ovation than it is the normal way of Norwegians to give. . . .

In the evening the Nobel committee gave its usual dinner. I held a speech for Marshall were I tried to emphasize the basis for awarding him the prize [aid East + West] much stronger than Hambro had done . . . The Women's League and the Norwegian Peace Council had refused to come. Both had sent letters to the Nobel committee that they were not minded to come to a dinner when this could leave the impression that they condoned the award to Marshall. They are not alone in disliking it. There are many pacifist circles who are against the award of the peace prize for Marshal and these have been joined by most of those who are against the Atlantic Pact"

1954

[Decision: prize reserved.]

1955

[Decision: prize for 1954 awarded to the UN High Commissioner for Refugees.]

1956

[Decision: prize for 1956 transferred to funds.]

November 11:

[Hungarian uprising—volatile times—not Indian (first vice-president Sarvepalli) Radakrishnan who has praised Soviets]. . . . "Naturally the situation today played a role. I mentioned the Women's International League for Peace and Freedom and said that after the woolen statement they had come up with about Hungary, I was unable to give the prize to them."

1957

[Decision: prize for 1956 transferred to funds; prize for 1957 awarded to Lester Pearson.]

October 3 or 4:

[Radakrishnan was discussed and . . .] "Tranmæl proposed Lester Pearson [Canadian statesman who helped to resolve 1956 Suez Canal Crisis], and Hambro and Mrs. Lionæs were of the same opinion. I said that there could be no question of awarding more than one prize and that under the circumstances I could accept giving the prize to Lester Pearson despite the fact that in principle I am against giving the prize to a former statesman whose activities under a potential "comeback" would be hard to foretell."

1958

[Decision: prize for 1958 awarded to Georges Pire.]

September 13:

"I was rather aghast that several of the committee members were fixed on Helen Keller [U.S. deaf and blind author] as their candidate for this year. I cannot really understand that she could possibly get the peace prize, despite being the unique and valuable human being she no doubt is. I thought there were good reasons to speak for giving half the prize to Fr. Georges Pire [Belgian priest who organized relief for refugees] and half to Norman Cousins [U.S. antinuclear advocate]. This I supported in the following way: We give one half to the one who has done such a great effort to heal the wounds of war. We give the other half to one who has done much to end the tests with atom and hydrogen bombs and for a ban on nuclear weapons. I said I did not think we could give the prize only to those who do humanitarian work, it should primarily be given to those who try to struggle against war in one way or another. I was not supported regarding Cousins, who they felt was too thin. After all he was only, as one of the committee members said, forty-six years old and none of the others believed that his activity in America had made any difference. I cannot resist noting a peculiar remark from Hambro; when I said I could not join [in supporting] the prize to Helen Keller, Hambro said: Schweitzer had not done anything for peace either, when he received the prize. I responded that Schweitzer had at least invested everything he had, his whole life, to promote the idea of brotherhood among nations and this not only in words, but also in action, and there is not one winner who has felt the obligation involved in receiving the peace prize as strongly as Schweitzer. He had not only felt the obligation, but had done a major job afterwards. They were surprised by this defense speech. I do not understand a thing. Decided to meet again later and not decide this now."

1959

[Decision: prize for 1959 awarded to Philip John Noel-Baker.]

1960

[Decision: prize for 1960 reserved.]

October 28:

"We decided not to award a prize this year. I could not, after what I had heard from [Linus] Pauling lately on Cousins, continue to support the latter. [Long debate Nehru . . . UN . . . Kashmir] . . . and then Hambro mentioned something at least I had not been aware of, but that had been mentioned in Norwegian papers and which implied that he [Nehru] had behaved with dictatorial authority and even sent soldiers against some Indian tribes living at the border of Burma and China. What is in this I do not know. I have not had the time to check, but in any case I stick to my view that no sitting prime minister should get the peace prize since it is never possible to know what they later may engage in."

1961

[Decision: prize for 1961 reserved; prize for 1960 awarded to Albert Luthuli; prize for 1961 awarded to Dag Hammarskjöld.]

1962

[Decision: prize for 1962 reserved.]

Autumn:

[Earlier meeting had shortlisted: International Commission of Jurists, Rockefeller Foundation, [U.S. Senator] William Fulbright, the Indian

Vinoba Bhave [advocate of nonviolence], Fenner Brockway [joint founder of Britain's Campaign for Nuclear Disarmament] and Linus Pauling, in addition to Mrs. Roosevelt.]

"I named these and asked Natvig-Pedersen to speak first. . . . On Linus Pauling he (Tranmæl) said that he was not very inclined and the background probably was that Pauling had shown himself too uncritical of the radical and communist-friendly flanks of the peace movements. In particular he mentioned that Pauling had been a sponsor for the meeting in Moscow this summer, a meeting organized by the World Peace Council.

Hambro was of the same opinion as Tranmæl, but all in all he preferred to wait till next year. Aase Lionæs again supported Eleanor Roosevelt and alternatively The International Commission of Jurists. I spoke last and commented on the different proposals before speaking at length on Linus Pauling.

I said: None of the others had in later years, nor in earlier years, been so determined to stop the nuclear tests as Pauling. This he saw as the start of complete disarmament. I tried to show how Pauling had been attacked in the United States, what methods the Congress Committee on Un-American Activities had used against him. I mentioned how he had collected 11,021 names—all scientists—to sign a petition to the UN against nuclear tests, told how he later had worked tirelessly for this, how he had traveled around giving lectures, how he had now initiated a lawsuit both against the United States and against the Soviet Union. I also mentioned the reassurance that had come here at home from Eker and Poppe as to the effects of radioactive fall-out. I reminded them of how Pauling had responded to [U.S. physicist Edward] Teller in the US. I further mentioned a newspaper story some days ago from the UN scientific committee, to study the danger of radiation. Here the dangers are emphasized and the tests warned against. I read Pauling's reasons for having sponsored the peace meeting in Moscow this summer, organized by the World Peace Council, and said that in addition to Pauling, other peace prize laureates too—such as Boyd Orr, Schweitzer and Russell, had been sponsors. I also read the letter he had sent me about the resolution that had been adopted at the end of [British antinuclear campaigner Canon John] Collins's peace meeting in London in 1961. I underlined as strongly as I could that the committee should not take political considerations into account, but exclusively point out the person who had done most recently in the struggle against war. When this is the question, I concluded, I cannot find any other than Linus Pauling."

1963

[Decision: prize for 1962 to Linus Pauling; prize for 1963 to the International Red Cross Committee and the Red Cross League.]

September (?):

"[Each member presented their preferred candidates] Perhaps I did a wrong thing in the first meeting. In the usual way I let the different members of the committee present their views on which of the proposed candidates they felt should have the prize. Natvig-Pedersen at once threw in a word for the Red Cross—the other prize he felt could wait until next year. But if it should be awarded he would not be much against giving it to Linus Pauling. Tranmæl used the expression that he wished to give the prize to those who had healed the wounds of war. This was in particular the Red Cross. The other he could be willing to consider was UNICEF. Hambro was for Red Cross and the other prize reserved for next year. Aase Lionæs voted for UNICEF and had much sympathy for The International Commission of Jurists.

It was then that I expressed my opinion: If we continue to give the peace prize to institutions that heal the wounds of war, I shall have to ask Stortinget to free me from the task as member of the Nobel Committee. The prize, I said, must first and foremost be awarded to individuals who have struggled for peace, and here two men have in particular excelled: Bertrand Russell and Linus Pauling.

There was some consternation among the members of the committee. I think it was Hambro who said that I had made it a question of confidence. No, I said, but as a free human being I must, when things happen against my most deep-felt conviction, be permitted to ask myself to be relieved from the membership of the committee. I added that I would not give Stortinget any reasons for my wish to withdraw. With this the meeting was adjourned till Oct. 10. [At this point Jahn added a short note, 1, admitting he had softened his ultimatum considerably.]

   1) Before the meeting adjourned I said that I could reluctantly be prepared to give one of the prizes for the Red Cross, but that I felt it ought to be sufficient that they had received the peace prize twice. I also added that I would appreciate it if someone else could be found."

October 10:

"I opened the meeting saying that in my understanding, we were agreed that one of the prizes should go to the Red Cross. I proposed that the prize for 1963 should go to this institution because of its centenary celebration. Then I let Natvig-Pedersen talk. At the end of a long discourse on institutions and individuals, he concluded by disagreeing with me that one should not give the prize to institutions. I responded that I did not oppose institutions *per se*, but we cannot really constantly give the prize to those who have healed the wounds of war. What is correct, and also in keeping with the will of Nobel, is to seek out individuals who have struggled for peace. Natvig-Pedersen now said that he could support the prize for Linus Pauling and postpone the other prize. Tranmæl continued with his position last time, that the prize in his opinion should go to UNICEF. Hambro said he could vote for Pauling even if he did not care very much about him, if I would be willing to withdraw my ultimatum. Aase Lionæs wished to award the prizes for Red Cross and UNICEF.

I then stated that in my opinion there were two people who could be possible to consider: Russell and Pauling. I quoted the two letters on Russell sent from Noel-Baker to Schou. Considering the content of these letters, I felt it would be difficult to let Russell have the prize; he was more communist-friendly than the two others that had been proposed. Hambro said that Russell was an old man, but [he] would, under the circumstances he had mentioned, vote for Linus Pauling to receive the 1962 prize."

1964

[Decision: prize for 1964 to Martin Luther King.]

DATE?

"[W]e had an easy decision this time. Even if there was alternative support from Lyng, who had the International Commission of Jurists as his first choice. It was Martin Luther King."

1965

[Decision: prize for 1965 to UNICEF.]

October 21:

Wikborg, meeting as deputy, was very well prepared. . . . "Everyone was present and they all were in favor of U Thant [Burmese secretary-general of the UN] as winner this year and UNICEF as the second choice. I could not vote for U Thant and made all the others drop him, and then it was UNICEF."

1966

[Decision: prize reserved.]

September 27:

[Discussion of U Thant, Bhave] . . . "I mentioned the commission working for birth control in underdeveloped countries, but that is a long-term project that does not bear directly on peace. The same could of course be said about Bhave, whose achievement essentially is social work."

October 9:

"This was a negative meeting actually, since we agreed not to award any prize this year, but reserve it for next year."

NOTES

CHAPTER 1

1. The figure for 2008, US$1,464 billion, is 4 percent higher than the figure for 2007, US$1,339 billion, which again is a 6 percent rise above the 2006 figure. In the 10 years since 1999, the increase is 45 percent, according to *SIPRI Yearbook 2009*. The 2009 expenditure of US$1,531 billion represents an increase of 6.9 percent in real terms compared to 2008 (SIPRI press release, June 2, 2010). See www.sipri.org/media/pressreleases.

2. Stiglitz, 2008. Stiglitz, professor of economics, received the 2001 Nobel Prize in Economics.

CHAPTER 2

1. Sohlman, 1983, p. 46.

2. C. J. Hambro, in the June 16, 1954, meeting in the Parliament of Norway, *Stortingsforhandlinger 1954*, p. 1939.

3. Sohlman, 1962, p. 51.

4. Ibid., p. 53.

5. Storheim, *Aftenposten*, November 4, 2003.

6. Sohlman, 1950, p. 74.

7. Sohlman, 1962, p. 53.

8. Nobel speeches, nominations (older than 50 years), and press releases are accessible at www.nobelprize.org. Documents relevant to the present book may be found at www.nobelwill.org.

CHAPTER 3

1. Knoph, *Norsk arverett*, 1930.
2. Lødrup, *Arverett*, 1995.
3. Storheim, 2003.
4. Fogelström, 1971, p. 168.
5. Jorfald, 1962, pp. 53–54.
6. "Tar ikke Nobel på alvor" [interview with Fredrik Heffermehl], October 12, 2007. See www.nettavisen.no, doi: 1385065.ece.
7. Friede, 2005, p. 35.
8. Fogelström, *Kampen för fred* [*The Struggle for Peace*], 1971.
9. Fogelström, 1971, pp. 60–61.
10. Ibid., 1971, p. 119.
11. Not surprising in view of the emphasis on the weight on parliamentarians in his article, the full title of which is: "For Whom Nobel Tolls? An Interpretative Account of the Migration of the Concept of Peace as Perceived through the Solemn Eyes of Norwegian Lawmakers," p. 583.
12. In her *Memoiren* (1909) von Suttner used a good German translation: Völkerverbrüderung.
13. Thanks to Professor Douglas Bulloch, London School of Economics (LSE), for making me aware of this.
14. Knoph, p. 168.
15. von Suttner, *Memoiren*, 1909, pp. 270–272.
16. von Suttner, 1910, p. 436.
17. Abrams, 2001, p. 8.
18. Abrams, 2001, p. 8.
19. Abrams, 2001, p. 27.
20. Ibid., p. 27.
21. Ibid., p. 31.
22. Garbo, 2004.
23. Parliament of Norway, *Stortingsforhandlinger 1901/1902* [Deliberations of the Parliament of Norway], December 10, 1901, p. 405.
24. Ibid., p. 615.
25. *Svensk ordbok* [Swedish Dictionary], 1999. *Ordbok över svenska språket* (1928) on the word "Förfäktare": "person that is in the front line in combat, fighting in the first line, person who is a follower or defender of someone." The current president of the International Peace Bureau (IPB), Tomas Magnusson, himself a Swede, writes that a common translation into English, "promoters of peace," is too weak an expression. "Champions for peace" is a closer translation. See www.ipb.org.
26. von Suttner, 1909, pp. 270–272; Biedermann, 2001, p. 47 [my translation from German].
27. von Suttner, 1897, p. 1 [my translation from German].
28. Memoiren, Ch. XXXVIII.
29. Biedermann, 2001, p. 57.

30. Ibid., p. 174, Letter March 18, 1896 [my translation from French].

31. IPB got the Nobel Peace Prize in 1910, and all 13 of its leaders have won individual peace prizes, from Passy and von Suttner in 1901 and 1905, to Linus Pauling (1962), Seán McBride (1974), and Alva Myrdal (1982). IPB made a successful nomination when the 1995 Nobel went to Pugwash and Joseph Rotblat.

32. In one remark, however, during an early stage of the first will's preparation, in a January 1893 letter to Bertha von Suttner, Nobel envisages "a prize for peace in Europe/making Europe peaceful" (pacification de l'Europe). See Biedermann, 2001, p. 122.

33. Http://nobelprize.org/nobel_prizes/peace/laureates/1983/presentation-speech. html.

34. A pathbreaking resolution in the Norwegian parliament on March 5, 1890, petitioning the Swedish king to enter into arbitration treaties with as many countries as possible may well have been decisive in attracting Nobel's interest in Norway as a peace nation.

35. Lundestad, *Aftenposten*, October 17, 2007.

36. See www.haguepeace.org.

37. Confirmed by two independent sources.

38. See www.barcelona2004.org/eng/queFue.

39. See www.worldpeaceforumbc.ca/themes.

40. See www.peace2.uit.no/hefp/announcement/background-notes.htm.

CHAPTER 4

1. Member of Parliament Hanna Kvanmo, interviewed June 2005 by Kjell Pihlstrøm, Høylandet film og TV-produksjon. See www.hftv.no.

2. Hovdhaugen, 1985, pp. 297–304.

3. In the following years, no prize was awarded: 1972, 1967, 1966, 1956, 1955, 1948, 1944–1939, 1932, 1928, 1924, 1923, 1918–1914.

4. Bulloch, 2008, p. 586.

5. We have to presume that the nominations of Cora Weiss and The Hague Appeal for Peace actually reached the committee, but the public will not be able to know before the period of secrecy expires in 2050.

CHAPTER 5

1. Heffermehl, *Aftenposten*, August 14, 2007.

2. Heffermehl, *Aftenposten*, October 18, 2007.

CHAPTER 6

1. See monographs by historians Stenersen, Libæk, and Sveen, 2000.

2. Member of Parliament and peace activist (later member of the Nobel committee) Bernhard Hanssen about professor of law Ebbe Hertzberg. See Jorfald, 1962, p. 126.

3. Libæk, 2000, p. 6.
4. Garbo, 2004.
5. Jorfald, 1962, p. 126.
6. Ibid., p. 127.
7. Abrams, 2001, p. 13.
8. Actually in the will there is no such division and indication of a "Paragraph one."
9. *Les prix Nobel, 1921,* p. 143.
10. Moe, 1932, p. 28.
11. Schou, 1950, p. 402. The view Schou took of Bertha von Suttner may have been influenced by Swedish professor, H. Schück. In Schou's first year as Nobel secretary, Schück had been commissioned to write the history of the Nobel prizes, even if he was hostile to the Peace Prize. See Jorfald, 1962, p. 129: "Professor Schück is still being criticized by many for his very subjective attitude, particularly when it comes to the causes of peace and feminism." According to Jorfald, Schück found it difficult to digest the fact that a woman could be behind the peace prize. It was incomprehensible to him.
12. Sverdrup, unpublished manuscript, The Nobel Institute Library, registered February 9, 1988. At that time, Sverdrup had held the position as Nobel secretary for 10 years.
13. Cohen, 2007.
14. A most revealing sentence, proudly mentioned as the internal motto of the committee to the author by a committee member, speaking in an off-the-record situation.
15. Oral information from Mari Holmboe Ruge, August 14, 2008, and confirmed by Ingrid Eide.
16. Eckhoff, 1973, p. 2.
17. Sjur Lindebrække, Helge Rognlien, and several deputy members; Helge Refsum, Erling Wikborg, Mona Røkke, Elisabeth Schweigaard Selmer, and Rakel Surlien.
18. Abrams, 2001, p. 22.
19. Lundestad, 2001, see www.nobelprize.org.
20. Biedermann, 2001, p. 47.
21. Moe, 1932, p. 2.
22. Ibid., p. 24.
23. Ibid., p. 25.
24. Ibid., p. 28 [my translation from French].
25. Schou, 1950, p. 477.
26. Lundestad, 2001, see www.nobelprize.org.
27. Lundestad, in an e-mail to author June 17, 2008.
28. Sverdrup, in an article (perhaps a lecture) found in the Nobel Library, not published or dated.
29. Stenersen, Libæk, & Sveen, 2001, p. 19.
30. Lundestad, 2001, see www.nobelprize.org.
31. Abrams, 2001, p. ix.

32. Ibid., p. viii.

33. Abrams, 2001, pp. 335–336. Abrams further makes a distribution by countries, where the following have got more than one prize (p. 337): USA (19), Great Britain (14), France (7), Switzerland (6), Sweden (5), Germany (4), South Africa (4), Belgium (3), Israel (3), Norway (2), Austria (2), and East Timor (2). Only one woman was awarded the prize in each 20-year period up to 1959, and then four between 1960 and 1987 and three between 1988 and 2001 (p. 338). In the years before 2001, only 10 women received the Peace Prize (9 percent of the 107). Since 2002, two of the eight prizes have gone to women (25 percent).

34. Abrams, 2001, p. 31.

35. Abrams, 2001, p. 22, column 1.

36. Stenersen, 2000, p. 35.

37. Ibid., pp. 35–36, mentions that the liberal Johan Ludwig Mowinckel after withdrawing from the Nobel committee (together with Koht) before the Ossietzky prize was announced, joined the chair of the conservatives, Johan H. Andresen, in a failed attempt to have the Foreign Affairs Committee of the Parliament of Norway adopt a declaration of friendship with the German people. The experience with the Ossietzky prize pinpointed the close connections between the Norwegian government and the Nobel committee and brought to a head the need to give a more credible impression of political independence.

38. Ibid., p. 15, for example, finds that the prize to British Arthur Henderson (1934) was motivated by a serious controversy between Norway and Britain over fishing rights; p. 22, 24, the prize for Argentinean Carlos Saavedra Lamas (1936) was an express wish from the United States, and favorable to the trades in fish and apples; p. 27, with the prize for a veteran of the League of Nations, Forbund Cecil (1937) some in the committee wished to bridge the increasing distance Norway was keeping to the world organization; p. 34, the prize for the Nansen International Office for Refugees (1938) was pushed by the foreign minister (Koht) and the president of Parliament and that "Opportunities are rare to survey such a prosess, with the peace prize so clearly being utilised as an element in the formulation of Norwegian foreign policy."

39. Stenersen, Libæk, & Sveen, 2001, p. 19.

40. Libæk, 2000, pp. 19–22.

41. Galtung, 2008, p. 34.

42. Johan Galtung in an e-mail to the author, January 25, 2008.

43. Mentioned several times in Stenersen, Libæk, & Sveen, 2001; and Abrams, 2001.

CHAPTER 7

1. Conversion rate for Norwegian kroner (NOK) throughout: US$1 = NOK 5.5.

2. A group named www.ukultur.org sent an appeal to Parliament requesting an initiative to prevent "any suspicion about improper use of friendship and double roles in our political life," but it was filed without action by the

presidency, led by Thorbjørn Jagland, who at the time combined his parliamentary role with the position of chairman of the board of former premier Bondevik's Oslo Center. Often criticized for a propensity to wear too many hats, Jagland since 2009 is in the chair of the Nobel committee, on the board of the Oslo Center, and at the same time is the Secretary General of the Council of Europe.

3. Heffermehl, 2006.
4. *Kampanje*, November 2, 2006.
5. Bye & Hoel, 1996.
6. Jorfald, 1962, p. 98.
7. See http://www.bilderberg.org/2005.htm.
8. The use of the title was temporarily changed for "professor of history" following the publication, in 2008, of *Nobels vilje*. Just a few months later the byline was again "director of the Nobel Institute." My criticism was not new: in 2003, in a phone call with the newly elected leader of the Nobel committee Ole Danbolt Mjøs, I complained that since the Lundestad newspaper columns had absolutely nothing to do with the Peace Prize, it was improper to let them sail under the Nobel flag. Mjøs responded that Lundestad had been such a valuable man to the Peace Prize that he did not wish to raise the issue with him. This might at the same time be a hint as to relative power in the Nobel system.
9. *Aftenposten,* March 26, 2008.
10. *Aftenposten*, April 3, 2008.
11. Press communiqué, August 20, 2008.
12. See www.mediaplanetonline.no (retrieved June 18, 2008).
13. Ibid.
14. Gelis, 2008.
15. *IKFFs årsberetning* [KKF Annual Report], 1939, "In an article in *Dagbladet* April 25 (printed in *Fred og Frihet*), Ursula Jorfald asked, *Er Nobelkomiteen bare for menn?* [Is the Nobel committee only for men?].
16. Mari Holmboe Ruge, *Norsk biografisk leksikon* [Biographical lexicon], 2002, p. 5.
17. Interview with Nanny Jahn Hayes (daughter), January 2010.
18. Eckhoff 1973.

CHAPTER 8

1. Jorfald, 1962, p. 49.
2. Jorfald, 1962, p. 52.
3. Jorfald, 1962, p. 52.
4. Heffermehl, 2000, p. 13, and 2005, p. 96.
5. Ibid., p. 103.
6. In Heffermehl, 2000, Kate Dewes and Alyn Ware explain the civil society effort to obtain an opinion from the ICJ on the legality of nuclear weapons,

and William R. Pace the civil society role in getting the International Criminal Court (ICC) established.

7. Alyn Ware in Heffermehl, 2000, p. 158.

8. See www.oxfordresearchgroup.org.uk. Elworthy has been nominated to the Nobel committee several times and would be an excellent choice.

9. Elworthy in Heffermehl, 2000, p. 54.

10. In Heffermehl, 2005, I developed the role of media in relation to nuclear weapons and disarmament in general.

11. Jody Williams in Heffermehl, 2000, p. 138.

12. Heffermehl, 2000, p. 76.

CHAPTER 9

1. United Nations, *Our Common Future*, 1987, Introduction to Chapter 11.

2. Report of the Canberra Commission, August 1996, executive summary.

3. Galbraith, 1996.

4. Farewell address, January 17, 1961.

5. Klare, 1995, pp. 3–18.

6. Chomsky, 1994, p. 22.

7. Heffermehl, Fit for NATO? *New York Times*, December 12, 1997.

CHAPTER 10

1. Sohlman, 1950, pp. 320–322.

2. Heffermehl, 2000, p. 24.

3. See www.2020visioncampaign.org/pages/336.

CHAPTER 11

1. A collection of links can be found at www.vidarforlaget.no: Boksøk [Search-box]: Heffermehl.

2. Räikkä, *Helsingin Sanomat*, October 17, 2008.

3. *Wall Street Journal*, October 11, 2008, p. A12.

4. Oberg, October 10, 2008, Google search: 780588: BlogPost:76936.

5. Farina, *Il Giornale*, June 7, 1999.

6. *Aftenposten*, October 2, 2008.

7. *Aftenposten*, news report, November 7, 2008.

8. *Dagsavisen*, November 27, 2008.

CHAPTER 12

1. Swanson, Consortiumnews.com, February 10, 2010.

2. Still, there is the problem that Nobel had individuals in mind.

3. http://nobelprize.org/nobel_prizes/peace/laureates/2009.

4. But Poland, the Czech Republic, and the U.S, arms industry seem to get compensatory missile programs.

5. See www.un.org/secureworld.

6. http://nobelprize.org/nobel_prizes/peace/laureates/1990.

7. http://nobelprize.org/nobel_prizes/peace/laureates/1995.

8. http://nobelprize.org/nobel_prizes/peace/laureates/1974.

9. All quotes from the Obama Nobel speech can be found at http://nobel prize.org/nobel_prizes/peace/laureates/2009.

10. *American Journal of International Law 1947*, 1946, p. 186.

11. Associated Press, news dispatch, February 18, 1999.

12. Heffermehl, 2000, p. 9.

13. E-mail from Bruce Kent (London) to author January 31, 2010.

14. Timmerman, 1991.

15. BBC.co.uk, September 12, 2001, Taliban offered extradition to an international court provided the US showed a *prima facie* case.

16. From memo, published in *Sunday Times* (London) May 1, 2005: "Bush wanted to remove Saddam, through military action, justified by the conjunction of terrorism and WMD. But the intelligence and facts were being fixed around the policy."

17. That the United States/NATO has no such authority is the underlying premise for the 1950 "Uniting for peace" resolution of the General Assembly of the United Nations. Res. 377 gave the GA a possibility to act when the SC was deadlocked.

18. Eskeland, 2005, lecture for Oslo Military Society [delivered in Norwegian], http://www.oslomilsamfund.no/oms_arkiv/2003/2003-10-06-Eskeland.html.

19. E-mail October 13, 2009, to Cherrie Daniels, Head of Political Economic Section, U.S. Embassy, Oslo.

20. Stenersen, Sveen, & Libæk, 2009.

21. http://www.dn.se, searchword: 1.1008456.

22. Sejersted commented on the purpose of the prize in several of his Nobel speeches and expressed, in a private conversation, an opinion to the author on *Nobels vilje*.

CHAPTER 13

1. *Aftenposten*, April 6, 2009.

2. http://nobelprize.org/nobel_prizes/peace/laureates/2009/press.html.

3. *Aftenposten*, February 27, 2009. Not posted on the newspaper's very comprehensive Web site aftenposten.no.

4. Letter, November 11, 1896 [original in French].

5. Cohen, 2005, p. 96 [my translation from German].

6. Friede, 2005, pp. 34, 35.

7. *Peace and Change*, Vol. 30, No. 1, January 2005.

8. Friede, 2005, p. 29.

9. von Suttner, 1910, Vol. 1, p. 340.

10. Fant, pp. 267–272.

11. Fant, p. 271.

12. Greve, 1964, p. 171.

13. Jorfald, 1979.

14. Pauli, p. 237.

15. Ibid., p. 229.

16. Stenersen, 2001, pp. 141, 151.

17. In 1930 the committee awarded the Peace Prize for 1929 to Kellogg.

18. The factual basis of this analysis of the early history of the Norwegian Peace Association is the master thesis of Mats Rønning, 2005, and conversations with historian Åsmund Svendsen (Moss, Norway) on his current unpublished research for the biography of Halfdan Koht.

19. This idea has been taken from Gunnar Garbo, at the end of his article on peace politics in Norway around 1900, Garbo (2004).

20. *The Daily Telegraph* (London) began publishing details from an inquiry in daily installments from May 8, 2009, showing flagrant and sometimes gross misuse of the expenses system for personal gain by many members of Parliament (including government and shadow cabinet ministers) across all parties.

CHAPTER 14

1. E-mail to the author, November 2008.

2. Henrik Syse, *Aftenposten*, December 16, 2009.

3. Borgen, 2009, pp. 229–258, has an analysis of the transformation of the "peace party."

4. Of course it was unacceptable to drop both parliamentary vice presidents and the chair of Parliament's Committee on Foreign Affairs from the guest list. The interesting point here is why these key people in Parliament where not invited. In *Dagens Næringsliv*, December 9 and 10, 2009, Geir Lundestad, speaking for the committee, explained that more than 30 seats at the banquet tables were used to reward financial sponsors of the Nobel Peace Center and the Peace Concert. Some chief executive officers (CEOs) could even bring communication directors and invite business partners from abroad, all with spouses. IBM had the biggest delegation (eight people); then Telenor (three directors, bringing two partners from India); Hydro (four); and then CEOs with spouses from the DnB Nor bank, Dagbladet, Statkraft, Orkla; Yara, KPMG, and Cisco. Under the bylaws, the Nobel Institute is supposed to be financially independent, but it tells a lot about a Peace Prize in the hands of commercial interests when the Parliament to whom Nobel entrusted the prize is pushed aside to give room for the corporate elite.

5. Garbo, 2008.

6. Borgen, 2009, p. 134; Borgen, "A small piece of Norway," 2006.

7. Heffermehl, 2000, p. 12.

8. Ibid., p. 13.

9. Melman, 1970, pp. 151–152, refers to Kraslow & Loory, 1968.

10. *Friede–Fortschritt–Frauen*, 2005, p. 117.

11. Some information is found in International Peace Bureau (IPB) publications. See Archer, 2006; Heffermehl, 2000; and www.peaceispossible.info. Here are some more examples from the landscape where the committee may find qualified persons, working for the global system change Nobel had in mind: Acronym Institute, Alliance for the Global Wellness Fund Treaty, Atomic Mirror, Canadian Consortium on Human Security (CCHS), Canadian Peace Alliance, Center for Defense Information (CDI), Common Dreams, Economists for Peace and Security (EPS), Fundació per la Pau, Geneva Centre for the Democratic Control of Armed Forces (DCAF), Global Article 9 Campaign, Global Facilitation Network for Security Sector Reform (GFN-SSR), Global Security Institute (GSI), Green Cross International (GCI), Hague Appeal for Peace (HAP), Human Security Commission (HSQ), Human Security Network (HSN), Human Dignity and Humiliation Studies, Institute for Disarmament Studies, Institute for Inclusive Security, International Campaign to Ban Uranium Weapons (ICBUW), International Network of Engineers and Scientists Against Proliferation (INESAP), Mouvement de la Paix, National Priorities Project (Cost of War), Nuclear Free Philippines Coalition (NFPC), Pacific Campaign for Disarmament and Security (PCDS), Pax Christi International, Peace Action, Peace Depot, Peace Majority, PeaceQuest International, Project Ploughshares, Rwanda Women's Network, Swedish Peace and Arbitration Society, Transnational Institute (TNI), United States Institute of Peace (USIP), Verification Research, Training, and Information Centre (VERTIC), Weeramantry International Centre for Peace Education and Research, and World Federalist Movement (WFM).

12. I first wrote about the need for a new, humane, and just foreign policy as a potentially unavoidable consequence of the mixing of ethnic minorities with the populations of the affluent countries in *Vanunu* (Heffermehl, 2005). Within two weeks my point was horrifyingly demonstrated by bombs on three London Underground trains and one bus on July 7, 2005. See also Beebe and Kaldor, 2010; in line with Alfred Nobel, they call for *human security* as the realistic alternative to military "security."

BIBLIOGRAPHY

NOBEL RESOURCES

1. *Nobelprize.org*: Nobel speeches and press releases can all be found at the following URL: http://nobelprize.org/nobel_prizes/peace.
2. *Les Prix Nobel*: Speeches from Nobel award ceremonies in Oslo and Stockholm, 1901–2007). Stockholm: Nobel Foundation/Norstedt.
3. *Nobel Institute Series*: *Det Norske Nobelinstitutts Skriftserie* [The Norwegian Nobel Institute Series]. Oslo: The Norwegian Nobel Institute.
4. *Nobelwill.org*: Material on the present book and the efforts to restore the Peace Prize to its legitimate purpose, as formulated by Alfred Nobel.

To get an idea of the content of referenced material in Scandinavian languages use translation tools on the Internet, for instance Google translate.

Abrams, I. (2001). *The Nobel Peace Prize and the laureates*. New York: Science History Publications.
Archer, C. (2006). *Warfare or welfare? Disarmament for development in the 21st century*. Geneva: International Peace Bureau.
BBC (British Broadcasting Corporation). (2001, September 12). *Bush: Culprits will be punished*. Retrieved May 11, 2010, from http://news.bbc.co.uk.

Beebe, S., and Kaldor, M. (2010). *The ultimate weapon is no weapon: Human security and the new rules of war and peace*. London: Public Affairs.

Bergengren, E. (1960). *Alfred Nobel*. Uppsala: Gebers/The Nobel Foundation.

Biedermann, E. (2001). *Chère baronne et amie—cher monsieur et ami: Der Briefwechsel zwischen Alfred Nobel und Bertha von Suttner*. Hildesheim: Georg Olms Verlag.

Bjørke, B. H. (1989). *Bertha von Suttner—i kamp mot våpnene* [Bertha von Suttner—struggling against armaments]. FMKs fredspolitiske skrifter. Oslo: Folkereisning mot krig.

Borgen, E. (2006). *Et lite stykke Norge* [A small piece of Norway]. Documentary movie. Oslo: Borgen Productions A/S.

Borgen, E. (2009). *Fredsnasjonens hemmeligheter* [The secrets of the peace nation]. Oslo: Manifest.

Brock-Utne, B. (1985). *Educating for peace: A feminist perspective*. New York: Pergamon International.

Bulloch, D. (2008). For whom Nobel tolls? *Millennium: Journal of International Studies, 36*(3), 575–595.

Bye, V., and Hoel, D. (1996). *Dette er Cuba—alt annet er løgn!* [This is Cuba—anything else is lie!] Oslo: Spartacus.

Canberra Commission. (1996). *Report on the elimination of nuclear weapons*. Canberra: Government of Australia.

Chomsky, N. (1994). *Secrets, lies and democracy*. Tucson, AZ: Odonian Press.

Cohen, L. (2005). *"Gerade weil Sie eine Frau sind . . ."* Vienna, Austria: Braumüller.

Cohen, P. (2007, October 14). The politics behind the Peace Prize. *New York Times*. Retrieved May 8, 2010, from http://www.nytimes.com.

Curtis, M. (2010). *Doublethink: The two faces of Norway's foreign and development policy*. Oslo: Forum.

Durand, A. (1986). The development of the idea of peace in the thinking of Henry Dunant. *International Review of the Red Cross*, January–February 1986, no. 250, pp. 16–50.

Eckhoff, T. (1973, December). *Stortinget og Nobels fredspris* [The Parliament of Norway and the Nobel Peace Prize]. (Unpublished legal report).

Eisenhower, D. D. (1961, January 17). *Farewell address to the nation*. Retrieved May 11, 2010, from http://www.informationclearinghouse.info/article5407.htm.

Elich, G. (2008). *How the Nobel Peace Prize was won*. Retrieved May 8, 2010, from http://www.transcend.org.

Ellsberg, D. (2003). *Secrets: A memoir of Vietnam and the Pentagon Papers*. New York: Penguin USA.

Eskeland, S. (2003, October 6). *Krig og fredsbevarende operasjoner: Lovlig, ulovlig eller straffbart?* [War and peacekeeping operations: Legal, illegal or punishable?] Oslo: Oslo Military Society. Retrieved May 12, 2010, from http://www.oslomilsamfund.no/oms_arkiv/2003/2003-10-06-Eskeland.html.

Farina, R. (1999, June 7). Why we Serbs have given in [Interview with Ljubisa Ristic]. *Il Giornale,* Milan. Referenced in Elich, 2010.

Friede–Fortschritt–Frauen: Friedenspreisträgerin Bertha von Suttner auf Shcloss Harmannsdorf. (2005). Internationaler Bertha von Suttner Verein. Wien: LIT.

Fogelström, P. A. (1971). *Kampen för fred: Den okända folkrörelsen* [The struggle for peace: The unknown mass movement]. Stockholm: Svenska freds och skiljedomsföreningen.

Galbraith, J. K. (1996). The autonomous military power: An economic view. *Disarmament,* 19(3).

Galtung, J. (2008). *Norge sett utenfra* [Norway seen from the outside]. Oslo: Kagge forlag.

Garbo, G. (2002). *Også krig er terror* [War is also terror]. Oslo: Self-published.

Garbo, G. (2004, April 15). Fredsaktivisme i Stortinget [Peace activism in Parliament]. *Dagbladet.* Retrieved May 8, 2010, from http://www. dagbladet.no/kultur/2004/04/15/395810.html.

Garbo, G. (2007, October 2). Krig eller fred: Fortsatt dominerer overtroen på militær makt [War or peace: The superstitious belief in military power still dominates]. *Klassekampen.*

Garbo, G. (2007, November 12). Militarismen er trusselen [Militarism itself is the threat]. *Bergens Tidende.*

Garbo, G. (2008, January 16). Stortinget I strid med FN [Stortinget in conflict with the UN]. *Verdens Gang.*

Gelis, U. (2008). Fredsprisen forplikter [The Peace Prize, an obligation]. *Fred og Frihet.* Oslo: Internasjonal kvinneliga for fred og frihet.

Greve, T. (1964). *Det norske storting gjennom 150 år.* Oslo: Gyldendal.

Heffermehl, F. S. (1988). Vår militære uvirkelighet [Our military unreality]. *Samtiden.*

Heffermehl, F. S. (1997, December 12). Fit for NATO? *New York Times.*

Heffermehl, F. S. (2000). *Peace is possible.* Geneva: International Peace Bureau. Available in 18 languages at http://www.peaceispossible.info.

Heffermehl, F. S. (2005). *Vanunu.* Oslo: Aschehoug.

Heffermehl, F. S. (2006, January 24). Vi kan ikke ha det slik [We cannot accept this]. *Dagens Næringsliv.*

Heffermehl, F. S. (2007, August 14). Fredsprisen i fare [The Peace Prize in danger]. *Aftenposten,* Part 2, p. 5.

Heffermehl, F. S. (2007, October 18). Nobel—ideen som forsvant [Nobel—the idea that disappeared]. *Aftenposten,* Part 2, p. 5.

Hovdhaugen, E. (1985). Gjest i Nobelkomitéen [Guest in the Nobel committee]. *Syn og Segn,* 4, pp. 297–304.

International military tribunal judgment. (Nuremberg, 1946, October 1). *American Journal of International Law 1947,* p. 186.

Jagland, T. (2008, October 2). Nobelkomiteen fornyes [Nobel committee being renewed]. The president of *Stortinget* interviewed. *Aftenposten,* Part 1, p. 4.

Jorfald, U. (1962). *Bertha von Suttner og Nobels fredspris* [Bertha von Suttner and the Nobel Peace Prize]. Self-published.

Jorfald, U. (1979). *Le prix Nobel de la paix. Pourquoi? Comment?* Angers: Forum.

Kissinger, H., et al. (2008, January 15). Toward a nuclear-free world. *Wall Street Journal.*

Klare, M. (1995). *Rogue states and nuclear outlaws.* New York: Hill and Wang.

Knoph, R. (1930). *Norsk arverett* [Norwegian inheritance law]. Oslo: Aschehoug.

Kraslow, D., and Loory, S. H. (1968). *The secret search for peace in Vietnam.* New York: Random House.

Kvanmo, Hanna. (2005). Interviewed by Kjell Pihlstrøm. Høylandet film og TV-produksjon.

Lange, C. (1906). Panamerikanisme. *Samtiden.*

Larsson, U. (2008). *Alfred Nobel: Networks of innovation.* Stockholm: The Nobel Museum.

Libæk, I. (2000). The Nobel Peace Prize: Some aspects of the decision-making process, 1901–1917. Chap. 2 in Nobel Institute Series, Vol. 1, No. 2.

Lundestad, G. (2001). *The Nobel Peace Prize, 1901–2000.* Retrieved May 7, 2010, from http://nobelprize.org/nobel_prizes/peace/articles.

Lundestad, G. (2007, October 17). Et vidt fredsbegrep [A wide concept of peace]. *Aftenposten,* Part 2, p. 5.

Lundestad, G. (2009, April 5). Hvordan tolke Nobel [How to interpret Nobel]. *Aftenposten,* Part 2, p. 5.

Lødrup, P. (1995). *Arverett* [Inheritance law]. Oslo: Self-published.

Melman, S. (1970). *Pentagon capitalism: The political economy of war.* New York: McGraw-Hill.

Moe, R. (1932). *Le prix Nobel et le mouvement pacifiste 1890–1930* [The Nobel Peace Prize and the peace movement 1890–1930]. Oslo: Aschehoug.

Nobel Finn. (2008, October 11). *Wall Street Journal,* p. A12.

Norsk Biografisk leksikon. (2002). Oslo: Kunnskapsforlaget.

Oberg, J. (2008, October 10). *Nobel committee's choice again a scandal.* Retrieved July 8, 2010, from http://www.internationalpeaceandconflict .org/profiles/blog/show?id=780588%3ABlogPost%3A76936.

Parliament of Norway. (1901/1902, 1906/1907, 1954). *Stortingsforhandlinger* [Negotiations in *Stortinget*]. Oslo: Parliament of Norway.

Räikkä, J. (2008, October 17). HS panel members do not fawn over Ahtisaari. *Helsingin Sanomat.*

Rønning, M. (2008). *Fredsfaar i gjentatt strid* [Peace sheep in recurring strife—the history of the popular peace movement in Norway before 1914]. Ph.D. Diss., University of Oslo.

Saue, G. G. (1991). *Fredsfurien* [The peace shrew]. Oslo: Aschehoug.

Schou, A. (1962). The peace prize. In H. Schück, *Nobel—the man and his prizes.* Amsterdam: Elsevier.

Schück, H. (1962). *Nobel—the man and his prizes*. Amsterdam: Elsevier.

Smith, M. (2005, June 19). The leaked Iraq war documents. *The Sunday Times*. Retrieved May 8, 2010, from http://www.timesonline.co.uk/tol/news/uk/article535913.ece.

Sohlman, R. (1950a). *Ett testamente: Nobelstiftelsens tillkomsthistoria och dess grundare*. Stockholm: Norstedt.

Sohlman, R. (1950b). Nobelstiftelsens tilkomst och dess grundare [A testament: The Nobel Foundation and its founder]. In *Nobelprisen 50 år: forskare, diktare, fredskämpar*. Stockholm: The Nobel Foundation.

Sohlman, R. (1950c). *Nobel—the man and his prizes*. Stockholm: The Nobel Foundation.

Sohlman, R. (1962). *Nobel—the man and his prizes*. Amsterdam: Elsevier.

Sohlman, R. (1983). *The legacy of Alfred Nobel*. London: The Bodley Head.

SIPRI (Stockholm International Peace Research Institute). *SIPRI Yearbook 2009*. Retrieved May 4, 2010, from http://www.sipri.org/media/pressreleases/2009.

Stenersen, Ø. (2000). The Nobel Peace Prize: Some aspects of the decision-making process, 1932–1939. Chap. 4 in Nobel Institute Series, Vol. 1, No. 4.

Stenersen, Ø., Libæk, I., and Sveen, A. (2001). *The Nobel Peace Prize: One hundred years for peace*. Oslo: Cappelen.

Stenersen, Ø., Sveen, A., and Libæk, I. (2009, December 6). Dolda motiv. *Dagens Nyheter*. Retrieved May, 8, 2010, from http://www.dn.se, doi: 1.1008456.

Stiglitz, J. E., and Bilmes, L. (2008). *The three trillion dollar war: The true cost of the Iraq conflict*. New York: W. W. Norton.

Storheim, A. (2003, November 4). Hvorfor ble det norsk fredspris? [Why a Norwegian peace prize?]. *Aftenposten*. Retrieved May 8, 2010, from http://www.aftenposten.no/fakta/nobel/article658516.ece.

Suttner, B. von. (1892). Lay down your arms. (translation of *Die Waffen nieder*). London: Longmans, Green. Reprint 1971, New York: Garland.

Suttner, B. von. (1897, January 12). Erinnerungen an Alfred Nobel. *Neue Freie Presse*.

Suttner, B. von. (1909). *Memoiren*. Stuttgart, Leipzig: DVA (Deutsche Verlags-Anstalt).

Suttner, B. von. (1910). *Memoirs: The records of an eventful life*. Boston: Ginn.

Sveen, A. (2000). The Nobel Peace Prize: Some aspects of the decision-making process, 1919–1931. Chap. 3 in Nobel Institute Series, Vol. 1, No. 3.

Sverdrup, J. (1988). *Alfred Nobel og fredsbevegelsen* [Alfred Nobel and the peace movement]. Unpublished manuscript, The Nobel Institute Library.

Swanson, D. (2010, February 10). *US ignores UK's Iraq War evidence*. Retrieved May 9, 2010, from http://www.consortiumnews.com/2010/021010a.html.

Tägil, S. (1983). *Nobel och hans tid: Fem essayer* [Nobel and his time: Five essays]. Stockholm: Atlantis.

Timmerman, K. R. (1991). *The death lobby: How the West armed Iraq*. New York: Houghton Mifflin Company.

United Nations. (1987, August). *Our common future: Report of the world commission on environment and development*. Retrieved May 9, 2010, from http://www.un-documents.net/wced-ocf.htm.

Weber, W. T. (1989). *Gandhi and the peace prize*. Retrieved May 8, 2007, from http://www.mkgandhi.org/nobel/nobelpeaceprize.htm.

INDEX

About the Author

FREDRIK S. HEFFERMEHL is a Norwegian lawyer and international peace activist. He is the vice president of the International Association of Lawyers against Nuclear Arms and served as president of the Norwegian Peace Alliance and vice president of the International Peace Bureau. He has served in Norway as a deputy judge, deputy consumer ombudsman, and as the secretary general of the Norwegian Humanist Association. Heffermehl has law degrees from the University of Oslo, New York University, and the College of Public Administration in Oslo. He edited *Peace Is Possible* (International Peace Bureau, 2000), a volume of 31 contributions by eminent peacemakers which has been translated into 18 languages.